AT GOD'S PACE

A biography of
Josemaría Escrivá de Balaguer
Founder of Opus Dei

François Gondrand

AT GOD'S PACE

A biography of
Josemaría Escrivá de Balaguer
Founder of Opus Dei

SCEPTER

London – New York

This edition of *At God's Pace* is published:
in England by Scepter, 1 Leopold Road, London W5 3PB; and
in the United States by Scepter Press Inc., 481 Main Street, New Rochelle,
    N.Y. 10801.

This is a translation of *Au pas de Dieu*, first published in 1982 by Editions
France-Empire.

With ecclesiastical approval

© Original – Editions France-Empire, 1982
© Translation – Scepter, 1989
© This edition – Scepter, 1989

British Library Cataloguing in Publication Data
    Gondrand, François
    At God's Pace: Josemaría Escrivá
    1. Catholic organisations. Opus Dei. Escrivá de Balaguer, Josemaría
    1902-1975
    I Title   II Au pas de Dieu   *English*
    267'.182'0924

    ISBN 0 906138 27 2

Cover design & typeset in England by KIP Intermedia, and printed in
Hong Kong.

Contents

Forgetting the course already run,
I go forward, straining with all my strength,
and I run toward my goal
thinking of the prize that God calls us
to receive on high in Christ Jesus.

Saint Paul
Epistle to the Philippians, (3:13-14)

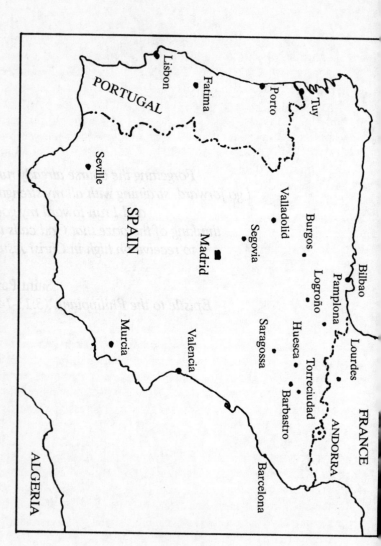

Map of Spain and Portugal

FOREWORD

On 26 June 1975, Monsignor Josemaría Escrivá, the founder of Opus Dei, died in Rome. He was known throughout the world as a pioneer of the apostolate of the laity and a tireless promoter of the quest for sanctity in everyday life for those living in the midst of the world. Less than six years later, the process of his beatification and canonisation was opened in Rome. The petitions for his canonisation came not only from important figures in the civil and ecclesiastical life of many different countries, but also from thousands of ordinary men and women who were witness to his sanctity and to his influence on their lives.

Opus Dei, *the Work of God*, was born on 2 October 1928. For Josemaría Escrivá it was the beginning of a remarkable spiritual adventure, one that has had far-reaching effects and opened up a way to God remarkable for its astounding vision. From that day until the day he died, he did not cease to promote the marking out of that way with all his strength.

Who was this remarkable man? What was the path he took, first of all to the priesthood and then to the founding of this Work of God? These are some of the questions I have tried to answer, basing my attempt partly on my own personal recollections and partly on such important sources as the writings of Monsignor Escrivá himself, as well as depositions and other documents which, once properly assessed and classified, constitute a mine of valuable information. I wish to thank all those who have given me access to these documents, especially Monsignor Alvaro del Portillo, the present Prelate of Opus Dei.

Opus Dei was born with a universal, and essentially lay, spirit: both these aspects were heavily underlined by the founder even in his very earliest writings. Nevertheless, despite all the approvals he obtained from the Holy See from 1943 onwards, it was not until 1982 that the Work received its definitive status – the configuration that exactly fitted Monsignor Escrivá's wishes, as being in perfect accord with what he had *seen* on 2 October 1928. Providence had willed that the founder should not live to see the culmination of that long journey, when Pope John Paul II set up Opus Dei as a personal prelature of the Catholic Church, worldwide in extent and with its prelatic church – in the central offices of the Prelature – in Rome. It was on this occasion that the Roman Pontiff made use, for the very first time, of a legal entity directly envisaged by the Second Vatican Council for the answering of special pastoral needs (see *Presbyterorum Ordinis*, no. 10).

The Apostolic Constitution, *Ut sit*, of 28 November 1982, recalled what had always constituted the aims of Opus Dei: the spreading in all milieu of society of a deep awareness of the universal call to holiness and apostolate, in and through each person's ordinary work. The Prelature is made up of a Prelate (who is the Ordinary of Opus Dei), his clergy, and laity – men and women, single or married – who freely join in answer to a divine vocation.

Opus Dei provides its members with the training and spiritual means they need in order to practise, with complete freedom and personal responsibility, the life of a Christian who wants to live in accordance with his faith in the middle of the world, in the realities that go to make up his ordinary activities.

'With very great hope, the Church directs its attention and maternal care to Opus Dei, which – by divine inspiration – the Servant of God Josemaría Escrivá de Balaguer founded on 2 October 1928, so that it may always be an apt instrument of the salvific mission which the Church carries out for the life of the world ...' In these, the first words of the Apostolic Constitution *Ut sit* mentioned above, Pope John Paul wished to stress the worldwide scope of the Work founded by Josemaría Escrivá, as well as the interest its personality should hold for Catholics throughout the world.

So many glories of France are glories of mine too! wrote Monsignor Escrivá. *And in the same way, much that makes Germans proud, and the peoples of Italy and of England ... and Americans, Asians and Africans, is a source of pride to me also. Catholic: big heart, broad mind The Way*, 525).

What can I do but recall these lines – for me, such a wonderful lesson in universal outlook – in the *Foreword* to this first edition of my book in English, *lingua franca* of the whole world!

F.G., 26 June 1989

I

MADRID: 2 OCTOBER 1928

The Work of God
was not thought up by any man ...
It was inspired by Our Lord, many years ago,
in a deaf and clumsy instrument
who saw it for the first time
on the feast of the holy Guardian Angels,
2 October 1928.

J. Escrivá[1]

It is early morning. A young priest of twenty-six is celebrating Mass in the house of the Missionaries of Saint Vincent de Paul, where he and five other priests are on retreat. The chapel is on the ground floor; the house – a large, imposing building – is situated on García de Paredes Street, near the northern outskirts of Madrid.

Today is the third day of the retreat. The liturgy celebrates the feast of the holy Guardian Angels; the Collect recalls this fact, as does the Epistle – "Behold, I am sending My angel before you, to guard you in your way and bring you to the place which I have prepared for you. Pay heed to him and hear his voice; do not resist him ... " (Ex 23:20-21) – and in the *Alleluia*; "Bless the Lord, O you His angels ... " (Ps 102:20). And before the Canon, the Preface: "Through Him the angels praise Your majesty ... *Sanctus, Sanctus, Sanctus* ... "

Then comes the supreme moment of the consecration, when the mystery of love that is Transubstantiation takes place: "This is my Body ... This is the cup of my Blood ... " After the invocation of the Most Holy Trinity, through Christ, with Him and in Him, follows the communion with the Body and Blood of Christ. Then, after again invoking the angels, the final blessing and the Last Gospel, that of Saint John: "In the beginning was the Word ... "

After the prayers at the foot of the altar, Father Josemaría Escrivá – for that is the young priest's name – removes his vestments, reciting the customary prayers, and begins a lengthy period of thanksgiving.

A frugal breakfast is taken in silence so as not to disturb the quiet and recollection of the retreat. The meal over, he returns to his bedroom, sitting at his table, from where he can scarcely hear the noise of the street under his window; he sorts out some little sheets of paper – notes taken over the last days and months, resolutions, short invocations ... and the record of repeated calls, of suggestions half-grasped from his prayer, and afterwards deeply meditated on.

He barely has time to re-read them. As he passes the sheets between his hands, suddenly everything fits together in a completely new way, in a completely new light – like a jigsaw puzzle whose pieces fall into place without his help, like a painting unexpectedly unveiled before him, when all he had seen before had been tiny details.

A reality long sought after, a vision sometimes glimpsed obscurely, and only partially: now it impresses itself forcefully on his mind and on his heart. Thousands – millions – of souls, covering the whole face of the earth, raise their prayers to God. Generation upon generation of Christians, submerged in all the world's activities, offer God their work and the thousand-and-one concerns of their daily lives. Hour after hour of hard, conscientious work: an offering that rises up like precious incense from the four corners of the globe ... A multitude of people, rich and poor, young and old, from every country and of every race ... Millions and millions of souls spread out in time and space covering the whole surface of the earth with their invisible influx ...

Thousands – millions – of souls, like an unending peal of bells echoing towards heaven, the chimes mingling as they echo up and up.

Bells ... yes, the echo of bells sounds now in the little room, from a church nearby. A couple of hundred yards away as the crow flies, the tumbling bells of the church of our Lady of the Angels, at *Cuatro Caminos*, are pealing out in honour of their Patron.

Benedicite Dominum, omnes angeli eius ... (Ps 102:20)

Thousands – millions – of heavenly creatures carry to God, through the mediation of the Queen of the Angels, the precious offering of all those lives lived totally for him, in Him; lived, in joy and in tears, with eyes fixed on Him. And the humble prose of those ordinary lives is transformed into heroic verse, into a magnificent poem of Divine love.

Lord, so that's *what it was!*

Joy, tears of joy! [2]

Here I am, because You have called me! (1 Sam 3:5,6 & 9)

The immensity of God's mercy and His greatness ... Glory be to the Father, glory be to the Son, glory be to the Holy Spirit! Glory be to the Most Holy Trinity. Glory to our Lady: to Mary, Mother of God.

An act of thanksgiving wells up: intense, deep, wide as a river that nears the sea, unending.

II

LORD, THAT I MAY SEE!

God writes straight with crooked lines
(European proverb)

1. BARBASTRO

Lord, so thats *what it was!*

At that instant, all the events he had lived through appeared in a new light: everything, from his early years in Barbastro and Logroño to the days in Saragossa and even these first few months in Madrid – everything had clearly been a preparation for what had just taken place in his soul.

As he thought back, his earliest recollections – despite later, darker days – were of care-free happiness, of loving and attentive parents.

When he thought of his father, the picture came again into his mind's eye: short hair, elegant moustache, calm expression, eyes that sparkled with intelligence and with a joy that was never quenched, not even by hard trials. Josemaría never hesitated to confide in him all his thoughts and ideas. He did not remember having ever been severely punished – save once, and if he was sorry it was less for the smack he received than for the distress he realised he had caused by his stubbornness.

He was proud to walk by his father's side along *El Coso* – the broad promenade at the top of the town, where people would stroll around greeting relatives, friends and neighbours. Sometimes, when he grew older, their steps would take them beyond the town wall, and they would speak of more intimate things.

When the end of Autumn brought the first chilly weather, Don José would buy a bag of roast chestnuts from a vendor. Josemaría could still remember the feel of his father's hand squeezing his own and the sound of his laugh when he tried to pluck the hot chestnuts out of the bag in his father's coat pocket – getting only scorched fingers for his pains.

Winter saw sheepskin-muffled shepherds guiding their flocks along the sunken, snow-covered lanes of the Pyrenean foothills in search of more clement pastures. A donkey would be laden with packs and bundles, including a large cauldron used to prepare meals and brew up first-aid potions. The dogs would run along beside them, barking excitedly. Sometimes one of the men carried a sick sheep on his shoulders, or cradled a new-born lamb in his arms.

His mother, who was called Dolores, was kind and gentle (he had seen how beautiful she used to be from a picture painted in the first years of his parents' marriage), but strong-willed for all her gentleness. It was to her – and to the good example his father was not ashamed to give – that he owed his simple, unaffected piety: he had never forgotten those simple prayers which his parents had very early on inscribed in his memory as a child. He would still draw each day on these treasures to revive his dialogue with Our Lord. *O my Queen, my Mother*, he would often say to the Blessed Virgin, *I offer myself entirely to you and, as a proof of my loyal affection, I consecrate to you this day my eyes, my ears, my tongue and my heart* ...[1]

His mother's lessons were always eminently practical. He still smiled when he thought of what she had told him once, when he was very small. He had hidden under the bed to escape from some family friends who wanted to see the boy of the family at all costs; she made him come out by lightly tapping the floor with a walking stick. When he finally sheepishly crawled out, his mother gave him this affectionate reproach before leading him into the sitting-room: "Josemaría ... you should only be ashamed of sinning!"[2]

Peaceful years

The family house, where Josemaría was born on 9 January 1902, stood near one end of the long market-place, where he would sometimes go and play under the colonnade that surrounded it. At other times he would get together with some friends in his father's shop on the other side of the square. As was common in the region, the shop had two sides to its business, in this case trading in cloth and making chocolate, so that there would be a penetrating smell of cocoa wafting up from the basement of *"Juncosa y Escrivá"*. The children also used to go to the shop next door, which belonged to Josemaría's uncle on his mother's side – with any luck you could come away with some honey, or a few sweets.

At the school run by the Sisters of Charity both he and his sister Carmen (two-and-half years his elder) learned to read and to count. He remembered more clearly the Piarist School, where he went from the age of seven. He used to walk there every day, taking the road which led from his house to the Cathedral.

When the holidays came round it was off to Fonz, a short drive away, to stay with their grandmother (his father's mother). Once across the river the road climbed gently among almond trees and grey-green olives until suddenly, as the car turned a corner, the whole town could be seen at a glance, the houses ranged in tiers around the dominating Romanesque church.

Not only grandmother lived at Fonz, but also his uncle Mosén Teodoro, who was a priest, and his sister Aunt Josefina. Uncle Teodoro owned a property, *El Palau*, an old house set amidst vines and olive trees that stretched away on all sides as far as the eye could see.

Something Josemaría enjoyed very much as a little boy was watching the bread being made. The dough would be kneaded vigorously after a little yeast had been added and the grey, pale mounds placed inside the burning-hot oven with a long wooden shovel. The children would wait impatiently for the moment the baking was over, when the cook opened the oven door and gave them the little pastry cockerel which she had slipped in with the loaves of bread.

From the bare hills that overlooked the town the eye could see row upon row of fields and orchards, cultivated in terraces to conserve the soil. Further off, the view took in valley after valley, on and on until the foothills of the far-off Pyrenees barred the horizon.

The start of the new term always came sooner than expected, and with it the procession of days, all of them more or less the same: classes at school, then running home to find his friends, games in the market-place, reading books (something that took up more and more time as they became longer and more interesting) and talking with his parents – childish conversations at first, but becoming more involved and serious as the years passed by.

Later on, when he had a greater perspective on his childhood and his adolescent years, he came to realise that the influence his parents had had on him stemmed from their availability – they had always had time for him – and from the trust they had always shown him: they had given him more and more of a free rein as they saw him mature, teaching him (by giving him very little pocket-money for instance, so that every penny counted) to "administer his freedom well".[3]

He did not, however, feel that he had been a very manageable child. Even when he had overcome his fear of some of his mother's lady friends who always wanted to kiss him (one of them had a prickly moustache!), he would occasionally flare up in rebellion, a part of his nature which took him a long time to master. There was the incident of the chalk and duster flung against the blackboard, for instance, when he thought that the mathematics teacher had mistakenly corrected him. Then again, his anger when he was accused – falsely as it happened – of having hit a little girl. He found the injustice of it all quite unbearable. There were the memorable protests against Latin – *Latin is only for priests and monks* [4] – as well as many other trifling incidents he now smiled at.

He also knew, though, how to keep any little upsets to himself. Bitten one day by a dog, and not wanting to alarm his mother by arriving home with blood on his leg, he went first to his aunt's to get bandaged up. There was the incident the day before his First Communion. On that occasion he hid the pain caused by a burn from the hairdresser's curling tongs, which were being used to make a wave in his hair. This time too, his mother did not find out about it – at least not until some time later.

These were part of an early apprenticeship in suffering: his first encounters with the Cross on a journey that had otherwise been happy and secure.

He had started going to Confession regularly three or four years previously. As soon as he had reached the age of reason, his mother had explained the idea of the Sacrament to him in simple terms; she had helped him prepare for it, and accompanied him to her own confessor. After he had confessed his childish faults, he heard the good priest tell him to eat a fried egg. Coming out, he told his mother about this penance. His parents, good Christians but not narrow-minded, laughed about this for the rest of the week!

A Piarist priest had prepared him for several months for his First Communion – the coming of Our Lord into his soul. He was always to remember and say that formula for spiritual communion the priest had taught him: *I wish, Lord, to receive You with the purity, humility and devotion with which your Most Holy Mother received You, with the spirit and fervour of the saints.*

His first experience of the Blessed Eucharist had been in Barbastro Cathedral. There, in the apse, in the centre of the great altar-piece, was an oval aperture surrounded by little flickering lights. Behind its pane of glass, his mother explained, was Jesus: mysteriously present, perpetually awaiting men's silent adoration. During these visits to the Cathedral they would also stop in the lofty chapel of *Cristo de los Milagros* to the left of the porch, to see its ornate baldaquin. In the south aisle they would contemplate the Dormition of the Virgin lying peacefully, hands joined as in prayer, in a shrine situated beneath a panelled reredos. Finally, they would pray before the little statue of Our Lady of *El Pilar*, a replica of the Madonna venerated in Saragossa.

The family usually said the Rosary together, often in a private oratory belonging to some neighbours; on Saturdays they would say it in the church of Saint Bartholomew during the office in honour of Our Lady.

In Barbastro, the piety of the people overflowed during the

feastdays throughout the year. There were the processions and presentations of flowers to Our Lady in May. Then in July, on the feast of St Anne, the little chapel in the market-place would be adorned with a profusion of blossoms. At Christmas there would be the crib, a new one made each year but always in a similar style, with its paper and cardboard mountains and simple figures grouped around the manger by the children. Everyone would gather together and sing the simple tunes – lively rhythms, or the melodious tones of a lullaby – that expressed the joy of men at the coming of the God-Child. At night, Josemaría and his sister would be allowed to attend Midnight Mass with their parents in the Cathedral, its vast nave towering up into the night.

Although he was pious, Josemaría did not see piety as anything out of the ordinary. Like all boys of his age, he was mischievous and full of life; he would playfully pull his sister's pigtails, or sit watching his friends in the market-place with his legs stuck through the railings of the balcony, long after his mother had called him to come in.

All told, he was an obedient child and would never have done anything to cause his parents grief. Before very long, however, the joy of the Escrivá household would be mingled with tears.

Trying years

Three sisters were born after him; the first, María Asunción, when he was three, the next, María de los Dolores, when he was five, and the littlest, Rosario, when he was seven.

A year after her birth Rosario was dead. Josemaría saw his parents' grief, though they tried not to show it: he saw, too, how they tried to assuage the sorrow he felt himself. Two years later it was the body of his second sister, Lolita, that he saw in the parish church. Her coffin, its handles made of white ribbons, was carried by girls, as was the custom for the burial of young children.

The family drew closer together. This time, he could see his parents found it more difficult to hide their grief; he himself felt for a second time the nearness of untimely death. Two sisters in heaven, close to God and to the Blessed Virgin, they had explained; despite his sorrow, he thought of their eternal happiness, as well as of their presence – in a new way at home. Scarcely more than a year later, as he was playing in the colonnade around the market-place, he was overcome with a sense of foreboding; he suddenly rushed back home – knowing that his favourite sister, María Asunción (nick-named Chon), was seriously ill.

How is Chon? he asked, when his mother came out to him.

"Chon is very well; she is already in heaven", she answered softly. This time it was too much for him: he threw himself into his mother's arms in floods of tears. It was only the calmness of her face and of her voice that helped him to accept this new wrench a little better.

Although the children were not allowed in, he had gone into the bedroom and wept for a long time before the body of the little fair-haired sister he had adored.

The sympathy of friends and of those close to the family deepened; but the Escrivás, far from remaining frozen in their grief, drew from it a deepening of their Christian life and a strengthening of their mutual love.

* * *

He could see more clearly now the heroic efforts his parents had made, so that nothing should disturb the atmosphere of joy and peace that he and Carmen had always known. His father and mother loved one another. That was their secret; and they were not ashamed to show it, simply and modestly, in front of their children.

Now, after all, he could see that there was a meaning to these events – one whose depths he had never even dreamed of. They had been a long and mysterious preparation for a divine enterprise, an undertaking in which he could now see the fundamental reason for his existence. By making him suffer – through the suffering of those he loved – Our Lord had, as it were, "worked" him: like the blacksmith who gives *one blow to the nail and a hundred to the anvil*.[5]

* * *

Chon's death had made such a deep impression on him that he began to say, *Now it's my turn!*,[6] for his three sisters had died in inverse order to their age, from the youngest to the eldest.

His mother reassured him: "Don't worry. You've been put in the care of the Blessed Virgin of Torreciudad."

And she told him how, when he was two years old, he also had fallen gravely ill, so ill that the doctors had given up hope of curing him. But she had spontaneously invoked Our Lady of Torreciudad, to whom she had a special devotion. One evening he had been hardly able to speak, or even to breathe, and the two doctors looking after him gave him only a few hours to live ...

"At what time did the child die?" asked one of the doctors the next day, ready to present his condolences.

"Come and see him; he's cured," replied Don José. "A few minutes ago he was jumping around, hanging on to the railings of his cot!"

A little later, when he had completely recovered, Josemaría found himself in his mother's arms again. They were making their way slowly – on horseback – along the rough tracks that led to Torreciudad: he was going to be presented to the Blessed Virgin, in gratitude for his cure which was clearly miraculous. His mother told him that she had been very frightened, riding sidesaddle along the precipices. It was their faith, and their gratitude toward the Mother of God, that enabled them to reach the shrine safely. The shrine itself was in a little rustic chapel that overlooked the Cinca valley, and took in views of the peaks of the Pyrenees.

The family's sufferings, however, were not to end with the death of his sisters. Another very different trial was awaiting them ...

One day they had to tell the children everything. Their father's business was going from bad to worse, and he would soon have to think of closing the shop.

In 1914 this is precisely what happened. Josemaría, now twelve years old, was already perfectly capable of understanding what was happening, and of appreciating his parents' concern. They were totally ruined.

His admiration for his father grew when he discovered that he had decided to pay back the creditors in full, instead of having recourse to the possibilities of compromise that the law permitted. This gesture of honesty and loyalty was all the more remarkable in that a determining cause of the bankruptcy was the dishonest activity of a partner. "Don José Escrivá is so good," said some, "that they've taken advantage of him and played dirty."

But not all the comments had been so favourable. Failure is not forgiven lightly in small towns, and gossip is free.

For Josemaría it had all begun with certain remarks made in his presence by friends and neighbours; then people avoiding their gaze; muttered words of sympathy that were hard to fathom; snatches of his parents' conversation accidentally overheard. A vague sense of foreboding gradually gave way to the conviction that something serious was going on.

He would have so much liked to help his parents!

He saw his father grow old before his eyes, but without ever complaining, without losing anything of his elegance, or of his smile.

The family lowered its standard of living. Doña Dolores took on all the household chores from then on, and kept a tighter rein on the household expenses – without a word of complaint. The grace with which they carried this new cross which the Lord had chosen to send them was one of the greatest lessons in courage and Christian resignation which he learned from his parents. So much so, that he would often make the comparison, when he had become more familiar with Scripture, between his father's situation and that of Job, the just man in the Old Testament who was mocked by those who had been his friends because he had the misfortune to lose his wealth.

Abandoned by everyone – even by those from whom he should have been able to expect gratitude or family solidarity – Don José Escrivá's only solution was to go out and look for new

work. He searched out his faithful friends and made several unsuc-
cessful journeys before eventually settling at Logroño, capital of the
Rioja district and a good deal further west from Barbastro, though
still near the Pyrenees.

Deep roots

For Josemaría, everything continued apparently unchanged:
school, games, reading and now some music as well. He also began
to mix with grownups, when he accompanied his father in the cultural circles of Barbastro or Fonz.

As time went on, his interest in the past was awakened and
deepened. From his father himself and from his father's conversations with friends he learned about his region of Spain, Somontano,
and got to know it better. Here, where the mountains of the
Pyrenees swept down to meet the plain, had been the setting for
commercial exchange and political battles.

It was at Barbastro that the Cortes united Aragon and
Catalonia in 1137. An episcopal see since its reconquest from the
Moors in 1101 by Peter I of Aragon, it had as bishop in the eleventh
century Saint Raymond Penyafort, who died in Andalusia by the
side of King Alfonso the Warrior. Saint Vincent Ferrer, too, probably lived in Barbastro. There were no pleasant memories left
behind by the troops of Duguesclin, Constable of France, in the
fourteenth century. On 2 February 1366 they sacked the town, burning to death three hundred people who had taken refuge in the
Cathedral tower.

His teachers at the Piarist College had spoken with veneration
of their founder, Saint Joseph of Calasanz (a remote relative of his,
born in Peralta del Sal), who had exercised his ministry as a young
priest in Barbastro.

He also learned of the history of the Escrivás. The family, ori-
ginally from Narbonne, had established themselves in Balaguer
(near Lérida) in the twelfth century, shortly after its reconquest

from the Moors. Landowners at first, his ancestors had moved into the professional classes in the seventeenth century as a result of the repressive centralisation of the Castilian monarchy. His great-grandfather on his father's side, Don José María Escrivá y Manonelles, had set up practice as a doctor at Fonz, only a few miles from Barbastro.

As for the cradle of his mother's family, the Albás, that was to be found in Ainsa, a stronghold of Upper Aragon and capital of the ancient earldom of Sobrarbe. One of Josemaría's great-uncles had been Bishop of Avila. Two uncles were priests: one of them was beneficiary of Burgos Cathedral, while the other, Don Carlos Albás, was archdeacon of the chapter of Saragossa.

Don Carlos, he had discovered, had not been very understanding towards his brother-in-law José Escrivá, reproaching him for his bad business sense – and for having put his family at risk with his excessive loyalty towards his creditors.

Don José spent several months at the beginning of 1915 in Logroño, settling down to work in a business fairly similar to the one he had given up. During that time he found and prepared a house so that the family could come and live with him.

For Josemaría there were a few more months at college, exams in Lerida, then it was off to Fonz again for the Summer, a visit that was slightly tinged with melancholy, although the family would in fact continue going there for the holidays for some years.

In September, the family gathered in Barbastro to make preparations for the move to Logroño.

Very early one morning they took the coach for Huesca, turning to look back just one more time, glimpsing the houses of the town which would always have a special place in their hearts. A couple of miles further on, and they prayed as they passed the shrine of Our Lady of Pueyo, perched on a spur in the middle of the plain of Cinca.

A page had turned in the lives of the Escrivás as they entered an unknown province.

2. LOGROÑO

The family drew closer together in Logroño, partly because of the situation in which they found themselves, but also through the efforts of Josemaría's parents to ensure that the calm and good-humoured atmosphere they had always known should not be disturbed by their bad fortune. At first the family home was on the top floor (the fourth) of a house on Sagasta Street, not far from the iron bridge over the River Ebro. Don José had found a job with a dealer in textiles and clothing, Antonio Garrigosa. His shop, "The Great City of London", was on the corner of a side-street and fronted on to the main shopping thoroughfare.

They had to settle down, to find new friends and new interests. It was not easy but, little by little, thanks to a colleague of their father's, they were received first into one family, then into others.

On Sundays they would go for a stroll outside the town, over beyond the Ebro, on the road leading to the neighbouring village of Laguardia. In the distance stood the hills, rosy or blue-washed, over which cold winds blew in the winter months. If they took the direct way home, over the iron bridge, they could see the town stretched out along the broad river-banks. It seemed almost overshadowed by its church towers − first, the twin towers of the Collegiate Church; then, further over to the left, three more steeples, two of them belonging to the church of Santa Maria de Palacio – one square and massive, the other Gothic, slender and sharp as a sword. The excursion would end with afternoon tea somewhere, or they would just sit together and discuss the day's news.

A time for friends

Josemaría continued his studies at the secondary school in Logroño, where he very quickly made a number of friends among his new classmates. The people of Rioja have a frank and open character, similar to that of the Aragonese, with the same egalitarian tastes and independent outlook. Their language is proverbial throughout Spain for its Rabelaisian vigour. It is that of the winegrowers of Rioja who, after the phylloxera plague had ravaged the vines around 1870, just as it did in France, had planted vine-stocks from the Bordeaux area.

The *Instituto* (or State School) was situated on a square at one end of Market Street. If he went through the arcade and along in front of the town hall and the Collegiate Church of Saint Mary-le-Round, Josemaría would reach the corner where "The Great City of London" had its shop windows. He could, if he wanted to, go in and see his father before going home along Sagasta Street. The shop's mezzanine floor had dark wood panelling, giving it an elegant appearance. Don José, who had pitted his good will against bad luck, soon gained a reputation for professional integrity and punctuality, as well as having a pleasant, helpful attitude towards his customers.

The classes at the State School were supplemented by study and revision classes in two other schools: one was run by the Marist Brothers and the other, San Antonio, shared some of its teachers – all laymen – with the *Instituto*. Josemaría was a lively boy, but rather more serious and mature than most of the other pupils in his year. One of his friends at the *Instituto* was Isidoro Zorzano, an intelligent student and a very hard-working one. He had been born in Buenos Aires, to which his parents had emigrated from a little village in the province of Logroño. When Isidoro was still very young, his parents had moved back to their native land with the whole family.

The most noteworthy building in Logroño was the Collegiate Church, the basilica of Saint Mary-le-Round, thus called because of the polygonal Roman temple that had once stood on the same site. Its two baroque towers rose above a high and richly ornamented portal. The side chapels and the ambulatory were full of art treasures, accumulated over the centuries.

A large painting in the south aisle depicts the future Saint Francis Borgia realising the frailty of human attachments on uncovering, with horror, the decomposing face of Queen Isabella of Portugal in her coffin. Around him all the people in the scene, a bishop at their head, turn away – holding their noses in a very expressive manner.[7] In a niche in the ambulatory is carefully preserved a small painting that is thought to be the work of Michelangelo.

Josemaría carried on his secondary-school studies without any difficulties. He began to take a particular interest in the classics – literature, history and philosophy. It was at this time that he learnt to love the poetry of the Middle Ages, the great Castilian mystics, and the classical authors of the Spanish Golden Age, especially Cervantes (he enjoyed the *Novelas Ejemplares* and, even more, *Don Quixote*), and never stopped re-reading them. In these first adolescent years he also became passionately interested in the great events he heard his father discussing with his friends. In 1916, he heard of the Irish Rising, a people's outburst for their freedom and their religion after centuries of persecution; in 1918 came the end of the Great War and the difficulties of re-establishing the international balance in a Europe bled white.

He also reached the age of going out with girls – which earned him one day a wise but amusing piece of advice from his mother: "Always try to behave well, my son. And if you're thinking about serious things – if you think of marriage one day – don't forget that proverb of ours, and look for a girl who is

'Not so pretty she enthralls,
Nor yet so ugly she appals ...'"

Inklings of love

In Josemaría's case, however, the first flights of the heart had, after much hesitation, taken another direction.

It was an event without much obvious significance that had set him thinking about all that a man could do, as long as his heart was full of God's love. It had been very cold for several weeks in Logroño during December 1917. The snow of the night before had covered everything as he set off along the high street. Suddenly he noticed footprints on the otherwise immaculate snow in front of him. And there was no doubt as to what sort of prints they were. They were the marks of bare feet! Looking up he could see in the distance a Discalced Carmelite, Padre José Miguel, who came from the monastery near Logroño.

The train of inklings and convictions that people call "vocation" always has something of a mystery about it. The discovery of an undreamt-of generosity had crystallised hitherto hidden impulses; and, over the days that followed, he could not put them out of his mind. It was becoming very clear that God was asking him to be more "available": but how could he put himself at His disposal? Would he have to become a priest? The very idea, not long ago, would have made him laugh.

He also thought of his future, and about what he would like to have studied. He had told his father that he wanted to be an architect. How could a few footprints in the snow be enough to put a question mark over the whole direction of his life?

Still without telling his parents, he went gone towards the railway bridge to visit Padre José Miguel on several occasions between January and March 1918. Their chats did not help him to see very clearly within himself as yet, save on one point: he did not think that the availability Our Lord was asking of him (He alone knew why) was compatible with the conventual life proposed by his, now, spiritual director. Padre José Miguel, with all the good will in the world, wanted to persuade him that the best way of responding to the call he felt in the depths of his soul would be to enter the Carmelite Order.

But Josemaría, even if he could not yet see where the call he felt would lead him, understood this much at least: it was not, in his case, a matter of monastic vocation, an invitation to withdraw from the world. He explained this to Padre José Miguel.

Although he did not know where his path lay, he did not try to smother the restlessness he had felt ever since seeing those footprints in the snow.

It was at this point that he began to intensify his ordinary acts of devotion. Moved by a desire to purify himself more each day, he constantly invoked Our Lord, generously mortified himself, made frequent Confession, went to Mass and Holy Communion daily: for him these acts were a kind of short-cut, uniting him more closely to the Lord and enabling him to see into himself more clearly.

Despite his initial repugnance, he came back to the idea of the priesthood. For him, however, the idea of becoming a priest was just part of an overall picture of *something* for which he had to be available, which the Lord was asking of him, but which he could not see ...

One day he took the decisive step: he would speak to his father about entering the seminary.

It must have been an unexpected shock. It was the only time he ever saw tears in Don José's eyes. After a moment's silence, his father looked at him seriously: "Think carefully about it, my son. Priests have to be saints ... It's very hard not to have a family, not to have a home, not to have a love on earth. Think about it a bit more ... But I won't oppose your wishes."

It was only later that he realised what heroism there was in that simple phrase. His father had suffered so much, and had already planned another sort of future for him. On Don José's advice he visited the Dean of the Collegiate Church, Don Antolín Oñate, and a military chaplain recently moved to Logroño, Don Albino Pajares – a man well-known for his piety and his wisdom. He was not very enthusiastic about the possibilities they conjured up: a country parish, a cathedral chapter, diocesan curia, director of a seminary ... He did not see himself "making a career for himself" in ecclesiastical circles! But his desire to respond to the call of Our Lord, pressing, yet still mysterious, was stronger still: he would be a priest.

As they had promised, his parents did nothing to make him go back on his decision. Without letting it be seen, they renounced their plans as well as their hopes that he might help them to recover the family patrimony.

On his side, it was not without some heartache that he decided to respond to the incomprehensible will of God by entering the seminary. As if to compensate for his leaving, he asked the Lord to send his parents another son to take his place in the family. Once he was gone, the only child remaining to his parents would be his sister Carmen.

A new era in his life was starting. But for him it seemed nothing more than a step forward, a step towards something else. "Why desire to be a priest, if you don't want to be a holy priest?" his father had asked him gravely. He certainly did not envisage the priesthood as separate from the search for holiness; but his call to serve souls was inscribed within another vocation, one no less precise but one which he had not yet come to identify. That was why, despite his decision (which, he felt, was the right one), he continued to feel a curious sensation, as if he were half-blind, forever seeking the "why"? "Why am I becoming a priest? The Lord wants something; but what?" And he began to repeat, like the blind man at Jericho when Christ passed by: *Lord, that I may see! "Domine, ut videam! Ut sit!" Lord, may 'that thing' be done, 'that' thing — I don't know what it is — You want me to do, ...* [8]

A change of habits

His life henceforth, from November 1918, was ordered in a very different way. In the mornings he would go to Mass at the seminary, which stood in one corner of the *Espolón* (a vast square in the centre of the town); he would come home for breakfast, and return to the seminary for classes until the end of the morning.

Acting on advice from the Rector of the Seminary and the bishop, he adopted a private plan of study which took into account the subjects he had been studying in college up until then, and laid great stress on Latin – it had finally come to that! – and philosophy. He was given tutors to help him in his studies.

In the seminary he limited himself that year to what posed the fewest problems: the history of the Church, archaeology, canon law, pastoral theology, French and sociology. The following year he got to grips with fundamental theology.

He did not find his new studies too difficult. Besides, his upbringing and his taste for the classics put him at an advantage in comparison with the other students.

The other seminarians found him a bit reserved, no doubt, but it was a time when he made great friendships, of the kind that do not fall away with the passing of the years. He often spoke to his fellow-students and his teachers about the secondary school he had just left, and about the urgent necessity of giving these young people, who in a few years would be intellectuals, leading citizens, men of great influence, a truly Christian spirit.

On Sunday mornings he would take part in the catechism classes organised by his fellow-students in the seminary church for the children of the suburbs of Logroño. He did this on his own initiative, for as an external student he was under no obligation to help. But he was a seminarian, just like all the others. And he would be a priest when the time came.

But there still remained in him the deep conviction that he had not entered the seminary "for that reason alone". There was a call to something else in the premonitions awakened in him by the sight of a few footprints in the snow in a street in Logroño; but what that something was he still could not see. He intensified his prayer still more.

Lord, what do You want me to do? he would repeat, making his own the cry of the prophets of the Old Testament, their generous response to Yahweh when he had burst into their lives, asking them to accomplish some great work with Him ... and he would add, again taking his inspiration from the Bible: *"Here I am, because You have called me"* (1 Sam 3:5,6 & 9).

At such moments it seemed as if God were playing with him, leading him where He wanted without his realising it. When the revelation finally came on 2 October 1928, he understood: everything was clear.

Some two months after he had entered the seminary his mother announced to Carmen and Josemaría that they would soon have a little brother or a little sister. His daring request had thus been heard! It was one more sign that what he was doing was part of a precise plan of Providence.

On 28 February 1919 his brother Santiago was born ...

The following summer he returned once more to Fonz, to his friends and to the countryside of his childhood days.

He had always had the idea of taking on the law studies his father had advised. During the academic year 1919-20 this project took a definite form, and he considered asking to be transferred to the seminary in Saragossa. He had obtained a half-scholarship for this course, and the help his family could give would make up the rest of the fees.

On Tuesday, 28 September 1920, he entered the majestic Major Seminary of San Carlos in Saragossa, leaving with the somewhat surprised porter the pipe and tobacco he had been using for several months in Logroño ...

3. SARAGOSSA

During his years in Saragossa the Lord led him by the hand and, as it were, closed His hand more tightly on Josemaría's.

He understood now the sufferings which had marked this stage of his life, and the consolations he had felt in his soul – *a set of graces which followed one after the other and which I did not know how to call. And so I said they were 'operative', for they had such a hold on my will that I hardly had to make any effort.* [9] They had but anchored still more firmly within him the call, irresistible and yet still shadowy, that he had felt since his adolescent years. These were months of interior maturing, intense prayer, increased penance, acceptance in advance of whatever a still-impenetrable Providence was preparing for him.

He had gone as soon as he could to lay his uncertainties at the feet of the Virgin of "El Pilar", well-known through all the towns and villages of Aragon. *Domine, ut sit!* had long been his plea, often repeated, asking God to enlighten him further: Lord, may it be! Now, before the little statue perched on its marble column (similar to the figure of Our Lady who, according to a tradition, had appeared to the Apostle James), Josemaría addressed this same prayer to the Blessed Virgin. My Lady, Our Lady, may it be! He had even, on the feast of Our Lady of Ransom some four years after entering the seminary, engraved these words – in what he qualified as *very low* Latin under the base of a plaster statuette representing the Virgin of El Pilar: *Domina, ut sit!* [10]

A difficult adaptation

Without his wishing it so, his manners clashed with the rather uncouth behaviour of many of his classmates who had come straight in from the surrounding countryside. He spent whole hours in the loft overlooking the immense baroque reredos of the chapel while they were asleep or playing sports. Their jokes made him suffer, as did the scornful nickname of "the mystical rose" that some of them gave him behind his back.

Despite these difficulties, he never wanted to see anything but the virtues and the generosity of his fellow-students in the seminary. Besides, he made some very close friends there.

These knocks had helped to mature him. His Canon Law lecturer in the University of Saragossa, Don Elías Ger Puyuelo, had tactfully made him realise this. The tutor had explained how, after fruitless efforts to get replacements from Germany for the millstones of a little cinnamon-grinder that had worn down, he had hit upon the idea of replacing them with little round pebbles picked from a stream, which had lost their rough edges as a result of constant friction. "I think you understand me, Escrivá?" Don Elías had said.

Josemaría never forgot that lesson in common sense, given in the style of a science lesson. From the friction between different characters the soul gains the "polish" that is needed in order to bring harmony to any group.

It was, on top of all this, the first time he had lived in a seminary as a boarder. He wore the uniform: a black sleeveless tunic and a red felt band over the shoulders. The band came to a point in front, the two ends being joined by a metal badge with a sun and the word *caritas* on it.

He also adhered to the strict timetable in full: half an hour's meditation in the morning, followed by Mass, breakfast and then classes at the Pontifical University; lunch, more classes at the University, recreation, study, Rosary and dinner. And before going to bed there were prayers and a short talk during which the points of the next day's meditation were announced.

The first two floors of the San Carlos building were used as a priests' residence. The seminary proper, called the seminary of San Francisco de Paula in memory of the patron saint of its founder, Cardinal Benavides, only started on the third floor.

According to a plaque fixed to the cloister wall, Saint Vincent de Paul had lived there while he was studying in Saragossa, although not everyone was convinced of this.

As in most old buildings of grandiose proportions, the corridors were cold and enormously long, and the majority of the rooms were large and poorly furnished.

On Sundays, Thursdays and feast days the seminarians went for a walk in the countryside around Saragossa. Apart from the times of recreation this was their only spell of relaxation.

Josemaría had forced himself to bend to a change in habits that was painful for him. But he put this ordered life to good use, deepening his interior life and broadening his religious culture. It was at this time that he drew a lot from his re-reading of the Castilian mystics – notably Saint Teresa of Avila, whose works he already knew. He had made a habit of reading the New Testament every day, trying to relive the Gospel scenes as if he were actually there, engraving the verses in his memory and on his heart. He also gained a greater understanding of the liturgy as well as greater ease in praying.

He studied hard. Although the curriculum was set at a higher level, it was similar to that of the seminary in Logroño. He obtained brilliant results in the various theology examinations at the Pontifical University.

That effort he had offered to God, asking Him for more grace so that His will – so cloudy and mysterious – might be revealed.

Why be a priest?

   Lord, he would repeat incessantly, *why do you want me here, in this seminary? Why do You want me to be a priest?* [11]

   His prayer would come back again and again to those familiar and insistent cries: *Domine, ut sit! Domina, ut sit!* [12] Lord, may *it* be! Our Lady, may *it* be!

   He would have long conversations, walking round the cloisters, with those friends of his who did not spend the recreation time playing with a ball in a room on the fourth floor.

   Four or five of them would meet in this way and comment on the little incidents of the day, or on events in the news. Josemaría would amuse them by reading out epigrams that he had composed (sometimes in Latin, sometimes in Spanish, caricaturing the style of some ancient Greek satirist or some author of the Spanish Golden Age) which he then wrote in a notebook. His facility in versification earned him one day the unsought for, but unavoidable, task of composing and reading in public a poem in honour of the auxiliary bishop of Saragossa, who was the president of the seminary. This he did with a composition which he entitled *"Obedientia tutior"*: it's safer to obey! It was the motto of the bishop ...

   His family was very happy to have him back in Logroño for the summer holidays. In the Summers of 1921 and 1922 he came back with a friend – who, in his turn, invited him to his own family home near Teruel. This fellow-student also happened to be a nephew of the vice-president of the seminary, Don Antonio Moreno. Josemaría was very much at ease in the relaxed family atmosphere; everyone was careful to take into account the fact that he was a seminarian.

   At the seminary he had been singled out, although he did not know it, by the Archbishop of Saragossa, Cardinal Soldevila, who questioned him about his studies and his family.

   Both Cardinal Soldevila and the Rector of the Seminary of San Francisco de Paula knew well the qualities of this seminarian, so that on his return from the Summer vacation of 1922, two years after entering the seminary of San Carlos, he discovered that he had been named *Superior*.

To be *Superior* he had to receive the tonsure. It was Cardinal Soldevila himself who conferred it on him, in the chapel of the episcopal palace, on 28 September of that year. From that day on he wore a cassock with a cape and broad-brimmed hat. Very often, when putting it on, he would kiss the cassock as a sign of his love for the priesthood he was preparing for. In December he received the four Minor Orders: Doorkeeper and Lector on the 17th, Exorcist and Acolyte on the 21st.

During his years as *Inspector* – from 1922 until he left the seminary – he always tried to make sure that the discipline did not weigh too heavily on the companions he had been given to look after. He felt he had achieved this. The younger ones were, by nature, rowdy; but an affectionate glance, an encouraging smile or a little gesture sufficed to quieten them down. In the dining-room he would dispense with the rule of silence whenever he felt there was a valid reason: the seminarians would immediately erupt enthusiastically.

Josemaría was allowed to go out more freely than the others. This permitted him to visit the basilica of "El Pilar" every day, though he always returned quickly and plunged once more into his programme of study or reading.

In the academic year 1922-1923 he put his original plan to study Law into effect. After obtaining the required permission from his superiors he enrolled at the University of Saragossa as an external student. At the beginning, because of the seminary timetable and his duties as an Inspector, he could not attend the course regularly. As he did not want to follow the two courses simultaneously, he sat his examinations at the Pontifical University in June, and for the Law exams in September. That Summer of 1923 he studied a lot in Logroño, where a friend of his father who was a registrar of mortgages gave him private lessons together with his own son. Thus, in September, he surmounted this hurdle without any difficulty.

Sad events

At the end of the year 1922-1923 there occurred an event that outraged not only Saragossa but the whole of Spain. On the afternoon of 4 June 1923, Cardinal Soldevila arrived at a school he had founded near Saragossa. Just as he was getting out of the car he was assassinated. It was soon discovered that the attack was carried out by members of an anarchist group.

Five days later, the solemn funeral of the Cardinal was celebrated in the basilica of "El Pilar" in the presence of the Spanish Cardinals and of the representatives of the Pope, the Parliament, the government and the municipal authorities. Josemaría was there with all the other seminarians. He prayed sorrowfully, still overcome by the loss of a man he had admired and who had always treated him with affection.

During the academic year 1923-1924 Josemaría was able to go to the faculty of Law on a more regular basis. As a result of this and of the private tuition he had received in the summer, he made quite rapid progress in his civil studies.

On 14 June he was made a subdeacon. His cassock did not pass unnoticed among the students, who at first showed their deference by keeping a distance he considered excessive. Nevertheless, he met good new friends there whom he tried to help to come closer to God. Although they had all been brought up in the Catholic faith, they were often lukewarm and neglected their devotions, or did them out of routine. He talked to them and would often carry on his conversations in the streets of Saragossa, or even in the seminary of San Carlos. He taught some of his friends Latin, as they needed it for their Canon Law subjects.

One day, towards the beginning of that same academic year, in October 1923, he had a fight with another seminarian, much older than himself. Some blows were struck. They were both punished − rather unjustly in his case, for the other seminarian had grossly insulted him and had struck him first. Josemaría had offered this humiliation to the Lord, using it as another means of purification to bring him sooner to a clearer understanding of God's will.

Then, in 1924, came another family tragedy, which affected him deeply ...

The summer before, to his great joy, he had been able to spend some time with his parents, his little brother Santiago and his sister Carmen. He had been struck, however, by the way his father had aged before his time. Despite everything, they had arranged to meet in December, when he would be ordained Deacon.

On 27 November, a telegram arrived at the seminary asking him to come to Logroño as quickly as possible: his father was seriously ill.

A shop assistant was waiting for him at the station. He told him how Don José had been taken ill that very morning. A few minutes before that, his father had meditated in front of an image of the Blessed Virgin of the Miraculous Medal, as he did every day. Then he had played for a little while with young Santiago.

Just before they arrived at the house Josemaría was told the whole truth: Don José had died that very morning.

Josemaría climbed the two floors to his parents' flat in silence; he entered and embraced his mother and sister, and knelt by his father's body.

He returned to Saragossa after spending a few days with his family, trying to meditate on the meaning of this new trial which had been added to those his family had endured over the past years.

The ceremony of the Diaconate in the baroque chapel of San Carlos had not, after all, been the joyful occasion he had been anticipating. He spent 20 December alone, offering God the disappointment of not being with his mother, his brother and his sister, who had remained in Logroño. He could not arrange for them to move to Saragossa until the beginning of 1925, when they settled in a small flat at Urrea Street, not far from the seminary of San Carlos.

Priestly ordination

Preparations for the great day, when he would become a priest forever, were at last begun.

On 18 March he and his fellow ordinands were on retreat before their ordination, meditating on the dignity of the priesthood and what it meant.

The ceremony took place on Saturday, 28 March, in the chapel of the seminary of San Carlos. After prostrating themselves before the altar, the ten ordinands, their stoles draped diagonally across their white albs, approached the officiating bishop to receive the laying-on of hands – the *matter* of the Sacrament of Holy Order. The officiating bishop then implored God's help and recited the long prayer of consecration before anointing the hands of the new priests, who then vested in chasubles and received the chalice and paten, concelebrating the rest of the Mass with the bishop.

For the first time, and with deep emotion, Josemaría had brought Christ onto the earth by pronouncing the words of the consecration: *"Hoc est enim Corpus Meum ... Hic est enim calix Sanguinis Mei"* – this is My Body, this is the cup of My Blood. In the name of Christ, in the person of Christ, he had carried out the Sacrifice of the altar by which the whole Church lives.

On the following Monday, 30 March, he said his first solemn Mass in the Lady Chapel of the basilica of "El Pilar". Because of their recent bereavement, only the family and a few close friends were present. His uncle, Don Carlos Albás, was conspicuous by his absence: he had not put himself out, either, for the funeral of his brother-in-law in Logroño. His sister, Doña Dolores, had come and settled with her children in Saragossa on the initiative of Josemaría, and Don Carlos Albás was annoyed that they had not asked for his advice ...

Another little occurrence kept the pinpricks of disappointment always present, even in the midst of his greatest joys. Like all young priests, he had dreamed of giving Communion first to his mother. But as he went down to her, another woman moved in front, obliging him to begin the giving of Holy Communion with her.[13]

Once a priest, he was at the disposal of his bishop, ready to fulfil any pastoral charge the latter might wish to give him. Given his family situation – he had his mother, his sister and his brother to look after – he would normally have been given a parish in Saragossa: this would have enabled him to give classes in his spare time in order to provide for them. However, three days after his ordination his superiors asked him to make his way to Perdiguera, a little village some fifteen miles to the north-east of Saragossa, to stand in for the parish priest, who had fallen ill.

He obeyed promptly. But it was obvious that there was something peculiar about this arrangement, which was so inconvenient for him ...

The life of a country priest

The next morning, 31 March, the Tuesday of Holy Week, found Josemaría on the road to Perdiguera, ready to grapple with this first occasion to serve Our Lord in the priestly ministry.

The twin towers and multiple domes of "El Pilar" had disappeared behind him. The road first climbed, then skirted around the grey hills which were brightened periodically by yellow splashes of flowering broom. He passed a village, then a Carthusian monastery looking down over vineyards and olive trees. More hills, more fields and, in the distance, the blue silhouette of the "Sierra de Alcubierre".

Soon the village appeared on the crest of a rise, lying as if asleep in the middle of its wheat fields and pastures. It was a poor little market town, numbering scarcely eight hundred souls in all. The white-washed houses had one, occasionally two, floors. When he arrived at the main square a young boy came up to greet him and offered to carry his suitcase. He was the son of the sacristan. His father, who was ill, had sent him in his place to try to help the new priest to find his bearings in the ceremonies of Holy Week – they could be quite disconcerting for a newly ordained young priest.

The church on the hill was tall and elegant, its square tower crowned with a circular gallery and decorated in the *mudéjar* style popular in Aragon.

Josemaría knelt in the nave before the Renaissance reredos that surrounded the tabernacle. The Madonna was an Aragonese matron holding the Child upright in her left arm, surrounded by scenes from the life of Christ and the Blessed Virgin. To the right was a primitive little confessional which could not be entered without stooping.

At first he would spend hours waiting for penitents and eventually they came: an old lady, then two, then three. A first man plucked up courage and others followed very quickly.

One day, however, he was hurt by a remark which he had overheard from the porch, just as he was leaving the church, unnoticed by a group of youths who were chatting noisily: "Be careful of the new priest: for two pins he'd have got me confessing even the bits I didn't want to say!"

He took his job as a country priest very seriously. Every day he sang Mass; in the evenings he presided over the recitation of the Rosary and Benediction; there was, as well, an hour's Exposition every Thursday. And then there were the catechism classes ...

The villagers repaid his affection. He found no difficulties in taking to them with complete trust as he visited them in their homes : in two months he had visited each family at least once.

He spoke to the sick, encouraging them and bringing them to the Sacraments, making himself available day and night.

The family with whom he lodged had kept the best room in the house for him; it was to the right of the ground floor passageway, next to the kitchen. It had a low ceiling and rudimentary furniture. The large iron bedstead had copper knobs which started to rattle against the other ornaments at the head and feet when one climbed into bed. One really had to climb because to make it comfortable they had put several layers of mattresses, eiderdowns, blankets and bed-covers on it ...

These good folk never knew that Don Josemaría slept on the floor most nights ...

So as not to put his hosts out, he also forced himself to eat whatever they prepared for him. Intending to please him they made him eat too much fatty food, which was not good for his health. As a result he put on a lot of weight in those first few weeks.

They had a boy who spent the whole day out in the fields with the goats.

It was from this lad, unexpectedly, that Don Josemaría learned a lesson which he was then able to put to good use in his interior life. One day, trying to make him understand what the joy of Heaven would be like, Don Josemaría had asked him:

What would you like to do if you were rich?

"What does being rich mean?", the boy had asked.

Being rich means having lots of money, having a bank ...

"What's a bank?"

So Don Josemaría had tried to explain things another way:

Being rich means having lots of land, and having very big cows instead of having goats. It means going to meetings, and changing your clothes three times a day ... What would you do if you were very rich?

The boy's eyes suddenly lit up

"If I was rich, I'd have wine with every bowl of soup!"

Human ambitions can be reduced to such little things![14]

Don Josemaría had indeed learned a lot in the course of the two months he had spent in this forgotten village. There were the moving answers of simple souls when the treasures of Christ's Sacraments were opened to them; there was the silent encouragement of Our Lord in the tabernacle; even the miserable gossip that, after a while, he realised was directed against him, probably because he was seen devoting time to prayer which others might have devoted to playing cards or chatting with the influential people of the village – the mayor, the doctor, the town clerk ... He had found out that he was uncharitably called "the Mystic", which revived some bad memories from his days at the seminary at Saragossa. It hurt him very much, for it meant a lack of reverence towards Our Lady.

He would never forget Perdiguera, with its dusty streets, its massive church, and the road he would often take as a short walk through the fields before arriving back at his house with its low, whitewashed walls.

Return to Saragossa

On 18 May 1925 he returned to the diocesan capital, recalled by his bishop.

In the course of the next two years he went again several times to the little villages around Saragossa, to supply parishes in need. His main pastoral work was, however, in Saragossa itself. He was thus able to lodge with his mother. After carrying out various pastoral tasks he had been given to perform, notably that of chaplain at the church of Saint Peter Nolasco, he continued with his Law studies in the evenings. He went to Saint Peter's every day to say Mass and, as at university, he found new opportunities there for apostolate.

He spent many hours hearing confessions there and carried out an extensive catechetical programme. On Sundays he would also accompany some young students who gave catechism classes to children in a suburb to the south-west of Saragossa, near the Casablanca district.

At the beginning of 1926, even before obtaining his degree, he was already earning some money by giving classes at a school which had just been opened by a young army officer. The "Instituto Amado" prepared students for entry into the military academies – Saragossa's had just been opened – and various subjects were taught relating to the curricula of other colleges and faculties.

Apart from his intense pastoral work, study and reading took up the rest of the day already well filled with prayer and administering the Sacraments.

But more than ever he was looking for an answer to that question still unanswered; *Lord, what do you want of me?*

At the centre of her chapel enshrined in the basilica of "El Pilar", Our Lady listened to his unceasing request: *Domina, ut videam!*

"I have come to bring fire on the earth and I have no greater wish but that it be enkindled." "*Ignem veni mittere in terram!*" (Luke 12:49) He would repeat these words with his heart overflowing with love for Jesus Christ. He would say them again and again, and even sing them to a tune he had made up, when he believed himself to be alone.[15]

The end of his Law studies in January 1927 gave him the possibility of thinking seriously about moving to Madrid. There, he would be able to round off his studies with a doctorate, something not then possible in Saragossa.

His relationship with his uncle, the canon, and his other relatives had been rather strained since his father's death. Going up to the capital would indeed be to enter an unknown world. But it would also mean more opportunities to serve souls, and probably to discover the more specific path to which God was calling him.

There had been no extraordinary revelation, no special call influencing his decision. God had made use of the ordinary ways of Providence. Having carefully considered the pros and cons, he had made enquiries and told his mother about his plans. Still unaware of the promptings in his soul that had moved her son to become a priest, she must have wondered about his future. So she went with her two children to Fonz, to stay with Uncle Teodoro until she could rejoin Josemaría in Madrid.

On 17 March 1927 Monsignor Rigoberto Doménech, the Archbishop of Saragossa, gave him written permission to move to the capital in order to finish his studies.

4. MADRID

"The Foundation for the Sick" occupied one section of a block on Santa Engracia Street, between Gallego Street and Marañón Road. It was an impressive building in the Mauresque style, its facade ornamented with mosaics and patterns picked out in projecting bricks. One side was taken up by the church where Don Josemaría said Mass every day for the sick and the poor, together with the nuns who looked after them and for other people of the district.

As soon as he had arrived in Madrid, Father Escrivá had gone to pay his compliments to the bishop, Don Leopoldo Eijo y Garay, who had read the letter of introduction from the Archbishop of Saragossa. He immediately gave the young priest permission to preach and hear confessions in the diocese of Madrid.

Every priest needs a livelihood, and Don Josemaría was soon appointed chaplain of the charitable institution "The Foundation for the Sick". The Congregation running it – the Apostolic Ladies of the Sacred Heart – had been founded at the beginning of the century by an Asturian noblewoman, Doña Luz Rodriguez Casanova.

Father Escrivá lived in a priests' residence in Larra Street which was also founded by the Apostolic Ladies. He was one of the youngest of the ten or twelve priests who lived there, which meant that he had the job of running little errands for the older priests, and sometimes of keeping them company! He had breakfast at the residence, but spent the rest of the day out and about, absorbed in activities which gave him hardly any time for rest.

Untiring activity

He had very quickly gone beyond the brief given him for the Foundation: to say Mass, take Holy Communion to bedridden nuns, give Benediction with the Blessed Sacrament ... He also looked after the sick, talking to them, encouraging them and trying to revitalise their faith.

He learned a lot from them, from those who came to the Foundation and from those he went to visit, often in the deprived suburbs and outlying districts. There he saw the extent of the misery, both of those who admitted their destitution and of the *shamefaced poor* who hid their poverty behind apparently middle-class apartment blocks. What a lesson it was for him![16]

Wealth does not always lie where one thinks. These people, poor as the world measures poverty, were sometimes living witnesses of the spirit of the Beatitudes.

As in Saragossa, he also taught catechism to the children from the "free schools" of Madrid; he heard their confessions and prepared them to make their First Holy Communion.

At the same time he worked on his doctorate in Civil Law. There were also the lectures he gave in Roman Law and Canon Law at the "Academia Cicuéndez" – a private academy similar to the "Instituto Amado" in Saragossa – providing him with extra means and at the same time giving him the chance to continue his apostolate with students.

At the end of 1927 his mother, sister and brother moved to Madrid, to Fernando el Católico Street, not far from the Foundation for the Sick, and he went to live with them.

Prayer, in a life brimful of activity, continued to take pride of place, and he persevered in it, repeating constantly: *Lord, that I may see! Domine, ut videam!*

Some glimmerings of an answer had appeared, from time to time, in this continual semi-darkness; but when put together they did not constitute the clear response he needed ...

2 October 1928

Why the light should have come during these days of recollection, in this era of this life when everything seemed, if not fixed, at least ordered in a more stable way, he had no idea. Why now and not earlier? Or later? Why in this moment of relative peace and not in one of greater pressure?

He was not able to say. God knows best. Divine Providence, working as it does through the most insignificant – sometimes the most bewildering – events, traces its path in the hearts of men, working at a pace that is neither slow nor fast but entirely its own; it was a pace, having at last seen clearly what it was he was called to do, he would from now on faithfully try to proceed at: *God's pace* .[17]

Ecce ego, quia vocasti me!

"Here I am, because You have called me!" (1 Sam 3; 5, 6 & 9)

III

AS WATER MAKES ITS WAY THROUGH THE MOUNTAINS

Hope sees that which is not yet, but which will be.
Charles Péguy

1. MADRID: 1929, 1930

Here I am, because you have called me! (1 Sam 3:5,6 & 9).

Don Josemaría often repeated these words after 2 October 1928.[1] At the same time he was well aware of the immensity of the task to be carried out, a task that was all the more overwhelming in that it did not, he was convinced, proceed from a sudden flash of inspiration but from a divine Plan of which he had been completely unaware. How puny the means appeared in the face of such a gigantic vision! Beginning with himself, he thought he was a *deaf and clumsy tool*,[2] who had been so slow to see what God wanted of him. All told, he had but his *twenty-six years, the grace of God and a sense of humour.*[3]

The grace of God would not fail him. That is why his first reaction after 2 October 1928 was to pray even more intensely, following that supernatural logic so remarkably different from poor human logic: *First prayer; then, atonement; in the third place, very much 'in the third place', action.*[4]

How could he be faithful to the divine Will, if God himself did not do the essential work? *Lord, I am worth nothing, I can do nothing, I know nothing, I am nothing ...*[5] These words, so often on his lips since the first stirrings of his vocation as a fifteen year old, he now said with even greater conviction. In return he obtained a feeling of great confidence in the future: "That which He has once promised, God can bring to fruition." (Rom 4:21)

Opening the breach

Interior purification, reparation for his lack of correspondence and for the sins of all the world, in union with Christ's sufferings on the Cross, so as to be as docile as possible to what God wants ...

Ignem veni mittere in terram! (Luke 12:49), Josemaría had sung in his teenage years, words which his young brother had learned by heart simply by hearing them so often ... Yes, it was a fire that must be enkindled and spread to the four corners of the earth! And how much strength he would need to ensure that this flame was *not a will-o'-the-wisp: an illusion, a dying fire, that neither sets ablaze what it touches nor gives off any heat.* [6] Such a fire could only spring from generosity. *How beautiful it is to give up this life for that Life!* [7] Love has to be shown in deeds. And there was so much to do! Indeed, everything: of that great task which God wished to achieve through him, nothing as yet existed.

So Josemaría undertook a series of mortifications – using a cilice, disciplines and fasting – which he made more severe each time, while he also intensified his work, offering his tiredness for that same intention.

Who claims that corporal penances belong to the Middle Ages? In the middle of twentieth-century Madrid, at the beginning of the so-called "mad years" – the 1930s – a young priest of twenty-six, feeling inexperienced and almost helpless before the immensity of what he was about to undertake, was opening a new path to God on the earth to the rhythm of his discipline and his prayers ...

But so many graces would be needed to open the first furrow in the as-yet uncultivated soil that he would have to obtain supernatural "reinforcements" from others.

Don Josemaría asked his friends to pray for "an intention very dear to him". Sometimes he would even approach a priest in the street, if his bearing led him to think that this was someone who lived his priesthood seriously. After the first moment of surprise the priest thus accosted would smile, acquiesce and pass on his way, still pensive, no doubt, at the daring of this unknown colleague ...

He also counted on the prayers of the poor and the sick, all-powerful before the Omnipotent if they but knew how to unite themselves to Christ the Redeemer. It was not without reason that Providence had brought him to the Foundation for the Sick as chaplain since his arrival in Madrid. It would be from these above all that the strength he needed would come. This plan of God would take shape and grow thanks to the scores of men and women who generously made over the alms of their prayers and sufferings to this young, unknown priest.

These would be the weapons with which to conquer! That was the treasure with which to pay![8] Those were the means to open up this new path of holiness in the midst of the world.

Lastly, action: last in the order of priorities only, not in order of time. From the very beginning everything worked together, since it was necessary to look for the people to do this completely new "thing"; those to whom he could propose the enthralling (though demanding) ideal of taking Our Lord into the heart of all human activities and raising them to Him through constant work, carried out in a spirit of self-denial, *facing God*:[9] the ideal of a life given drop by drop – without holding anything back.

But, on the other hand, why create something new? Could he not seek to unite his efforts to those of some institution that already existed and with similar aims and spirit to those God was asking of him, and where he would be able to serve, obeying? It would, after all, be a way of fulfilling the divine Will without adding yet another foundation to the many that already enriched the life of the Church.

At the same time as he looked around him to see if there might not be some Christians capable of responding to this new vocation, he also carefully studied the statutes of a number of lay associations which already existed or were just being formed. He wanted to see if the aims of one or other of them might fit in with the plan that God had shown him on 2 October 1928.

Towards the end of 1929 a number of documents arrived from two other countries in Europe. There was nothing that provided, even remotely, what he was looking for. The aims and objectives of the groups were high, but limited. There was nothing about moving Christians to pledge their whole lives to the service of Christ, with the specific vocation to holiness in the middle of the world. And so, despite hesitations (which, in his humility, he attributed to weakness), he soon had to admit that God wanted him to follow the most difficult route – to open up a new path of sanctity in the Church.

Seeking out the first vocations

More than ever, the goal seemed out of proportion, an act of complete madness! But a madness willed by God ... Thus, overcoming his initial reluctance to be the founder of anything, Josemaría had no doubt about starting on different lines, and set to work with the only help on which he could rely: God's, because it was He who had asked him for *this*, and with the intercession of Our Lady and of the angels and saints ...

He had been thinking since 2 October of the people he knew: pupils in the Academia Cicuéndez, office workers, students, labourers, young people related to his family circle, friends, priests ...

Visits, conversations, letters, soon followed ... He sought out souls one by one, testing them and encouraging them first of all to be more sensitive to the demands of Our Lord. For the moment it was not a matter of talking to them straight away about this specific plan of God's, the existence of which he alone knew. So he had to prepare, with patience, those whose human qualities and solid Christian life would predispose them to accept, some day soon, this new "madness" of divine love – if such was their vocation. He had to lead them along the ways of the interior life: prayer, the Sacraments, penance. Thus they might grow stronger and fall so much in love with Jesus Christ that they would be ready to give Him their will, for whatever He might want of them. Only in this way, in soil turned over and fertilised by prayer and sacrifice, could he plant the divine seed conserved so carefully in his soul. Only then could he reveal to them the call to be *an apostle of apostles* [10] in the midst of the world, without their having to leave the place where they were, without changing the exterior of their lives of work or study, but divinising everything they touched because, step by step, despite repeated falls, they would become more "of God".

There were few people to whom Don Josemaría could speak about the mission he had received from Our Lord. He had, it is true, revealed it to Padre Sánchez Ruiz, a Jesuit who was held in high esteem, and who later would be his confessor; although he would always be careful to distinguish the domain of advice received for his soul from that of the tasks required of his mission as founder, and in which spiritual direction would have no reason to interfere.

In June 1929 he also told one of his friends from Saragossa, José Romeo, about it.

He said nothing to his own family. His mother, brother and sister noticed that he was exerting himself more and more, with journeys across Madrid to see the sick in their hovels and to visit the hospitals, holding long conversations at home or in the streets with groups of friends or with some young men he was guiding in their spiritual life, whom he would sometimes meet at a bench in the park of *El Retiro* .

The Father, as some began to call him, had a special attraction, with his kind, broad face. He was of medium height. He wore the horn-rimmed, round spectacles of the period. He was always very careful with his appearance, at home or in the street; when he went out he would wear a cape and a wide-brimmed hat of the type worn by the Roman clergy.

He had an open and pleasant character and a contagious cheerfulness. When he talked, he expressed his ideas with a fervour that was manifest in the firmness of his voice and accent, typical of his native Aragon. The strength of his conviction earned him the support of others who quickly realised, just by listening to him, that they were dealing with a man of God.

Often, in his smile or in his keen glance, full of warmth, there was that "something" which inspired trust and, at the same time, seemed to be an invitation and an encouragement to become better.

Those who approached him would have understood the influence he had over them better if they had known that when he was alone with God, feeling himself so young, so tempted to let his exuberance burst out, he would ask the Lord for *eighty years of dignity*:[11] an outward sign, to him, *of the order and purity of the life within.* [12] Or if they had known of his prayer and his generous mortifications for each one of them ... if they had seen how he would not address himself to the slightest problem without placing himself heart and soul in the presence of God, often kissing a little crucifix he would lay on the table he was working at, so as not to lose sight of the supernatural point of view ...

Attracted by the Father's influence, many people came to confide in him and to ask him for advice regarding aspects of their interior lives.

One day in 1929 he discovered a convenient meeting-place – a "chocolate parlour" by the name of *El Sotanillo*, situated in the central street of Alcalá between Cibeles and Independencia. It was the sort of place where you could chat without bothering, or being bothered by, anybody.

The Father would meet friends there, exchanging views and impressions in a relaxed manner about the news or professional matters: it was like the *tertulia*, a form of get-together that was almost an institution in many Spanish towns. He would also invite the young men with whom he was in contact to meet at the Sotanillo.

The tone of the conversation you might overhear in this particular group, formed round a priest, would probably not have very much in common with the conversations going on around them. From the thousand-and-one little events of daily life – the Father was very amusing, and knew how to bring out the comical side of things – the mind would be drawn to the most elevated of considerations. The expressions on their faces would pass from laughter to gravity as Don Josemaría spoke about living a demanding Christian life: about prayer; about reading the Gospels so as to get get to know the Master better; about addressing the Blessed Virgin and the guardian angels; about getting to know Our Lord better through mental prayer – *each day try to find a few minutes of that blessed solitude which you so much need to keep your interior life going*;[13] about frequent attendance at Mass, *centre of the interior life*;[14] about the Holy Eucharist – *Communion, union, conversation, confidence: word, bread, love.*[15] *When you approach the Tabernacle remember that He has been awaiting you for twenty centuries*;[16] about frequent recourse to the Sacrament of Penance, so as to be purified and win the graces needed to renew the interior life …

The Father did not yet speak of that *Work of God*[17] he was trying to found; he first wished to broaden the spiritual horizons of the people he was speaking to. With all the warmth he could summon, he evoked the greatness and the depth of a Christian vocation lived in the midst of each one's daily job – it was there that they would find Christ. Those who are young must start working towards this ideal even now, while they are still students, for *an hour of study, for a modern apostle, is an hour of prayer.*[18] Theirs would be a deep and serious study, worked at to the point of heroism, in preparation for the exercise of their profession, which would then derive its worth and dignity from the grace of God.

It was in the depths of the heart that resolutions would be born, with his encouragement – the right word at the right time – and with the support of his prayer, and yet more penances .

Help from the poor and the sick

He asked some of the students who came from well-to-do families to accompany him on his visits to the suburb of Tetuán or the working-class district of Vallecas, where families lived crowded together in appalling conditions; sometimes in mere holes in the ground, with no water and no sanitation. Their hearts sank at the sight of so much misery: for it is a truism that knowing and seeing are not the same thing. It was this sort of shock that permitted eye-opening conversations; there was certainly the question of the social responsibility of intellectuals – this gave a new dimension to study! – but there was also a call to live a truly Christian life of reparation and constant union with God, the foundations for an intense apostolate in the very heart of society, making it more just and humane, converting it fundamentally, but from within.

In this way, too, the poor themselves helped without knowing it.

One day a medical student told the Father of the terrible conditions in two hospitals he had to visit, the San Carlos Clinic and the Provincial or General Hospital. The General Hospital dated from the end of the eighteenth century. It was ill-adapted and, above all, not large enough to cope with the expanding population. The sick were crowded together in conditions of doubtful sanitation. The corridors were lined with rows of beds. All of this, combined with the lack of resources, tended to depress the patients and the atmosphere was almost unbearable.

These poor people, cut off from others in their physical and moral misery, were well known to him, for he had visited them in the slums and outlying suburbs of Madrid. When he heard about the state of these hospitals, however, he thought of these young people around him. What better way was there to make them think about others and bring them closer to the Heart of Christ, to form them and give them the supernatural vision they lacked, the *third dimension: height, and with it, perspective, weight and volume*?[19]

Prayer, self-sacrifice, giving oneself to God and to others: this is what the poor and the sick would teach these students. *The limited, miserable happiness of the egoist – who withdraws into his ivory tower, into his shell – is not difficult to attain in this world. But the happiness of the egoist is not lasting.*[20]

You are too calculating. Don't tell me you are young: youth gives all it can, it gives itself without reserve.[21]

The Father and the students went first of all to the General Hospital, which was near Atocha Station and the Church of Saint Elizabeth. The religious Congregation that looked after the hospital willingly gave its consent: it had its work cut out in the existing atmosphere where anti-Christian feeling was running high. From then on, every Sunday afternoon, Don Josemaría's lads went from ward to ward speaking to the patients, trying to cheer them up, bringing them some little treat – and also taking on jobs neglected for lack of staff: washing them, cutting their nails and emptying their chamber pots ...

One day the Father followed a young engineer as he went to empty out one of those chamber pots. Luis Gordón had given an involuntary shudder of disgust at the sight of it; so the Father decided to follow him to the wash-room and do this disagreeable job himself, but when he arrived he saw Luis empty the chamber pot and clean it out with his hand, saying something to himself ...

Don Josemaría, who had overheard what he had said, would later evoke in *The Way* that moving scene:

Isn't it true, Lord, that you were greatly consoled by the childlike remark of that man who, when he felt the disconcerting effect of obedience in something unpleasant, whispered to you: 'Jesus, keep me smiling!'? [22]

For his own part, the Father tried to help the sick on a spiritual level. He saw in each man a soul that had to be saved. Some rejected him violently. Others, however, were moved that a priest should show an interest in them, abandoned as they were by everyone. Their hope was renewed and they learned how to turn their suffering into prayer, rediscovering the path of the faith. And what lessons the destitute sometimes gave him!

A gipsy fatally wounded during a brawl taught him one such lesson. Don Josemaría asked to be left alone with the dying man. Gently he explained to him how grave his condition was. The man was moved and wanted to make his confession. After giving him absolution, Don Josemaría brought to the gipsy's lips the crucifix he always carried. The gipsy turned his head away, crying:

'I can't kiss Our Lord with this filthy mouth of mine!'

But listen, very soon you are going to embrace him and give him a big kiss in heaven! [23]

And the Father, deeply moved, thinks: *What will I myself say? Lord! How can I kiss you with my filthy mouth?*

Clearing the land is hard work

The young people would tell the Father about their impressions at the end of these visits. And he, taking their emotions as a starting-point, would try to help them discover a new meaning in their lives, to be generous in the big things and especially in the little duties and small renunciations of each moment. *Many who would willingly let themselves be nailed to a Cross ... cannot bear with a Christian spirit the pinpricks of each day!*[24]

The Father did not talk to them about vocation. But he opened new horizons for them: working for God, spreading Christ's kingdom ... And in order to do so, letting oneself be "nailed" to the Cross in the sanctification of one's ordinary work, carrying it out as perfectly as possible and making it into an offering, a holocaust ...

Many of these young men, without realising it, had changed profoundly. They started going to Mass during the week. Sometimes they would attend Don Josemaría's Mass in the chapel of the Foundation for the Sick in Santa Engracia Street, which he said with such concentration that it almost made them tremble. They brought their friends, who were soon attracted by the warmth of this young priest whose direct way of speaking made a deep impression on them. And the immense panorama the Father revealed to them bowled them over: it was an ideal to give direction to a whole lifetime, one to change the world.

Some of them, however, drew back when they realised that it was an invitation for them to leave everything and follow Christ, without abandoning the world. How many of them were "rich young men", like the one in the Gospel! Their eyes bespoke a boundless generosity: but they turned sadly away at the moment of truth.

Souls slipped through his fingers *like eels in water.*[25] Some of them had the courage to admit their weakness; others simply took French leave ...

Yet God's Will must be fulfilled. If only even one would stay! Then everything could start.

But the Father did not feel he was alone. His mother, sister and brother came to live with him in the little chaplain's flat in the Foundation for the Sick in September 1929. He did not lack friends.

And above all he had *the conversation of the great Friend who never lets you down* [26] – Jesus Christ ... And always, deep down in his heart, burned the unwavering flame that urged him to carry on and open up the path without becoming discouraged. The Will of God would be carried out, because it was His Will. *Is that what you want, Lord? ... Then, it's what I want also!* [27]

At the beginning what he had undertaken did not even have a name. To those who were close to him the Father would speak of his apostolate as *la labor*, ("the labour", a word with all the implications of effort and perseverance implied by its Latin root), or he would talk about la *Obra* (the "Work", also in the sense of a job, an *apostolic task*). Then one day around the beginning of 1930 his spiritual director, Padre Sánchez Ruiz, asked him in passing:

"And how is that work of God coming on?"

Something clicked. If it needed a name, this was it: "the Work of God" – in Latin, *Opus Dei*, also implying working in an ordinary sense. *Opus Dei, operatio Dei* :[28] God's work and working for God! Professional work, ordinary work, carried out without forgetting the world's concerns and noble ambitions. Work converted into prayer, praise of God, following all human paths. *Opus Dei*. What better name could there be for the work that God had asked him to do?

Apostolate with priests

Don Josemaría also spent a lot of his time and energy encouraging priests and advising them in their spiritual lives. They were often older than he was, but they trusted his ability to direct them because they knew him to be a man of God.

He had been concerned for the holiness of priests ever since he had been a seminarian. Now he knew he could propose to some of them the vocation he himself had received on 2 October 1928: the call to holiness in their ordinary activities – in their case, their priestly ministry, to which they would dedicate themselves more completely, with greater generosity, with all the good for souls that could result from this.

These priests would also be able to look after the spiritual and sacramental life of the first lay people who asked to join the Work. These members would be men who agreed to give their lives to serve God, without giving up their secular mentality and situation in life, and who would try to exercise the virtues and values of the Gospel in all environments.

The priests had indeed already been there on 2 October 1928, when he had seen the whole of the Work in the silence of his room in the residence of the Saint Vincent de Paul Fathers. In what legal form they would be there he did not know as yet, but there they would be: they *were* already there!

The task was even more difficult than with laymen. When you speak to a priest about the interior life or about holiness, he may rather feel that you are preaching to the converted and that he, being something of an expert in such matters, has nothing more to learn about them ... And besides, what could this young colleague teach them?

That is what some of them thought, for they saw in Don Josemaría's proposal merely yet another "good work" in which they were being asked to help. And that is leaving aside those who began to think – or even to say – that Don Josemaría was crazy ...

However, others listened with real interest as he spoke of this new type of apostolate, describing it as *a sea without shores*,[29] and explaining it with an enthusiasm and a precision of detail that could not but impress the listener and give him the impression that things had, indeed, to happen this way. Some priests decided to follow him and help him in his work of formation. One of them was Don José María Somoano, who had been given several posts by the Bishop of Madrid (including that of chaplain of *Porta Coeli* , a home for young delinquents). Without doubt he was one of those who best understood and who would become more interested in the still-crystallising apostolic work.

The birth of the Women's Section of Opus Dei

Laymen of all types, a few priests by their side to give them spiritual help: the Work was beginning to take shape according to the original plan. But would it be right to include women among the laity? Certainly not! thought Don Josemaría. Never ...

It was certainly a possibility from a purely human point of view; but it did not fit in with what God had shown him on 2 October 1928. *There will never be women in Opus Dei – not even as a joke!* [30] he had written early in February 1930, when he received some documents relating to an institution made up of both men and women.

A few days later, on 14 February, he went to Alcalá Galiano Street to say Mass at the home of the dowager Marchioness of Onteiro, the mother of the foundress of the Apostolic Ladies. The little oratory was on the first floor of the house, just a stone's throw from the well-known avenue of *La Castellana*. Just as he was receiving the Body and Blood of Christ with the great devotion he always felt and with all the fervour he was capable of, he was aware of Our Lord "coming into" his life again, to ask something else of him, another thing, but in line with what he had seen on 2 October 1928: the call to live the fulness of the Christian life must be extended to women as well ...

There could not have been a clearer contrast to what he had thought and written ... Another proof that the Work was not his own, but was truly "of God".

His confessor confirmed it at once: "This comes from God like all the rest", Padre Sánchez Ruiz had said.

How clear it was that God was doing everything! He could even *write with the leg of a table* ... [31]

Around this time he wrote down the following reflection on a piece of paper: *The holy Saint Teresa, in Chapter II of the Foundations, points out as one sign of the divine Omnipotence that of giving boldness to the weak, so that they can carry out great things in His service. I subscribe to that boldness, and to that weakness ...* 2 October 1928 – 14 February 1930. [32]

2. MADRID: SUMMER 1931

Outside Atocha Railway Station the passengers came and went. Don Josemaría walked among them without a glance, on his way to catch the tram which would take him home to Viriato Street, where he and his mother were living. Now he was alone with her in Madrid, for he had just been seeing off his sister Carmen and his brother Santiago at the station. They were on their way to Fonz for the summer.

The atmosphere in Madrid was so tense you could have cut it with a knife. The signs had been growing for more than a year now: there was a storm coming, the convulsions of a society whose political fabric, it was common knowledge, was beginning to come apart at the seams.

On 21 January 1930 General Primo de Rivera had demitted office. No government had been able to solve the monarchy's grave crisis; on 14 April 1931 Spain was proclaimed a Republic for the second time in its history. These were times of uncertainty for the present, of hope for the future – and of tension too, for Spain's anticlerical tendencies were gathering their forces, giving rise to demonstrations of unheard-of violence. On 11 May gangs of fanatics took to the streets of Madrid, setting fire to churches and monasteries. The same scenes were repeated that day and the day after in other towns in Spain. Priests were regarded with suspicion if not actually insulted, as happened in the working-class districts and suburbs where Don Josemaría still went to visit the poor and the sick. People there often threw stones at him.

The Father was careful to refrain from any political remarks. But his heart was heavy, even if he remained certain that Our Lord would never allow anything irreversible to happen.

He had averted the possibility of a profanation of the Blessed Sacrament on 11 May, in the Foundation for the Sick, where he was still living. A colonel, a very old friend of the family, came looking for him at Santa Engracia Street bringing a suit of clothes for him to wear so that he could get away. Don Josemaría had gone to the chapel, opened the tabernacle and had consumed nearly all the Sacred Hosts in the ciborium. Then, as time was pressing, he reverently wrapped up the ciborium containing the rest of the hosts with a piece of paper and took it to the colonel's house in a taxi the colonel had ordered.

Things seemed to calm down over the following few days. But the storm clouds were still in the air, and no one knew where the lightning would strike next.

After spending a few days with his brother in the colonel's apartment, Don Josemaría moved to Viriato Street with his mother. He had in the meantime resigned as chaplain of the Foundation for the Sick, so as to be more available for the foundation that God had asked of him.

You are My son

The circumstances were hardly favourable for the founding of a work as important as this one: Don Josemaría realised this only too well. But when he took the tram home he was thinking that it would, in the end, become a reality, even if it seemed absurd.

At times when, humanly speaking, things were very difficult, in which, nevertheless, I was convinced that the impossible would be done ... I felt the action of the Lord, who prompted me to say with my heart and with my lips, with the strength of something imperatively necessary, this tender invocation: Abba, Pater! [33]

The passengers who on that day were crammed together on the tram rattling its way from Atocha to Cuatro Caminos must have been astonished to hear the young priest in their midst stammering out words they could not understand, his face suddenly lit up with joy.

Joy, and deep peace. I am a son of God! Nothing else matters ...

"You are My son, today I have begotten you." (Ps 2:7) A whole lifetime would not suffice to exhaust the deep meaning of these words from Psalm Two, which he now saw in a new light.

Joy. Identification with Christ, the only Son of God, the Well-Beloved of the Father. As with the just men of the Old Testament, as with Mary in the *Magnificat*, an answer sprang from the depths of his heart on the wings of other words from Scripture: *"Abba, Pater, Abba, Pater! Abba! Abba! Abba! Abba!* [34]

"And the proof that you are sons is that God has sent into our hearts the Spirit of His Son, crying Abba! Father! You too are a son, not a slave; a son, and therefore an heir of God." (Gal 4:6-7) "You have received the spirit of adoptive sons, the spirit that makes us cry Abba! Father! The Spirit himself joins with our spirit to attest that we are children of God, heirs of God, and co-heirs with Christ, since we suffer with Him that we might also be glorified with Him." (Rom 8:15-17)

Thank you, Paul, thank you great Paul, thank you for having disclosed this truth to us and for having reminded me of it now! [35]

What confidence, what peace and optimism, to know, surrounded as we are by difficulties, that we are children of a Father who knows everything and can do everything! [36]

Don Josemaría got off the tram, almost without realising it, and wandered through the streets still repeating mentally, and perhaps out aloud as well, regardless of passers-by: *Abba, Pater! Abba, Pater!*

This grace was too exceptional to be reserved for him alone. It was surely for others, for those who were to come. So that they might know always how to see the Cross of Christ when they were in difficulties; so that they might know that to meet the cross *is to meet happiness, joy. I see the reason for this more clearly now than ever: it is that to have the Cross is to identify yourself with Christ, to be Christ and therefore to be a son of God.* [37]

The light of 2 October 1928 shone even more intensely at particularly difficult times. The fact that this clear sign of divine sonship should have been received in the middle of a street – in a tram – was a clear sign that Christians can, and should, be saints in the middle of their ordinary occupations: indeed, thanks precisely to those very occupations themselves.

The street does not stop our contemplative dialogue. The bustle of the world is, for us, a place of prayer. [38]

"Why this tumult among the nations? Why this idle grumbling among the peoples? The great ones of the world plot against the Lord and His Anointed ... enthroned in His Heaven He laughs at them ... You are my Son, this day have I begotten you. Ask of me and I shall give you nations for your inheritance, the ends of the earth for your realm ..." (Ps 2)

The Father, as he was called spontaneously by those who meet him, arrived home with his heart bursting with joy and confidence in the future, whatever might happen. From now on this awareness of divine sonship would be even more of a central theme in his preaching. *We've got to be convinced that God is always near us ... He is there like a loving Father. He loves each of us more than all the mothers in the world can love their children – helping us, inspiring us, blessing ... and forgiving ... We've got to be filled, to be imbued with the idea that our Father, and very much our Father, is God, who is both near us and in Heaven.* [39]

Lord! – say it to him with all your heart! – I am a son of God! [40]

The first vocations

Don Josemaría's apostolate among priests and young people continued. Increasing the amount of time he spent hearing confessions, he broadened and deepened the foundational work necessary for a real beginning to the Work of God.

The confessional allowed him to start directing women, mainly young women, whom a priest could not meet in the same circumstances as he could men. He advised some of them to go to *La Ventilla*, a very poor suburb of Madrid, and give catechism classes to the children.

He fashioned souls, one by one, cutting them like diamonds, patiently, waiting for them to respond.

But he was no longer alone in the secret of this madness, this fire, the first spark of which God had passed to him nearly two years earlier. Some of those around him seemed to understand. Among them was someone whose name had immediately sprung to mind after the foundation of the Work: his old class-mate from the state school in Logroño. Isidoro Zorzano was a good Christian, an upright man with a big heart. He would certainly be able to understand this demanding ideal and with the grace of God, dedicate his life to it.

He had not entirely lost sight of Isidoro, although they had not met for several years. He knew that he was still unmarried, and that after studying engineering he had gone to work in Málaga for the Andalusian Railway Company.

At the beginning of the summer of 1930 he decided to write to him. It was a very short letter: *Make sure you come and see me when you are around; I have something to tell you that you may find interesting.*

A few months later, on 24 August, Don Josemaría was at the bedside of an architectural student whom he visited regularly. He had only just arrived when he had a feeling, without knowing why, that he should return home. He left, and not far from the Foundation for the Sick made a slight detour from the most direct route he always took. Suddenly, as he was walking along Nicasio Gallego Street, he saw someone he recognised coming in the opposite direction – Isidoro!

'I've just been to see you,' explained Isidoro, 'and when I found you weren't at home I was going to look for a restaurant and then catch my train. I'm going up North; my family are already there for the summer. It's odd, but I had the strangest feeling that I would meet you if I turned down this particular street ...'

They returned to Don Josemaría's rooms in the Foundation for the Sick. Even before he could broach the subject he had alluded to in his letter, Isidoro took the initiative.

'Josemaría, I came to see you because I wanted to ask your advice on something.'

What's troubling you?

'I feel unsettled. I believe God is asking something of me, that I've got to 'do something'. But I don't really know what it could be. I thought that maybe God was calling me to join some religious order: but I can't see that clearly. I've got my job as an engineer, and I'm perfectly happy with it. I don't know what to think. I need some guidance from you.'

Don Josemaría listened in astonishment. Then he said:

Do you remember my letter? Well, it was precisely because I wanted to talk to you about a work I've started ...

In broad strokes, he began to describe the wide scope of sanctifying work in everyday life. The life of an engineer like Isidoro, for instance.

'I can see the hand of God in this coincidence,' answered Isidoro. 'You can count on me. As far as I'm concerned, my mind's made up.'

It had all happened so quickly that Don Josemaría did not quite know what to do. He asked his friend to wait a little before giving his final answer, for he would be setting the course for the whole of his life ... Isidoro left, and said he would come back after lunch.

As he waited, the Father reflected on everything and asked Our Lord for light. It had all happened so fast. For one thing, Isidoro could not be transferred to Madrid immediately, and it would be difficult for them to meet in order to assure the necessary formation. On the other hand it all seemed so straightforward, so providential.

Isidoro returned. They talked on and on, until the time came for him to go and catch his train. From now on he would consider himself bound to Our Lord, irreversibly, to serve him in this Opus Dei in which he would be, in fact, the first member to persevere.

From that day on, Josemaría his one-time classmate, had become, for him, *the Father*.[41]

Convictions and contradictions

Although the fruit was slow in coming, 1930 had been a year rich in work and joy. Above all, there had been, on 14 February, the unexpected birth of the Women's Section of Opus Dei. Don Josemaría's apostolic work now followed a triple path: lay men, lay women, and priests.

Things were far from easy. In times of crisis such as these, people are deeply concerned and are stirred to political action. The ideal proposed by the Father was a far higher one. It was an ideal that necessarily included the noblest of aspirations and undertakings, but they were seen with the eyes of faith, with all the demands that this imposed: interior life, formation, moral consistency, unity of life ...

Don Josemaría usually conveyed to his listeners something of his own enthusiasm. He helped them to rediscover passages of the Gospel with new clarity (he himself had copied out a hundred or so verses from the New Testament, and reread and meditated on them time and time again). Others, however, smiled at the unbelievable audacity of the very idea of Opus Dei. Nor did they content themselves with making comments behind his back; they were also kind enough to inform him of their scepticism, with an "understanding" condescension. (Often, unfortunately, they were his brothers in the priesthood!). What an absurd idea! Proposing to ordinary men and women, to people who are not "consecrated" to God, who haven't taken vows and do not have a vocation to the religious life, to aim for holiness! These laity are immersed in the turbulence of the world, with so many opportunities to dirty their hands, to lose their souls: isn't it enough that they be saved at all, "yet so as by fire"? How can one dare to tell the first Christian who comes along: *Your duty is to sanctify yourself. Yes, even you. Who thinks that this task is only for priests and religious? To everyone, without exception, Our*

Lord has said: "Be perfect as my heavenly Father is perfect." [42]

The young founder suffered from these misunderstandings. In a sense, though, they did not surprise him: what he was preaching was certainly so new, so mad indeed. But he was quite certain that it came from God. He would not renounce it whatever surprise, whatever reserve some people might show. On the contrary, they made him all the more certain that he was not the inventor of an extravagant "idea", but the instrument chosen by God to open up a new *way* [43] on earth. This work was not just one more "good work": it was *the Work of God* which he had been shown glimpses of since his youth. That was why it was no surprise to meet with obstacles. It was up to him to lift them out of the way or to cast them aside, hand in hand with Our Lord! Heaven was, in a sense, *bent on its being carried out.* [44]

* * *

In 1931, on the feast of the Transfiguration, celebrated on the 7 August in Madrid, Don Josemaría celebrated Mass in the Church of Saint Elizabeth. As he silently formulated the intentions of the Mass, he suddenly realised the deep change that had taken place within him since his arrival in Madrid, over which he seemed to have had no control. So he renewed his resolution to direct his whole life towards the fulfilment of the divine Will for him: the Work of God.

The moment of the Consecration came, he wrote in his diary the same day. *At the moment I raised the Sacred Host, ... some words of Scripture came to my mind with extraordinary force and clarity: "et ego si exaltatus fuero a terra, omnia traham ad meipsum." (John 12:32) Normally, in the presence of the supernatural I am afraid. Then comes the "Ne timeas!" It is I. And I understood that it would be the men and women of God who would raise the Cross, with the teachings of Christ, above the summit of all human activity ... And I saw Our Lord triumphant, drawing all things to Himself ...*

I should like to write books of fire that would run across the earth like a living flame, passing on their light and heat to men, transforming their poor hearts into burning coals to offer to Jesus as rubies for His royal crown ... [45]

3. MADRID: SEPTEMBER 1931 TO FEBRUARY 1934

Before Don Josemaría had time to realise what was happening, the man had hurled himself upon him. He could not free himself from those hands that seized him violently. At the same time a torrent of abuse was pouring from his assailant's mouth. A few moments more and the priest would not be able to breathe.

But almost at that very instant someone came to his aid and the attacker let go of him. While Don Josemaría was getting his breath back he heard the young man who had rescued him murmur with a smile, "Mangy donkey!" Before he could react, the young man had disappeared into the crowd.

* * *

How could the young man have known? Don Josemaría went on his way to nearby Saint Elizabeth, his soul filled with a mixture of desire to thank God for having got him out of a nasty situation, and a strange sensation he had never felt before. For very few people knew the most intimate depths of his soul, and even fewer knew that, in his conversation with Jesus, he had no other wish but to be His *mangy donkey*, unworthy to receive Him, to represent Him and to carry Him among men.

The incident over, he was filled with an overwhelming sensation of peace. But he felt a great desire to go and speak with Our Lord in the tabernacle. What had just happened was so inexplicable! It was as if it had been a nightmare, were it not for the noonday sun blazing down on the street, where passers-by continued to come and go as if nothing had happened ... [46]

In the confessional at Saint Elizabeth

Every day since September 1931 he had been going to this district near Atocha Station, to the Church of Saint Elizabeth. Its classical dome and porch gave onto a little piazza tucked between a convent and a girls' school.

The convent was a community of enclosed Augustinian nuns, who had been granted the building by the Crown at the beginning of the eighteenth century. Their income derived from a royal foundation, which also provided for the College of Our Lady of the Assumption, on the other side of Saint Elizabeth's (and which was looked after by another order of nuns). Don Josemaría had offered to act as chaplain to the Augustinian nuns and said Mass for them every day at eight o'clock. The nuns were present behind a grille, studded with thick spikes, to the left of the altar looking from the aisle. He also officiated at the other liturgical ceremonies, particularly Benediction.

He knew Saint Elizabeth's already from his previous months of hearing Confessions there. The nuns were delighted with their new chaplain, for they were impressed by his piety, his good-humoured nature and his availability. If one of the nuns was sick, he would bring her Holy Communion after Mass. On his way back he would exchange a few words with the nuns in the corridor or the convent yard.

He spent a lot of time in prayer before the altar with its great baroque altarpiece. These were moments of trusting conversation between a son, entirely aware of his own weakness, and his Father God.

Lord, here's Your little donkey! [47] he cried again one day. And he then heard an interior voice: "An ass's colt was my throne in Jerusalem." Those words which had affected him so deeply – were they, too, from God? Were they not rather the fruit of his imagination?

In order to reassure himself, he immediately compared, mentally, the words he had heard with those he remembered from Scripture. The prophet Zechariah does indeed speak – he seemed to recall – of the Messiah to come, saying: "Behold, your king cometh unto you; gentle, he is mounted upon an ass, on a colt, the offspring of a beast of burden ..." (Zech 9:9) But recalling the passage did not entirely remove his doubt: Our Lord could have ridden the ass and not the colt ...

When he arrived home he looked up the Gospel of Saint Matthew (21:1-5), where he found Zechariah taken up: it says, in fact, (three verses before the entry into Jerusalem,) that Jesus had asked His disciples to fetch in preparation for his entry into the Holy City an "ass with her colt by her", but that was all. He turned next to Saint Mark, Saint Luke and Saint John: none of them mention an ass, only an ass's colt, "on which no man in the world had yet ridden" (Mark 11:2, Luke 19:30, John 12:14-15). Our Lord had clearly ridden the colt, then.

This detail removed all his doubts – and exemplified the prudence he had always shown in the presence of possible supernatural interventions. God had wanted to give him a tiny share of His divine wisdom, and had given him an affectionate encouragement that he would not forget.

See how humble Jesus is: a donkey was his throne in Jerusalem! [48] he wrote during the next few days, so as not to forget the lesson, and so that other souls might profit from it in the future. *Ut iumentum factus sum apud te!* (Ps 72:23). *Before You, Lord, I am nothing but a little donkey!* He repeated that, too, in his prayer and in his preaching.

His work at Saint Elizabeth's permitted him to spend long hours in the confessional, receiving men and women of many different backgrounds, for the church was open to the public. It was a good opportunity for him to continue giving spiritual direction to some young and older women he knew. He encouraged them to live an intense Christian life, in the midst of their habitual occupations. Soon a little group was forming: a student, a secretary, a nurse, a secondary school teacher ...

Those he considered ready to receive the grace of a vocation to Opus Dei he asked to go to Confession with one of the other priests attached to Saint Elizabeth's. He himself devoted his time to their spiritual direction in the strict sense of the term. As with the men, he spoke to the women about their duty to sanctify themselves in their everyday work, and, above all, of the need to be united to Our Lord in all circumstances, through prayer and the frequent reception of the Sacraments, in order to be able to carry out a useful apostolate in their surroundings.

The ideal he proposed to them was, from the start, the very highest. He spoke of Mary Magdalen, Mary of Cleophas and Salome, who kept close to the Mother of God at the foot of the Cross. All the disciples had fled save John, the disciple whom Jesus loved ... *Woman is stronger than man, and more faithful, in the hour of suffering ... With a group of valiant women like these, closely united to Our Lady of Sorrows, what work for souls could be done in the world!* [49]

Some of them seemed to understand the allusion. They deepened and strengthened their interior lives, in contrast with the sentimentality so easily fostered by the prevailing religious atmosphere on the grounds that they were women and thus by nature more attracted to piety than the menfolk ...

Don Josemaría's invitation was a challenge: it was big enough to take up a whole life and make it shed its light over the whole of society.

As always from the very beginning, it was the sick who would help the first fruits to ripen. In 1931 Don José María Somoano asked a young girl in the King's Hospital, a tuberculosis ('TB') case, to offer her sufferings and prayers for a special intention of his which would be for the good of a great number of people: it was a truly universal good that had need, and would continue to have need, of constant prayer and sacrifice in order to become a reality. 'Pray for it and don't stop,' he had told her. After that, every time María Ignacia saw him she would ask him how that intention he had spoken of so enthusiastically was getting on.

The Republican government had in fact abolished the post of

chaplain, along with the salary that went with it. Don José María Somoano was only standing in as voluntary chaplain, and it was proving difficult to find priests to look after the contagious sick who were treated there.

The Father, alerted to the situation, soon offered to look after the post himself without pay. In order to be accepted he had first to conquer the reluctance of several of the hospital directors, who were opposed to the idea of a priest coming to visit the sick unless the sick themselves had expressly asked for one!

The serenity, courage and good spirits of the young priest impressed everyone, especially the Sisters of Saint Vincent de Paul, who were sorely tried in these exceptionally difficult circumstances. They saw him come several times a week; without being discouraged he tried to come close to those of the sick who had most need of him. His arrival helped to raise the morale of those destitute patients, many of them incurables – often 'TB' cases who suffered all the more because their illness meant complete and unavoidable isolation.

The atmosphere of the hospital was quickly transformed. The sick could be seen facing their deaths with a peace – or even a joy – that was, humanly speaking, unexplainable.

On Sundays, weather permitting, Don Josemaría would say Mass in the open air, at a portable altar set up on a terrace in the garden.

Only Jesus in the tabernacle of Saint Elizabeth's heard the confidences and pleas of Don Josemaría, physically and morally worn out by his constant travelling to and fro, from one end of Madrid to the other. It was the constant prayers of the Father which obtained these miracles of grace from God, the deathbed conversions that surprised so many of the nuns in the hospital. The sick in their turn, by the mysterious interchange that takes place within the Mystical Body, obtained grace upon grace from heaven for Don Josemaría and for the newly born Opus Dei of whose existence they were quite unaware.

And what an example he received from these men and women, the forgotten of society! And from humble folk too, whom he happened to meet, like that milkman who had greatly puzzled him when he first arrived at Saint Elizabeth's. As Don Josemaría sat in the confessional he would hear a tremendous clattering as the church door opened, at the same time every day. One day, when he was on his own, he went out to see what was going on. The man, without any hesitation, explained how every day, before beginning his daily round, he would come into church with his cans and go down on one knee in the doorway, facing the tabernacle, just long enough to say: "Lord, here's John the milkman!"

Such simplicity in his interior life made the Father feel envious, and even a little ashamed. He made the resolution of doing the same himself and he told the anecdote to some of the people he directed, to help them simplify their interior lives and to be more spontaneous in their prayer.

How many hours of peace and contentment he spent at Saint Elizabeth's, where everything was an invitation to recollection and conversation with God! The paintings and sculptures were in good taste; some of them were even of undoubted artistic merit, gifts received by the royal foundation over the centuries. He was particularly enchanted by a sculpture of the Child Jesus. He discovered it on Christmas Day and, ever since, had asked the nuns to leave it at the revolving door, at the entrance. It was a dark-skinned baby, like a little gipsy, with eyes half-open and arms crossed on his chest as if to implore protection.

The good sisters had wrapped him in linen to protect his nakedness. He was the God-Child, all helpless.

He has become so small – you see: a Child! – so that you can approach him with confidence. [50]

Unity of life

At the end of 1932 his mother, along with Carmen and Santiago, moved to 4, Martínez Campos Street, in the Chamberí district of Madrid. This would allow him to bring together the young people he was directing and give them a more intense formation.

The level he demanded was still high; there were no

concessions to "taking it easy", although he helped each one of them to make progress at his own speed, leading them up an inclined plane. Only thus, by *an overflow of their 'life within'*,[51] would they feel a keener desire to give themselves to the others. The visits they made to the hospitals helped them to come to grips with their own consciences. *Don't let your life be barren,* he would repeat. *Be useful. Make yourself felt. Shine forth with the torch of your faith and of your love.* [52]

This way of thinking, as foreign to activism as it was to pietism, must have appeared all the more surprising, not least because of the degree of political ferment around them. Something in the air seemed to indicate the imminence of violent action, even a coup d'état. There were clashes between rival political groups at the university, and frequent fighting on the streets of Madrid.

Although Don Josemaría never discouraged – quite the opposite – those who wanted to take up their responsibilities in these difficult times the country was going through, he himself refused point blank to descend to the specific solutions that are a matter of individual free choice. It was for the same reason – respect for people's freedom in temporal matters – that he was not at all taken by the idea of a Catholic Party, though the project was very much in the air.

If anyone ventured to ask his opinion, or tried to put him in a position where his words might appear to suggest a taking of sides, he would cut them short in a tone that did not admit of argument. A student who had met Don Josemaría around that time remembers that on one occasion he wanted to satisfy his own curiosity on what was his political view, and asked what he thought of one of the outstanding figures of that time. His answer was quick, immediate: *Look, they will never ask you here about politics; the people who come around belong to all sorts of groups: Carlists, Popular Action, Monarchists of Spanish Renewal ... And yesterday*, he added by way of an example, *the President and the Secretary of the Association of Basque Nationalist Students were here*. After a moment's pause, he would continue with a smile: *On the other hand, they will ask you some "awkward" questions. They'll ask you if you pray, if you make good use of your time, if you keep your parents*

happy, if you study, because for a student it is a serious obligation
... [53]

He preached this doctrine untiringly, at the risk of putting off some who were more attracted by movements that provided an opening for immediate action. And he wrote it down as well: his papers would henceforth serve as guidance for those who would come after. From the very beginning, the founder of Opus Dei wanted the objectives and the means to be clearly defined.

He explained to the young students in 1932 that they should not consider themselves as belonging to a special group, and that they should not look to him for anything other than a stimulus for their interior lives and a spirit that would move them to carry the Christian faith to wherever they were, as well as − why not? − wherever they could make themselves useful. It was essential that there should be room for a healthy pluralism among them, whether or not they formed part of the little kernel of those who had committed themselves to serve God in Opus Dei.

In a letter dated 1932, he recalled yet again that the bond uniting them *is exclusively spiritual in nature ... There is a bond between you, and each one of you shares the whole of the Work with the others precisely in the area of the search for your own holiness, and in the area − also strictly spiritual − which consists in bringing the light of Christ to your friends, your families and those around you. You are citizens who fulfil their duties and exercise their rights; and who are only associated with Opus Dei in order to receive help to seek holiness and carry out apostolate, with specific ascetic means and apostolic methods. The spiritual aims of the Work make no distinction between races, or between peoples. They see only souls; they exclude every party, every political idea and plan.* [54]

In practice, he recommended that they completely avoid talking politics − in the sense of having political arguments − when they were with him.

Our pluralism is no problem for the Work, he had written as early as 1930, no doubt in answer to an objection. *On the contrary, it is a manifestation of good spirit, proof of the uprightness of our joint efforts and of our respect for the legitimate freedom of all men.* [55]

Those to whom these words were addressed would never

forget the lesson. Nor would they forget the Father's call not to limit the Christian life to what one might call "pious practices" such as going to religious ceremonies or reciting various prayers.

But pluralism is not abstentionism. On the contrary. The life of a Christian must have enough coherence for him not to be able to remain uninterested in the fate of his fellow-countrymen. *Unity of life* was a constant refrain in the Father's preaching. There should not be a double life, spiritual on the one hand and professional or social on the other, a family life and a civic life each separated from the other in hermetically-sealed compartments. One is a Christian twenty-four hours a day.

Have you ever stopped to think how absurd it is to leave one's Catholicism aside on entering a university, a professional association, a cultural society, or Parliament, like a man leaving his hat at the door? [56]

In certain situations – as was indeed the case in Spain at the time – the abstentionist attitude is the easiest. But Christians cannot be indifferent to public affairs. Some people adopt an attitude of indifference simply because no one has ever explained to them that *the virtue of piety – to say nothing of the cardinal virtue of justice – and the sense of solidarity among Christians are also exercised by 'being involved', by taking stock of the community's problems and helping to solve them.* [57]

At the same time he put those around him on guard against the easy temptation to "professionalise" the apostolate, something that was, thanks partly to the prevalent atmosphere, quite widespread at the time: young men would throw themselves body and soul into various activities to such an extent that their studies suffered, thus effectively ensuring that their wings were clipped for future action in society because of their lack of professional prestige. That was why the meetings organised by Don Josemaría in his mother's house lasted only long enough to ensure that some ideas would stick in the minds of those who came, serving to strengthen them in their daily interior struggle. At the end of the meeting the Father would make a short and practical commentary on a verse from the Gospel, normally from the Mass of the day.

Time and God's grace would do their work. The founder was

quite convinced that patience was the best guarantee that the Work of God would grow quickly: better to begin slowly than to build on doubtful ground. Inevitably it was from this little nucleus of generous young men that the first vocations would be born. Yet they would need to be the right kind of men, not over-pious Christians or "holy Joes" but strong characters, gifted with enough human qualities to withstand all difficulties. Building on that premise they would learn how to pray and how to give their lives a supernatural meaning, so that when a call came from God they would be ready to respond.

One day, towards the beginning of 1932, Juan Jiménez Vargas, a young medical student, was introduced to the Father by some fellow students. Juan was very heavily involved in political battles in the university. He had heard a lot about this young priest, and was very impressed when he met him; but the message he was preaching – Juan told his friends – did not really fit in with what he had expected. There were other things to do, he thought, while the country was on the brink of disaster ...

When they told him of Juan's reaction, Don Josemaría smiled. It was, after all, so natural in a young man of that age, considering the difficult times Spain was going through. However – and perhaps sooner than he thought – he would one day realise that if priority is given to a solid doctrinal formation, and to an intense spiritual life in union with Christ, society will be transformed in a more lasting and effective way than by an improvised and hasty activism.

Luis Gordón, the young engineer who had accompanied the Father round the hospitals, was one of those whose characters had matured in contact with suffering and under the influence of the Father's teaching. After university he had taken over the management of a small firm near Madrid – and soon afterwards decided to answer God's call.

These world crises are crises of saints. [58] Don Josemaría was absolutely certain of this. Difficulties only spurred him on in his striving to open up in modern society this new path of sanctity which God wished to make him see.

4. MADRID: 1932-1933

The year 1932 was to bring Don Josemaría a stream of joys and sorrows, in the midst of which Opus Dei would continue to grow. It also brought the warning signs of the upheaval that would degenerate into civil war.

The apostolic work went ahead on all fronts. There were now meetings every Monday for the priests. The founder tried to make them understand each of the specific aspects of this new path to the fulness of Christian life in the middle of the world.

Some of the priests were young and enterprising: Don José María Somoano and Don Lino Vea-Murguía went, like him, to visit the sick and give catechism classes in the suburbs on Sundays. Others were considerably older, but they too could help the Father, through spiritual direction, to make the Work grow at the speed God willed.

These priests began to grasp, some quickly and others more gradually, with greater or less penetration and profundity, what the Father was driving at with his idea of a new spirituality. Don José María Somoano was the first of them to appreciate thoroughly what the spirit of the Work was, and this led to his decision to commit his whole life to the enterprise, without ceasing to be accountable to his Bishop as his only superior in everything concerning his priestly ministry.

The vocation of an incurable

The Father's hours in the confessional in Saint Elizabeth's continued to allow him to widen and consolidate the base of what could be a beginning of the Women's Section of Opus Dei.

Providence was to arrange that one of the first stones of the foundation should be a poor sick girl who never left her hospital bed. María Ignacia García Escobar, a 'TB' case in the King's Hospital, was, without knowing it, praying for the Work. Don Josemaría knew that she was incurable. All the same, he unfolded to her this royal road to holiness in the middle of the world, to which he had dedicated his life since 2 October 1928. Despite her illness, María Ignacia decided to offer the time still remaining to her for this ideal.

Two days later she wrote in her diary: "This 9 April 1932 will never be effaced from my memory. Again You have chosen me, good Jesus, to follow Your divine footsteps ... From this moment on I promise, with Your help, to give You my all in the place You have put me because all the glory must be reflected back to You."[59]

The young women being helped by the founder of Opus Dei along the paths of the interior life took turns to spend time with María Ignacia, receiving from her a marvellous lesson of abandonment to God's will.

A dramatic death

Despite the difficulties, and despite the slow start to this Work willed by God, the Father did not lose his serenity. He continued to pray and labour ceaselessly.

Nevertheless the news he received on the morning of 17 July dealt him a real body-blow.

Don José María Somoano had suddenly fallen ill four days earlier. The Father spent a long time at his bedside, praying intensely for him to be cured. The rumour running through the wards was that he had been poisoned. It was quite a plausible possibility, in those days of really vicious anticlericalism. The Father thought of this on hearing that Don José María had died.

Although he was convinced he did not need it, the Father prayed a lot for him and would ask his sons to pray for him for many years.[60]

Once again he had to know how to accept without understanding, how to suffer while keeping in his heart the hope that a Christian can never lose, not even when the sky seems darkened for good. Over the years, he had learned the steps towards total acceptance of the divine Will: *to be resigned to the Will of God; to conform to the Will of God; to want the Will of God; to love the Will of God.* [61]

All situations are open to apostolate

While all this was going on, events were moving very fast in Madrid. It was just over a year since the proclamation of the Republic. Then, after the burning of churches and convents, riots broke out.

On 10 August 1932 General Sanjurjo attempted a coup d'état in Seville, which failed. Some students who had been demonstrating in the streets of Madrid were imprisoned in the Cárcel Modelo, to await trial. Among them were several of the young men to whom Don Josemaría was giving spiritual guidance. As soon as he heard about the arrests, he went to the prison, in his cassock, to speak to them, encouraging them not to remain idle and not to lose their Christian joy and hope. He went on to talk about prayer, reminding them that they were sons of God ... *With abandonment, therefore, you will not have to worry, since you will rest in the Father.* [62]

The Father also advised them to say the *Our Father* many times during the day, meditating particularly on the first two words: "Our Father" ... He encouraged them to go frequently to the Blessed Virgin, reciting the prayers they had learnt as children, or saying the Rosary, and to go to Confession and Holy Communion as often as they could, and also to maintain a cheerful atmosphere among themselves and with the rest of the prisoners. They and their companions would need this, for there were calls for nothing less than the death sentence against them ...

The young men thanked the Father from behind the grille in the visitors' room. They knew that his words were not just said for form's sake; they came from the heart to give them the only comfort they could hope for in such difficult circumstances.

In the end, their months in captivity provided not only an opportunity for interior progress but also taught them a lesson in charity and mutual understanding with the anarchist-syndicalists who were imprisoned with them. After a little while, Catholics and anarchists who a few weeks earlier had faced each other, weapons in hand, on the streets of Madrid, began to play football together in the prison courtyard during the recreation hour.

Don Josemaría, to whom previously these lads had admitted being, not unnaturally, a trifle apprehensive on that score, had encouraged them to fraternise, suggesting to them that not all play on the same team, but on opposing sides, so as not to reproduce political differences on the playing-field. He also told them it would be an opportunity to tell these men a little about Christian doctrine, of which they were, without necessarily there being any blame on their part, entirely ignorant. The Father brought a catechism to help them with this new-style apostolate.

A new trial

In October 1932, four years after the foundation of the Work, the Father again spent a few days in silence at a Carmelite monastery in the outskirts of Segovia. The mediaeval town stretches out behind the prow of its Alcazar or fortress silhouetted against the sky.

In a conventual chapel lies the body of Saint John of the Cross. It was there, in the course of his prayer, that the founder placed the apostolic work of Opus Dei under the protection of the archangels Saint Michael, Saint Gabriel and Saint Raphael and of the Apostles Peter, Paul and John.

A little while later, Luis Gordón also fell ill. Don Josemaría was told that he was getting worse, and after a few days – at day-break on 5 November – he died. The Father, who had remained in prayer at his bedside, immediately said Mass for the repose of his soul in the parents' private oratory. Once again the divine Will was beyond the understanding of the human mind. Luis was a young man, but had already acquired a very considerable professional reputation; with his faithfulness and his spiritual refinement he could have been an invaluable help for the Work. However, God had decided otherwise. Once again he had to accept without under-standing ... The Work would go on developing without any sup-port, without any material means.

Accepting the Will of God wholeheartedly is a sure way of finding joy and peace: happiness in the Cross. Then we realise that Christ's yoke is sweet and that his burden is not heavy. [63]

After losing those human consolations you have been left with a feeling of loneliness, as if you were suspended by a mere thread over the black emptiness of the abyss. And your cries, your shouts for help, seem to be heard by nobody. You deserve to be forlorn. Be humble, don't seek yourself, don't seek consolation. Love the Cross – to bear it is little – and our Lord will hear your prayer. And calm will be restored to your senses. And your wounded heart will heal. And you will have peace. [64]

A book of prayer and action

These lines were written by the Father for himself, and for all those who over the centuries would come close to the Work.

To provide those who had already come close to him with an added stimulus in their interior struggle, he had begun to put down in writing some aspects of his preaching and of his work of spiritual guidance: words of encouragement, intimate experiences from his continuous dialogue with Our Lord, extracts from letters, advice. It was not as yet a book, though it would ultimately become one.

During the December of that same year, 1932, he had a number of copies duplicated under the general title of

Josemaría, aged 19.

As a seminarian in Saragossa.

Consideraciones espirituales (Spiritual Considerations): *These are things I am whispering in your ear, in confidence, as a friend, as a brother, as a father.* They were things which would revive the memories of those he had advised and directed, because *God is listening to these things said in confidence.* [65]

The points for consideration were brief and very practical. They were, as his preaching was, inspired by Scripture, imbued with love for the Church and the desire to carry the fire of Christ to the ends of the earth. Their aim was to move the reader to make specific resolutions to improve his life as a Christian. Later, little by little, these points were amplified with other considerations, taken as always from his interior life or from his direct experience with souls. They constituted a plan of interior life and ascetic struggle for everyone: character, obedience, prayer, purity of heart and soul, the theological virtues ... and a series of basic devotions: Holy Mass, devotions to the Blessed Virgin, presence of God ... Added to these was an explanation of the way of spiritual childhood, that shortcut taken by souls in love with God, and a consideration of the sense of divine filiation whose richness the founder of Opus Dei knew well, particularly since that day in the summer of 1931 when he had been returning home from Atocha in a tram.

And everywhere, of course, like a recurring motif in the divine tapestry he was inviting each man to weave with the grace of God on the warp of his life, was the central theme of his preaching since 1928: the invitation *to sanctify your work, sanctify yourself in your work and sanctify others through your work,* [66] fulfilling as perfectly as possible the duties that daily life brings with it.

Do you really want to be a saint? Fulfil the little duty of each moment: do what you should be about and keep your mind on what you're doing. [67]

With this perspective the most ordinary occupations acquire a third dimension, the supernatural dimension, *and with it weight, contoured relief and volume.* [68]

The Cross on your breast? ... Very well. But you must bear the Cross on your shoulders, you must feel the Cross in your flesh, you must keep the Cross in your mind. You will then live for Christ, with

Christ and in Christ; only then will you be an Apostle. [69]

He proposed, without hesitation, the most demanding ideal to the generous students around him: martyrdom. But a martyrdom within arm's reach, in the most normal circumstances of their ordinary lives: *To shine like a star ... desiring to be a lofty and sparkling light in heaven? It is better to burn like a hidden torch, setting on fire everything you touch. That is your apostolate; that is why you are on earth.* [70]

This was, after all, the lifestyle of the first Christians, who were "not different from the rest of men in nationality, speech or customs", as a second-century document, the famous *Letter to Diognetus*, explains: "they do not live in states of their own, nor do they use a special language, nor adopt a peculiar way of life ... Whether fortune has given them a home in a Greek or foreign city, they follow local custom in the matter of dress, food and way of life; yet the character of the culture they reveal is marvellous and, it must be admitted, unusual ... In a word, what the soul is to the body, Christians are to the world."[71]

These words could very well also be said of the members of Opus Dei. They too have heard the call of Jesus to his first disciples. *To sow. The sower went out ... Sow the seed generously, apostolic soul. The wind of grace will spread it further afield if the furrow it fell upon was not worthy ... Sow and you can be sure that the seed will take root and yield its harvest.* [72]

The reader of *Spiritual Considerations* is not only encouraged to dream with very high ideals, but also to discover a detailed plan of God's to which he can respond by giving his life, by pledging himself fully, wherever he might be, without yielding to the temptation of changing places and running away from his present situation.

The book was not addressed only to members of Opus Dei, of that time or of those that were to come, but its publication would certainly help to broadcast the Father's preaching and thus move people's hearts, so that a vocation to the Work (or to some other path of holiness) might grow and mature within them.

With the eyes of the soul

Some had faltered, others had failed him. Luis Gordón and Father Somoano had suddenly died. But the founder refused to let himself be discouraged. He knew that others would come, and that their faithfulness would be the foundation upon which the Work of God would be built over the centuries, *for as long as there are men on the earth.* [73]

Spurred on without knowing it by the prayers of the poor and the sick whom the Father visited, one by one, there came vocations to Opus Dei, strong vocations based on firm convictions.

Don Josemaría had noticed for some time now a young man of twenty-three or twenty-four coming regularly to his Mass in the church of the Foundation for the Sick. His behaviour and piety made the Father think that maybe he would understand his message. He found out that he was called José María González Barredo, and that after taking his chemistry degree he was following a specialisation course at university. One day he approached him and asked him to pray for an intention of his. The young man agreed to do so, and even thanked the Father, probably out of sheer surprise. The whole encounter lasted no more than a minute or so.

Soon afterwards Don Josemaría ceased to see him at Mass. He learned that he was now a teacher at Linares Grammar School in the province of Jaén. He was sure he would see him again one day and carried on praying for him.

The young man came back to Madrid in December 1932, to spend Christmas with his family, and delayed his return because he wanted to do some research at the University. He wanted to continue his scientific training, among other things because he was worried by the agnosticism of some scientists and he wanted to help to show the harmony which exists between science and the Faith.

Shortly before Christmas, as he went down the Gran Vía towards the Plaza de España, José María González Barredo caught sight of the Father coming towards him in the opposite direction. He later admitted trying to avoid being noticed, for he was afraid that what had already happened with other priests he had known would happen again: they had talked him into enrolling in movements and associations which had been, he felt, a waste of time for him. But Don Josemaría had already seen him, and greeted him warmly. They exchanged a few words, and then the Father told him that he would like to have the opportunity to talk with him at greater length ...

The proposition the founder of Opus Dei put before José María that evening was an unbelievably perfect response to his deepest aspirations. *You worry only about building up your knowledge. And what you have to build up is your soul. Then you will work as you ought – for Christ. In order that he may reign in the world, there must be some people who, with their eyes fixed on heaven, seek to acquire prestige in all human activities, so that they can carry out quietly – and effectively – an apostolate within their professions.* [74]

José María González Barredo had indeed discovered an apostolic perspective worth dedicating his life to. Before he decided, however, he asked the Father's advice on something:

"I've been to Confession several times with this priest I know, who is a religious. Do you think I could consult him before I commit myself, just to be sure?"

You're free to do as you wish.

Encouraged by this advice, he went to ask this priest for advice. But he found his opinion rather unconvincing:

"If this Work you speak about is in its beginnings, wouldn't it be better to go for a more fully developed institution? After all, it's better to work in a library that's already organised, rather than in one that is in the process of being put together."

José María González Barredo thought: what difference did it make if the Work was just beginning? That wasn't the point; he wanted to know whether or not it was an ideal worth living.

When he returned to the Father, his mind was made up. The answer was yes![75]

The Holy Spirit was also at work in other souls. During the same Christmas holidays, the Father also talked about the Work to the medical student to whom he had been introduced at the beginning of the year. He had an intense conversation with Juan Jiménez Vargas. Saying nothing about it to Juan, he asked the Paraclete to give this young man light and counsel over the next nine days. On 3 January 1933, Juan gave a definitive "yes" to Don Josemaría's proposal.

Eighteen days later the two of them visited the *Porta Coeli*. In this Home the Sisters were striving by teaching and guidance to put back on the right track a number of orphaned or homeless children. Don Josemaría had been going there for some time, hearing the confessions of these boys who had just escaped a life of begging or even of downright delinquency. He thought the visitors' room, despite its rather unwelcoming appearance, could serve as a meeting place for the students he was gathering around him, and it would enable him to give them a more intense and regular formation. He invited a number of students to the first meeting, for which the Father had high hopes, having asked the first members of Opus Dei to pray for it.

But he was to be disappointed: only Juan and couple of medical students, both friends of his, turned up. It didn't matter. He certainly had no intention of cancelling it.

A small picture of Our Lady presided over the class. Two years earlier, as he was passing through the working-class district of Tetuán, he had discovered this picture, an illustration from a catechism, crumpled up on the ground under a tree. To make reparation for what he interpreted as an act of contempt, Don Josemaría had reverently picked up the little picture and had it framed, setting it on a background of gold tissue.

The meeting was brief and, as usual with the Father, very much to the point. It consisted of a commentary on the Gospel, an exposition of a particular aspect of the interior life, some points for an examination of conscience ...

The Father addressed those three students with the same assurance as if he had been speaking to a much larger group. After the final prayers, he invited them into the chapel of the Home. Dressed in surplice and stole, he knelt before the altar, then opened the tabernacle and carefully recited the prayers for Benediction of the Blessed Sacrament. As he turned to bless the three young men with the monstrance, he saw, behind them, all the others that would come later: *three hundred, three hundred thousand, thirty million, three thousand million ... white, black, yellow, of every colour, of all the combinations that human love can produce ...* [76]

* * *

A few months later another student asked to join the Work: it was Ricardo Fernández Vallespín, who was just finishing his architectural studies.

To make a little money he was giving lessons to some of his colleagues. Don Josemaría knew one of them, and his family. One day he had gone to visit him and had entered the room where Ricardo was teaching. The young man known to the Father introduced them, but Don Josemaría, so as not to interrupt their work, suggested that they just carry on. He brought out his breviary and started reading it over by the window until they finished the class.

Ricardo was so struck by that first encounter that he wrote in his diary that evening (14 May 1933): "Today I met a priest, very young and enthusiastic; I don't know why, but I think he will have a great influence on my life."

On 29 May they met again, this time at Don Josemaría's house. The Father spoke at length and was full of enthusiasm. He did not venture into the burning political issues of the moment; instead he opened up for him supernatural perspectives that were a revelation to Ricardo, and were in fact extending to him a pressing invitation to improve his spiritual life. As Ricardo was about to go, the Father got up, picked out a book from a shelf, and wrote a few words on the first page: *May you seek Christ. May you find Christ. May you love Christ. Madrid 29-V-33.* [77]

The book was the *History of the Sacred Passion* by Father La Palma.

Formation, prayer and sacrifice

The meetings – which were real classes of formation – continued, at the house in Martínez Campos Street. It was easier to transmit the spirit of the Work in family surroundings than it had been in the austere Orphans' Home.

Doña Dolores soon became accustomed to seeing groups of young men in her sitting-room, presided over by a picture of Our Lady with the Child in her arms.

All the same, she found all this coming and going a bit surprising, even though she had long been aware of her son's apostolic zeal. He gave cautiously indirect answers to her discreet enquiries about the reason for all this intense activity. In order not to alarm her, he had in fact decided not to say anything about what had happened in his soul on 2 October 1928. She accepted it all, without understanding, and even helped him in her own way along with her daughter, Carmen, often preparing an afternoon snack for the visitors.

"Josemaría's boys scoff the lot!" his young brother Santiago would mutter indignantly, on finding that the food had disappeared.

The visits to the hospitals continued. Now they went to the Princess's Hospital, a nineteenth-century foundation endowed by Queen Isabella II. It was a vast building, two stories high, in the centre of Madrid; there were two thousand patients there, crammed two or three hundred to a ward. Don Josemaría went from one long room to another, speaking to the sick, hearing their confessions and bringing them Communion.

Another activity was added during these visits. Just as some young women were doing in other areas, the Father encouraged the men students to teach catechism to children deprived of a religious education in Tetuán de las Victorias district. They tried to prepare this work very carefully, seeking to deepen their faith so that they were better equipped to pass it on to the children in their care.

To help them the Father gave – or arranged to be given to them – classes on Christian doctrine. He also proposed that they spend a few hours in silence every month, on a day of recollection in which he would comment on practical points of piety or morality, and, as always, invite them to draw practical consequences and resolutions to help them to improve in their daily life. He himself made his retreat, alone as was his habit, at the Redemptorist house in Madrid from 8-16 June.

He had been thinking for some time of how to increase his

apostolic work. It would require adequate organisation and suitable premises on which he could rely. He was sure that one day soon, thanks to everyone's efforts, he would find a solution to this material problem.

María Ignacia García Escobar continued to support him from her hospital bed. Her illness, tuberculosis of the stomach, was getting worse in spite of the treatment by quartz lamps to which she was being subjected. By the end of August she was in a serious condition and in constant pain; her body was deformed by the illness and covered with sores. Yet she did not lose her serenity; closely united to God, she offered her sufferings.

She was constantly visited by the young women Don Josemaría knew and who kept her company all the time. He himself tried to go and see her every day; when this was not possible, he telephoned for news.

At the beginning of September the doctors gave María Ignacia only a few days to live. The Father told her how seriously ill she was, and asked her if she wanted to receive the Anointing of the Sick: he administered it to her himself, in the presence of her sister. Afterwards he slowly read out the liturgical prayers to recommend a soul to God. Then he asked her, with great fervour, that once she was in heaven she would not forget to pray for this Opus Dei to which she had given the last months of her life. Once more he spoke of the future apostolate of the Work, spread out over the world in a panorama which she would soon be able to contemplate from on high.

On 13 September he came running to the hospital when María Ignacia's sister told him of her death. After Don José María Somoano and Luis Gordón, this was the third vocation in flower thus plucked by Our Lord. Three intercessors the more: three solid supports from which the Work of God could be launched over the centuries – a priest and two lay people, a man and a woman, prefiguring all those who would carry the word of Christ with them in their passage through all the crossroads of the earth.

The birth of a project

A little later, after another conversation with the Father, the young architect Ricardo decided in his turn to follow the way so clearly laid out before him. *Another crazy fellow for the asylum!*[78] was the comment Don Josemaría made, as on other occasions, with his infectious enthusiasm.

But although he was happy, he was not satisfied with this slow progress: the Work of God needed to grow more quickly, and for that he needed to get to know more people.

Don Josemaría was still thinking of a flat reserved exclusively for the apostolate, to which he could give the specifically secular tone proper to the spirit of Opus Dei. A sort of "Academy", where they could organise talks and lectures on cultural and professional subjects, as well as classes on Christian doctrine and other spiritual activities. The human and religious formation of many young men could thus be carried out in "symbiosis". And the young men would then be ready to give witness to Christ wherever they might find themselves.

For that he needed to find the necessary resources. But those around him, with the exception of Isidoro and José María González Barredo, were not yet earning their livings. He persuaded them to look for other means, trying to arouse their interest in this project, which would quickly enable them to enlarge their circle of friends. He invited them to pray, to ask God for the necessary courage.

Some will say it is another act of madness, he told them. *Take no notice., Madness has always been the term that 'prudent' people apply to God's works. Forward! Without fear!*[79]

"God", "daring ..."

Three capital letters were engraved on the iron plate which they put up outside the first floor flat at number 33 Luchana Street: DYA. These were the initials of the academy's official name: *Derecho y Arquitectura* (Law and Architecture). But over and above that, they were the initials of the motto that the Father had often recalled to the students around him: *Dios y Audacia ...* [80] (God and Daring).

5. MADRID: 1934

From December 1933 onwards, most of the apostolic work began to take place at the DYA Academy. Thanks to the scant savings of the Father, and those of Isidoro and José María, and thanks also to the help of a number of acquaintances, they had managed to pay the first instalment of the rent and set up the flat. Ricardo, the young architect, at the request of Don Josemaría, acquired some furniture at the *Rastro*, the Madrid flea-market. The rooms for visitors, get-togethers, reading and talks, as well as the Father's study, were arranged to look as inviting as possible, taking their limited means into account. But the house was so small that the kitchen (which was also the chemistry laboratory) was sometimes used by the Father for hearing confessions.

The Academy really came to life in the afternoons, with students coming to attend lessons in mathematics, physics and chemistry (which were common entrance subjects for a number of special schools and for university), architecture, foreign languages and various legal specialities.

The students paid their share; but they often had to ask for an especially generous effort from those of them who better understood the apostolic importance of the work carried out there. The Father had to appeal to his friends for more money: not only those who had contributed first time round, but others as well ... He himself, with the permission of the Bishop of Madrid, gave classes on Christian doctrine. He was helped in this by another priest, Don Vicente Blanco. Naturally, apart from going to those classes, anyone who wanted to speak with Don Josemaría about the spiritual life was free to do so.

How many graces were obtained during those conversations with the Father, in the different rooms of the Academy or in the Father's study, which only had a table, two chairs, a wooden cross and a prie-Dieu! How many times would these young men of good will begin and begin again in their lives as Christians!

Without making any easy concessions – the Academy was not a place to go to for amusement, but to be formed, to work, to study, to talk about serious things – the Father made the atmosphere of the Academy not only pleasant but cheerful for "a sad saint is a sorry saint indeed ..."

They did not have to wait too long for results. One student brought another, and soon the Academy was full. The Father's working day became busier and busier; it was second nature to him anyway, a habit he had picked up in his parents' home, where he had never seen his mother idle. Besides, the job to be done was immense: they had to open a new divine path on the earth; they had to bring the Gospel's call to holiness to thousands and thousands of men and women, wherever they might be.

The publication of 'Spiritual Considerations'

To help those he was advising and forming, Don Josemaría had decided to publish the notes he had accumulated over the years. All they had had until then were machine-duplicated copies.

On 3 May Bishop La Plana of Cuenca, a distant relative of the Escrivás of whom he had asked his advice on how to print the book as economically as possible, gave his *imprimatur* to *Spiritual Considerations*. It included four hundred and thirty-eight points for meditation, each one the fruit of his pastoral experience and his interior life, and aimed at giving the reader that uprightness of mind and soul which would lead him to live as a Christian should in all circumstances, with the three symptoms of the *divine craziness of the apostle ... : hunger to know the Master; constant concern for souls; perseverance that nothing can shake.* [81]

The Father explained to those around him that their *silent and effective mission* [82] could not be limited to a restricted circle, which would soon turn into a ghetto of "right-thinking" Christians living their faith at the margins of society. They had to spread the fire they bore to other souls; each had to try to be *an apostle of apostles*,[83] radiating out like the stone which, falling into a pool, sends out ripples in ever-widening circles over the whole surface of the water.

Those who were already engaged in the service of God in his Work, or who were thinking of being so, should not be so naive as to judge *from the smallness of the beginnings* ... [84]

On earth every big thing has had a small beginning. What is born big is monstrous and dies. [85]

So that the idea might really sink in, he would repeat to those first members of the Work that they were not there to carry out *a human undertaking, but a great supernatural enterprise. From the very first beginnings it has seen accomplished in itself, to the letter, everything needed for it to be called, without any presumption, the Work of God.* [86]

He put this idea down in a document addressed to them and to all those who would come to Opus Dei until the end of time, in order to convince them of the specific nature of their vocation. They would have to be *like an intravenous injection into the bloodstream of society.* [87]

Contrary to what some might think, given the turbulent times they were living in, Opus Dei was not invented by any man *to resolve the lamentable situation of the Church in Spain during the years after 1931. It was inspired by Our Lord many years ago in a deaf and clumsy instrument who saw it for the first time on the feast of the holy Guardian Angels, the second of October of nineteen twenty-eight.* [88]

We are not an organisation born of circumstances ... Neither have we come to answer a particular need in a particular country or era; Our Lord wanted His Work to be, from the very first moment, radically universal, Catholic. [89]

That is why the birth and growth of Opus Dei owed nothing to human means, but everything to prayer and penance.

Let them not become paralysed at the thought that they were only poor instruments. God realised this before they did and he would communicate to them the graces required so that his Work be done, as long as they were docile to his divine Will. Obstacles would only make them grow stronger!

The founder's writings carried a marked supernatural imprint, even when they were addressed to a much larger public than the members of the Work, as was the case with *Spiritual Considerations*.

The Rosary, a powerful weapon

Another book was soon to appear. One day while sitting in the church of Saint Elizabeth, on the right hand side of the altar and facing the conventual grille, during his thanksgiving after Mass Don Josemaría wrote out, at one go, a brief commentary on each of the fifteen Mysteries of the Rosary.

The sentences had poured out as if he were confiding a secret, *which could well be the beginning of the road that Christ wants them to follow*, [90] to many souls: in order to become big, be small; and for that you have to *believe as children believe, love as children love, trust as children trust, pray as children pray.* [91] Especially is it true that *a trusting love for the Blessed Virgin is the beginning of that road, the end of which is to be carried away by love for Jesus.* [92] This is why you should not let yourself be stopped by a misplaced scruple: a fear of routine. Those who love one another are not ashamed to say the same things over and over again.

To help his readers avoid the risk of *making mere noises like an animal, with a mind very far from God,* [93] he advised them to contemplate, slowly, one by one, each of the Joyful, Sorrowful and Glorious Mysteries, to introduce themselves into the Gospel scenes

as if each one were just another character: to live the life of Jesus,
Mary and Joseph.

Practised like this, the Rosary would become a *powerful
weapon* [94] to win in the interior struggle, opening the way to the
contemplative life.

Jesus, souls! [95]

In December 1934 Don Josemaría took the place of the Rector of the Foundation of Saint Elizabeth. He had already moved
with his family into the chaplain's house in February.

It was the rector's responsibility to see to the Foundation's
administration, so that the House of the Augustinian sisters and
also the adjoining school now came under his care.

His working days were well occupied: Mass in Saint
Elizabeth's, confessions, visits to hospitals, more confessions at the
Porta Coeli home; other calls and visits in the city, and, in the after-
noons, meetings with the students at the DYA Academy.

Being at the church of Saint Elizabeth also allowed him to follow up the formation of the first members of the Women's Section
of Opus Dei. This more difficult task was carried out mainly
through spiritual direction in the confessional, and by giving meditations and homilies for small groups in the church or in another
chapel.

Little by little, he widened the horizons of these young
women, showing them the way to seek holiness in the midst of the
world through work, and with the fully lay and *secular* [96] spirituality
of Opus Dei. He helped them widen their circle of acquaintances
and encouraged them to invite their friends to take part in the formation they were receiving.

He had to insist, firmly, that they could be saints, *like the
saints you raise altars to ... I won't stand for anything less.* [97]

There were serious obstacles, as was the case also with the
Men's Section, although the problems he had to face there were of
a different kind. So he turned to the Blessed Virgin to give the

impetus needed for the development of the Women's Section of the Work, asking her to be herself the Foundress.

In 1931, in the course of his visits to the General Hospital, he had got to know a sculptor, Jenaro Lázaro, who had since started to come to him for spiritual direction. Knowing his talent, and his piety, the Father commissioned from him a statuette of Our Lady which could be passed from house to house, a custom frequent among Christian families at the time. In this way he would obtain the filial prayers of those girls for the future growth of the Work.

In any moment of difficulty, it was always to the Mother of God that he turned to resolve the situation. The streets of modern Madrid, with their tall buildings facing each other all the way along Gran Via; the old streets of traditional Madrid, with their gas lamps fixed to the fronts of the houses; the "elegant" Madrid of *La Castellana* and *Chamberí*, with their carefully planned avenues and impressive junctions and roundabouts; working-class "fringe" Madrid with its squalid suburbs: they all saw Don Josemaría passing by, wrapped in his cape, piously saying his Rosaries – *whole fifteen-decade Rosaries* [98] – punctuated, in more difficult moments, with silent cries from the heart, entreaties to his Mother, always his last resort: *Most sweet Heart of Mary. Mother, my Mother! Don't abandon me!* [99]

Nor did he forget his constant concern, the apostolate among intellectuals. Not without reason, he explained to those around him, did Jesus use the image of the fish and the catch: *Men, like fish, have to be caught by the head. What evangelical depths there are in the 'intellectual apostolate'!* [100]

He himself preached a retreat over several days in May for university students and prominent figures in Catholic public life, in a church in Madrid: this was in response to a particular request. The main thrust of his preaching was no different from the one he had developed for the students at the DYA. He referred to the need for them to complete their formation, because professional prestige would then become *a 'bait' as a 'fisher of men'.* [101] At the same time they needed to intensify their life as Christians, so as to help spread the kingdom of Christ: *Today, with the extension and intensity of modern science, the apologists have to divide the work among themselves, if they want to defend the Church scientifically in all fields. You ... cannot shirk this responsibility.* [102]

A step taken in the right direction

The months passed and the Work continued to grow. But was it growing with the rhythm and at the speed God wanted? Those who were around the Father certainly thought so. Great was their astonishment, then, when not long after setting up the DYA Academy he was already starting to talk about the possibility of moving house the following year, so as to be able to undertake a fuller and more profound work of formation.

One of the priests who assisted him was thoroughly alarmed. There was no money. Had they not already gone too far in opening the Academy? Surely it would be far more prudent to go back to Don Josemaría's mother's flat? Setting up a new Academy now would be "like jumping out of a plane without a parachute"!

* * *

You have but little love if you are not zealous for the salvation of all souls. You have but poor love if you are not eager to inspire other apostles with your craziness. [103]

The Father began to speak to his sons about his new project. The idea now was to open a small students' residence, and transfer the DYA Academy there as well. At the time there were only two residences of this type in Madrid, so this new residence would be a service to students from the provinces, and would give them and their friends a chance to improve their Christian lives, thanks to the atmosphere and the means provided by the Academy.

Don Josemaría was also thinking of another advantage to having a stable base to work from: they could have Our Lord present in an oratory, and thus all the students who came could go to Him, confiding in Him all their worries and their will to fight, and keep Him company as Martha, Mary and Lazarus kept Jesus company in

Bethany.

The founder of Opus Dei was not unaware of the difficulties inherent in such an undertaking. The reaction of the "prudent", therefore, came as no surprise to him. But he was following a different logic – the logic of the "folly" to which God was pushing him in asking him to carry out His Work on earth. And he often meditated on these words of Saint Paul: "The love of Christ urges us on." (2 Cor 5:14)

6. MADRID: SEPTEMBER 1934

Doña Dolores and Carmen listened with growing fascination as Josemaría spoke, calmly, but making no attempt to conceal from them the passionate nature of his involvement.

He spoke clearly about the task the divine Will had entrusted to his hands on 2 October 1928, and into which he had put all his strength to bring it to completion. He explained the aims of the Work, the spirit that animated it and the immense apostolic horizons it opened up ...

Suddenly they could understand many things in his behaviour since 1928 which had baffled them until now.

Josemaría then revealed the reason for telling them all these things. He was asking whether they could sell their family property at Fonz, which they had inherited when his paternal uncle had died. The money raised from the sale would enable him to meet the needs of the residence he wanted to open in October ...

He realised that he was asking his mother and sister for an act of exceptional detachment, as well as of faith in God. He was the head of the family, after the death of his father, and he had very few resources for their livelihood; his brother was a boy of fifteen still at secondary school. He was asking them, therefore, purely and simply, to abandon their only patrimony.

He had hesitated a long time before asking his own family for such a sacrifice. But it was the only way he could see of carrying out what God was asking of him.

He had not over-estimated their generosity. Thanks to their consent, given on the spot, an apartment could be acquired and furnished.

The new project takes shape

Before the summer holidays he had asked the departing students who went to the Academy not to forget, during the coming months, to pray for him, and to pray that the apostolate in which they were taking part could develop in the new academic year. He had also given them good advice, so that this time of relaxation which they were going to spend with their families might not mean a period of neglect, but another opportunity for them to make progress in their interior lives. Finally, he had asked them to write.

When he received the first letters in July, he replied with four machine-duplicated sheets to everyone, giving each of them news of the others so as to maintain a link between them.

At the beginning of the first sheet there were always a few words in his own handwriting:

At last ... here is some news! I received your letters and you – all of you – deserve my warmest congratulations, for I see that you haven't forgotten my advice: you have been going about things the way a Christian should. Your holiday plans add up to living a life of piety and work: that's the way! Stick to it, and do not get lazy about writing us letters. [104]

During this time the first members of the Work set out to look for a flat, as they had the Summer before, and thought about the possible setting up of a residence and about its working budget.

This last point was the trickiest: Isidoro had arrived in Madrid to study the problem with Don Josemaría, and they had come to the conclusion that they needed at least twenty places for the residence to be reasonably viable.

By August they had found what they wanted: three flats on the third and fourth floors of number 50 Ferraz Street, near West Park.

The furniture from Luchana Street was moved there in September, with everyone helping. Ricardo, who had just finished his studies in architecture, directed by Don Josemaría, supervised the decoration of the flats and, in his capacity as technical director, asked for authorisation for the residence from the municipal authorities. Don Josemaría would be only the spiritual director.

The DYA Academy was set up on the fourth floor, while the residence proper took up the two flats on the floor below. A lot of problems still remained to be dealt with when they moved in. An important one was the financing of the project, which would necessarily run at a loss at the beginning because there would not be a sufficient number of students to start with.

To add to the money the Father had obtained from the generosity of his family, all the members of the Work asked their friends for all the help they could give, explaining how much would be done to form young people at the centre. Many were quick to respond in spite of the general air of political uncertainty prevailing at the time. Some families, fearing that the disturbances would increase, had already left Madrid.

They all looked for students for the residence, but by the end of October, there was only one definite application. They could not count on the students from the DYA Academy they had known in previous years, for those who lived in Madrid stayed with their families, while those from the provinces were putting off their return until the capital was calmer. On 3 October 1934 the various extreme left-wing movements called a general strike, to put pressure on the moderate government which had been returned in the recent elections. On 19 October the army occupied the Asturias mining basin, where there was a revolution brewing.

By January 1935 they had still only eight residents. But the Father was sure that they were coming to the end of their financial difficulties. Besides, he had found a new support in Heaven, in the person of Saint Nicholas of Bari, a holy bishop who had once had the happy idea of leaving a sum of money on the window-sill in the house of three young women, who could not marry for lack of a dowry.

If you get me out of this mess, I'll name you Intercessor of the Work! [105] he told him mentally one day, while he was preparing to say Mass at Saint Elizabeth's. But before he had even got to the altar he repented of this lack of trust: *And even if you don't, I'll name you Intercessor just the same!* [106]

For him, prayer and mortification were always the surest ways of reaching the ends he had set. So he carried on his extraordinary mortifications to an even greater degree. Ricardo would put his hands over his ears to shut out the muffled sounds coming through the bathroom wall into his bedroom. He knew the noise was made by the strokes of the discipline that the Father used for what seemed to Ricardo an interminable length of time.

A new apostolic platform

The financial position of the residence, though hardly rosy, gradually improved. The main effort up to the end of March was concentrated on setting up the oratory. They all put their shoulders to the wheel, the Father foremost among them all.

On 13 March 1935 he was able to ask the Bishop for permission to open the oratory. He said Mass there for the first time on 31 March, the fourth Sunday in Lent. Beaming happily, he addressed a few words before Communion to those present.

A few days later, on 2 April, he wrote to the Vicar-General of the diocese: *Holy Mass was celebrated in the oratory of this house last Sunday, and His Divine Majesty has been reserved here, making it possible for us to see fulfilled desires that go back many years (to 1928).* [107]

It was the first tabernacle in a centre of Opus Dei, the first link in a long chain which would stretch around the world.

The Father invited the students to approach Our Lord present in the Eucharist with confidence, and to come often to visit him in the tabernacle, where he had been waiting for them *for twenty centuries.* [108] He taught them to love the liturgy, the austere simplicity of which *carries you to God ..., brings you closer to God,* [109] to

penetrate with more understanding into the deeper meaning of the
rites and to learn how to sing Gregorian plain chant correctly (a
priest friend came to give them lessons).

Unfortunately, residents were slow in coming. By April there
were still only fourteen. The Father had already decided in February, much to his regret, that they would have to abandon the fourth
floor and bring the Academy and Residence together on the third
floor.

So as not to discourage the first members of the Work, and to
help them acquire a supernatural outlook, he had broken the news
to them in the oratory. In life, he told them, you have to know how
to get around difficulties, and sometimes you have to step back a
little in order to jump further. That is the moment to reinforce your
faith and to grow on the inside as you wait for the obstacles to be
overcome. *God's grace will not fail you: "inter medium montium per-
transibunt aquae!" You shall pass through the mountains! Does it
matter that you have to curtail your activity for the moment if afterwards, like a spring which has been compressed, you will reach
incomparably farther than you ever dreamed?* [110]

Everyone made greater efforts to bring their friends to the
Academy. And it was, naturally, something everyone was praying
for.

Soon students came flocking, won over by the atmosphere of
the modest but pleasant flat. They helped with the installation, they
moved furniture, did repairs ..., and in this way the house became
their home. That was why they returned, and brought their friends.

All were encouraged to make headway in their interior lives,
apostolate being but a consequence. The Father warmly recommended that they read Dom Chautard's *The Soul of the Apostolate* ,
which develops this theme. He encouraged them to pray, to turn
their hours of study into prayer, and to bring their friends closer to
God.

In so doing, some students would find their vocation to the
Work; others, depending on their generosity, would learn how to
draw from the riches of its spirit. The apostolate was spread very
widely: *All souls are of concern to us,* [111] the founder repeated often.
He also used to say: *There is no soul in which Christ is not*

interested. Each soul is worth all the Blood of Christ. [112]

His preaching and spiritual direction were demanding and clear without beating about the bush. He addressed himself to everyone, to those with the *vocation for marriage* [113] (at the time this expression raised eyebrows), as well as to those who felt that Our Lord was asking something more of them. The former he advised to place themselves under the protection of the archangel Raphael, who would lead them to a marriage *with a girl who is good and pretty and rich* [114] – he would say with a smile – as the Bible tells us Raphael did with young Tobias. Among them were some who would one day be able to receive a vocation to the Work – when the moment was right. In May, keeping always in mind the things he had seen on 2 October 1928, Don Josemaría began to put down on paper the broad outlines of the apostolate of these married men and women. Absolutely identical to their fellow citizens, for that is what they were, they would carry the light of Christ into the very heart of human activities, in their professional, family and social lives, wherever men work and meet together.

The formation of the first members

For the moment, however, he put the greater part of his efforts into directing those who could answer the call to apostolic celibacy. These vocations were indispensable if Opus Dei was to receive its first great impetus, for they would be fully available to offer all their time and their lives to serve the Work.

Those who saw these first members of the Work with the young Father Escrivá often wondered just what they did.

In fact, they did nothing out of the ordinary. Nothing, that is, that would have singled them out fundamentally from their colleagues at university or at work. And it was precisely this which was the special characteristic of their vocation: to be ordinary citizens like the rest, spreading a Christian spirit in their surroundings. They would make their impact without any brilliant feats, without any shattering declarations, but without concealing the plain truth that the source of their happiness was to have found God and given Him everything. And starting from there, they would endeavour to sanctify their ordinary work, wanting to share this treasure with their friends, with their families and with the other people God placed in their company. Thus, simply by talking with them, their friends would also discover the spiritual adventure of being with Christ, and begin to move *along the way of prayer and of Love.* [115]

Be *men and women of the world, but don't be worldly men and women.* [116] Remain very united to Our Lord through prayer, *wear an invisible cloak that will cover each and every one of your senses and faculties: praying, praying, praying; atoning, atoning, atoning.* [117]

There was no other secret! Simple though it might be, it was all you needed: it was that firm fulcrum which Archimedes claimed was all he required to move the earth.

Any Christian could do as much, some would say. But how to start doing it, that was the point! How to start seeking a real, heroic holiness, without settling for mediocrity? "Be perfect as your heavenly Father is perfect ..." (Matt 5:48) Don Josemaría proclaimed, because he was convinced it was true, that this call of Christ is addressed to everyone and not only to those who have received a vocation to abandon the world: *All noble and worthy work in the human order can be turned into divine work ... There is no need to do extraordinary things in order to love God and to serve Him.* [118]

Some of those around the Father decided to respond with generosity to the call, without giving up the professional vocation which was theirs already. On the contrary, in Opus Dei they would find a stimulus and encouragement to persevere and make progress in their job, living the particular spirituality that the founder had passed on to them. That is why he asked them for a serious commitment, one that would need to be carefully thought over. And that is also why vocations came slowly, one by one.

Another two vocations

The Father's prayer, penance and apostolate slowly bore fruit. In January 1935, a young man at the Madrid School of Civil Engineering brought one of his student friends, Alvaro del Portillo, to meet the Father. He had first of all invited him to accompany him on visits to the poor and to teach catechism to children.

Alvaro's conversation with the Father was very short. It happened, however, that an aunt of his had met Don Josemaría at the Foundation for the Sick and he had asked her whether she knew of any young people in her family, or in those of her friends, who might be interested in this ideal that he wanted to promote in all levels of society. She then had mentioned her nephew Alvaro, of whom she was very fond. Since then, without having met him, the Father had been praying for him.

Alvaro was surprised by the kindly interest this most likeable priest showed in him. They did not, however, meet again until several months later: an earlier appointment fell through because of a last-minute hitch.

On 6 July, just before leaving for his holidays, Alvaro del Portillo decided to pay a farewell visit to Don Josemaría, whose personality he had found so striking despite the brevity of their conversation.

Their talk this time was much longer. As usual it touched on holiness in the midst of the world, and on the supernatural aspect of work – the indispensable means to rise towards God and bring others to Him.

The next day Alvaro came to a day of recollection at the Father's invitation. Never in his life had he been to an activity of this sort, and he was visibly moved by Don Josemaría's preaching. Without waiting for any indication from the Father, a member of the Work took Alvaro aside and suggested, without any more ado, that he commit himself for life to the service of God in Opus Dei.

Alvaro was somewhat surprised; he had not expected any such suggestion at a moment when a perfectly ordinary career was opening out before him. But without a second's hesitation he decided to answer *yes* to what he saw as a divine call like that addressed by

Jesus to the fishermen as they repaired their nets by the Sea of Galilee. He immediately went and told the Father of his decision.

At another day of recollection three Sundays later on 28 July, another followed. He was a student at the School of Mines this time, an open-faced youngster named José María Hernández de Garnica. He had made his appearance in the Academy one day, elegantly dressed. The Father had greeted him cordially, and without further explanation had put him to work ... José María found himself in his shirt-sleeves, with a hammer in his hand, fixing a canopy over the altar of the oratory! He would never forget that first encounter with the founder of Opus Dei when he had been taught – first without any words at all – what he could do there, the formation he would receive, and a general concern for the care of the house ...

Faithfulness to the mission undertaken

The Father's apostolate was never-ending. When he had finished work at Saint Elizabeth's he would start talking to people who came from all backgrounds; with many others he kept up the same purposeful kind of conversation by letter. When he got back to his little study in Ferraz Street, he received, one by one, a steady stream of the students he guided in their spiritual lives.

After several months under this regime he fell ill through exhaustion and the Vicar-General of the diocese had to insist that he take some rest.

He had no regrets about having over-exerted himself. He was convinced it was right to subordinate everything to the fulfilment of the divine Will, to do Opus Dei, even at the risk, it seemed, of upsetting some people. For his intense apostolate had inevitably attracted attention and his name had been put forward for some important positions, which he had consistently refused. The young President of Catholic Action, Angel Herrera Oria, for example, had wanted him to take the post of Director of the central house of the Counsellors of the movement.

Don Josemaría rejoiced to see the new impulse given to the apostolate of the laity by Pope Pius XI, but he had nevertheless replied "no", while thanking Angel Herrera warmly for having thought of him. Obviously this particular post offered great apostolic opportunities, for the priests he would have had in his charge were the future chaplains of the different "movements", the élite of the Spanish clergy. But it was impossible for him to accept without compromising the growth of the Work that he knew God had asked of him. Certainly he had to *serve the Church*, but *in the way the Church wants to be served.* [119]

Similarly, remembering the conclusions he had come to in 1929, he had rejected proposals for the fusion of Opus Dei with certain other organisations. Even if they joined at the summit – in the love of Christ – in the apostolate, the different spiritualities were like *the mixture of various liquids, which are good in themselves, which may be pleasant but which in combination can also turn out to be poisonous.* [120]

He continued to stick to his line in spite of the consequent unavoidable criticism and lack of understanding. And vocations came to Opus Dei as such, thanks to those who had prayed and offered their sufferings for that intention for so many years.

The Father thanked Saint Joseph, to whom he had entrusted his concerns when he was setting up the oratory in Ferraz Street, as well as to Our Lady, who had not stopped gaining grace upon grace for him. It was around that time, in thanksgiving and in order to deepen his Marian devotion, that he decided to join his first two names – José and María – together, thus uniting in a single word – Josemaría – the Immaculate Virgin and the holy Patriarch who was head of the Family of Nazareth.

On a small desk in the residence stood a little statue carved in wood, a representation of the Blessed Virgin with the Child Jesus in her arms: not a day went by which did not see him bending to kiss the statue's feet when he entered or left the house. Opus Dei, now beginning to take its first steps, had truly been born and grown *under the mantle of Our Lady.* [121]

All the glory for God

Between the 15th and the 21st of September 1935, when Don Josemaría made his retreat, alone as every year, at the Redemptorist residence in Madrid, he was able to give thanks to God for the many gifts He had given him.

He spent the days in prayer, without any preaching to help him, and refused with a smile the suggestion of the monks that he speak a little to make his solitude easier.

It was a time of interior deepening and purification.

My God!, may I hate sin and unite myself to you, holding tightly to the Holy Cross, so that I in my turn may fulfil your most lovable Will, stripped of every earthly attachment, without any other desire but your glory ... with generosity, without keeping anything for myself, offering myself up with you in a perfect holocaust. [122]

* * *

He could recall very vividly how, on 22 June 1933, while deeply absorbed in prayer in that same church of the Redemptorist Fathers, Our Lord had submitted him to a strange and painful test in which he clearly and vividly experienced that the Work was God's.

As he was thinking hard about the future growth of the Work, a thought had suddenly come into his mind: were his motives for acting not purely human – a desire to shine, to exercise a personal influence over the souls of others? Was he not deceiving those who had approached him with so much trust?

Was he really acting truly *for pure Love, solely and exclusively to give God all the glory?* [123]

The doubt lasted long enough to put a question-mark over everything he had worked at with such driving energy all these years. And yet he knew in his heart that he had done it only for God; the mere idea that he might have done it for any other motive was unbearable.

So, to extract an answer from Our Lord – whatever the

consequences – he put his whole soul into his fervent cry: *Lord, if Opus Dei is not here to serve you and the Church, destroy it right now!* [124]

Scarcely had he made his request, ready to give up everything though it would tear him apart, than he was filled with an immense peace and joy, so strong that it was already an answer.

This type of feeling, he had learned, was an infallible sign of the divine presence and the divine Will.

This severe test had been, perhaps, the hardest he had undergone since the Work was born. What was the fatigue occasioned by unremitting toil and prayer, what were the external obstacles, compared with the anguish of that test?

In any case, Our Lord had permitted the temptation for his benefit. Don Josemaría thanked Him, humbly, like a grateful son, for having purified his intention.

This new grace spurred him on to put his hand to the plough and set off anew, to deepen the furrow that had, as yet, hardly scratched a trace on the surface of the earth.

7. MADRID: JANUARY 1936

In the first months of 1936 the storm-clouds loomed darker still. Spain was deeply divided politically between the "People's Front", becoming more and more revolutionary, and a bloc of combined parties of the political centre-right. As election day (16 February) drew near, demonstrations in the streets ended more and more frequently with the burning down or looting of churches and convents.

Things were becoming overheated. The students who came to the Academy-Residence DYA were not immune to the mounting fever, but there they found a haven of peace, where they could pray and become more mature. One thing struck them: there was never any conversation there – let alone arguments – on political matters. Don Josemaría contented himself with reminding them of the Church's teaching and of the duty of every Christian to take up his responsibilities in society.

Just as he would have done in any other circumstances, he encouraged these young men who lived in an atmosphere of hatred to put into practice the precept of charity, even if it meant heroic efforts. This is of the essence of Opus Dei; but in those times it acquired a special significance. He forewarned them against the temptation to succumb to sectarianism in the work they might be doing.

He would vigorously repeat the words of Jesus recorded by Saint John: "I give you a new commandment: you are to love one another. Even as I have loved you, so, too, must you love one another. By this sign will all men know that you are My disciples: by the love that you bear one another." (John 13:34)

To help them engrave these words in their minds, he had the complete verse copied out in Latin on a piece of imitation parchment, which was framed and hung on one wall of the study of DYA when it was in Luchana Street. Later he put it in the "piano room" in the Ferraz Street residence.

I have often thought, he would tell them, *that after twenty centuries it is still a new commandment, for very few have have tried to put it into practice; the rest, the majority, have preferred and prefer to ignore it.* [125]

The Father himself gave an example of serenity which could only be explained by his deep interior life and his immense trust in divine Providence. The Work has to carry on, at God's pace, in any country and in any political situation. He was thinking about the next steps of a further expansion, to other Spanish cities, and he was already considering going to Paris ...

The next stage: Valencia, Paris ...

Besides, it was precisely now that the first fruits of the apostolate were beginning to show themselves fully. The coiled spring, long compressed, had suddenly been released.

In the November of the previous year, two other students, Francisco Botella and Pedro Casciaro, had asked to join the Work. And the Residence had been full since the beginning of the academic year 1935-36. All tried to bring their friends along to the Academy for the formation that was given there. So much so that the flat soon became too small, and they had had to find another. As the fourth floor, which they had left for lack of money, had since been taken by a lodger, they chose the neighbouring house, 48 Ferraz Street, to set up the Academy on its own. The Residence stayed where it was on the two third floor flats of Number 50. They moved in September. But the Father was already thinking of the new steps that would have to be taken in order to broaden the apostolates of the Work. He talked to his sons about three specific projects which they would carry out that very year and the next. The founder had first asked them to offer their daily Mass and the little sacrifices of every day from then on for these intentions. He also asked some friends to help him with their prayers.

The first project concerned the Residence itself, which would have to be moved into a larger and permanent building. But they should look further afield, too: to other cities, and even to other countries ... This greatly surprised those around him ... But the Father was more precise: the first city would be Valencia, the first country, France, and Paris in particular. And all this, God willing, in 1936 ...

Why go to the capital of France? Because he knew that whatever was said and written there would sooner or later have repercussions in cultural circles, first in Europe and then all over the world. Don Josemaría had not forgotten his earlier concern for the apostolate among the intellectuals, which had been strengthened by his vocation to Opus Dei. This was why, despite the political tensions in France and the threat of war with Germany, he did not hesitate to make this wager on the future. The Work had been born universal, and it was good that this should be made clear as soon as possible.

Perhaps too, though this was not the determining reason for his choice, what he had of French blood rejoiced to see that the land into which he was going to cast the precious seed placed in his heart by Our Lord seven years earlier, was the land that stretched north and east from the Pyrenees of his childhood days.

The founder had even thought already of the members of the Work who would be able to move to Paris.[126] As for Valencia, it would mark the beginning of the Work's growth within Spain. In Valencia it would not be difficult to open a students' residence similar to the one in Madrid. Ricardo Fernández Vallespín would be the Director and Isidoro Zorzano could ask for temporary leave of absence from the Andalusian Railways and return to Madrid to

Above: Residence of the Missionaries of St Vincent de Paul and the Basilica of the Miraculous Medal (right) in Madrid. It was here that Monsignor Escrivá founded Opus Dei on 2 October 1928, while on retreat.

Below: Don Josemaría with students of the DYA Academy.

Left: Father Josemaría in civilian clothes, during the Spanish civil war.

Below: One of the early meeting places in the 'thirties – a chocolate bar called *El Sotanillo* in Madrid.

look after the Residence of Ferraz ...

Once the apostolic targets had been fixed, they got on with the job in spite of the worsening political situation. They had begun looking for an entirely new building for the DYA in the first months of 1936. They soon found one, in Ferraz Street itself, opposite the Montaña Barracks. It was near the Plaza de España and the university halls of residence were not far away. What is more, the owner was willing to sell at what seemed a fair price.

Anxious days in Madrid

The furore of agitation in the capital did not die down. As the rector's house in the Foundation of Saint Elizabeth was no longer safe, Don Josemaría decided that his mother, sister and brother should leave immediately. In March they moved into a house on Doctor Cárceles (now King Francisco) Street, very near Ferraz. The Father continued in Saint Elizabeth's, looking after the Foundation, hearing confessions in the church and providing from there the necessary momentum to the Women's Section of Opus Dei.

His many journeys across Madrid gave him an opportunity to pray in atonement for so much hatred, shown particularly to priests who went about (as he did) in cassocks. Many days he ate nothing. He slept very little. To economise, he went around on foot, using shoes thrown out by the residents of Ferraz because the soles were worn, although the uppers could still be polished and looked presentable.

He continued to preach to groups of students. At the Academy of 48 Ferraz Street there were many students and the Residence at number 50 was completely full. There was so much material work to be attended to that the Father, with the help of the few members of the Work who lived there, whenever they could manage it, had to look after the household jobs: make the beds, repair the furniture or set the table before meals ... And all this without the residents realising it.

From the 10th to 13th April the Father preached a retreat in the Residence. It was the first retreat in a centre of Opus Dei.

On the 12th, Vicente Rodríguez Casado, a student reading History and Law, asked to join the Work.

The plans begin to take shape

The Father paid his first visit to Valencia after Easter, on 20 April, accompanied by Ricardo Fernández Vallespín. On their way they crossed the strange rocky landscapes of Cuenca and the rows of orange trees of the orchards on the outskirts of Valencia. From time to time they glimpsed a typical country cottage of that area with its thatched roof and whitewashed walls.

As soon as they arrived they went to see various people who were friends of their friends. The Auxiliary Bishop received Don Josemaría and Ricardo warmly, and promised to help them.

They left after three days, convinced that they would have to return soon, this time to search for a house for the projected Residence.

Circumstances, however, were becoming less and less favourable. At the beginning of May a slanderous story was spread around Madrid: groups of monks and nuns were said to be giving out poisoned sweets to workers' children ... On 3 May religious houses and churches were sacked and set ablaze. Many monks and nuns fled their monasteries and convents and sought refuge in private houses.

There had been more than four hundred attacks of this sort since the beginning of 1936, and in sixty cases at least, the buildings had been totally destroyed. Strikes and acts of vandalism multiplied. The government had shown itself powerless to stop political crimes. There were rumours of a possible coup d'état, or of a revolution. Everyone by now apprehensively expected matters to take a tragic turn.

For Don Josemaría these sad events were a new stimulus. As always he prayed, and also asked the students, the priests he knew and his friends, to pray. By May he was so exhausted that the same

Vicar-General of Madrid, Don Francisco Morán, who had a great affection for him, advised him to see a doctor and to take a rest. Some of his sons who were doctors looked after him, but he was not able to take the rest ... [127]

Soon the Father considered it no longer a good idea to carry on the meetings of formation in the DYA Academy, where there was a risk of forced entry and confiscation. This did not stop him, however, from arranging a period of intense formation for July, for those going to Valencia and Paris.

He devoted a great deal of time to the first members of the Work. *Increase, therefore, your faith in God, and also have a little faith and trust in your Father,* [128] he told them, putting great emphasis on the divine origin of the Work, the guarantee of its permanence through the centuries to come.

He saw himself as nothing more than a simple instrument. Knowing that he might well disappear at any moment, on several occasions he took a son of his aside and asked:

If I were to die , would you carry on with the Work? [129]

The replies showed that they had indeed realised the supernatural nature of the commitment they had taken on:

"Yes, Father, I would carry on the Work ... "

He spent several days in June with the young vocations in Madrid, hurrying up their formation. The negotiations for the purchase of the new residence in Ferraz Street were concluded. Isidoro's arrival in the capital in July meant they could go ahead with setting up the residence, while Francisco Botella left for Valencia to look for a house there.

In Madrid, the strikes and assassination attempts were increasing, and the political situation got worse every minute. The Government was no longer in control. On 13 July a right-wing leader, José Calvo Sotelo, was assassinated.

By the 16th, several people were already living in the new Residence at 6 Ferraz Street, though it was largely without furniture.

Francisco Botella sent word that he had found a house in Valencia. Ricardo went at once to the city of Turia to arrange the conveyancing of the property. But the negotiations with the owner were broken off when it was announced on the radio that the Spanish Army in Africa had risen in rebellion.

Communications with Madrid were cut and the military ordered to report to barracks.

The Spanish Civil War had begun.

8. MADRID: 20 JULY 1936

Very early on Sunday morning, 19 July, sympathisers with the rebels poured into the Montaña Barracks just opposite the Residence.

Alerted to the situation, the National Guard and militiamen set up road-blocks on the streets surrounding the barracks in the early afternoon and ordered all passers-by to show their papers. At dawn the next morning the mobs attacked the barracks; there was constant gunfire and sometimes stray bullets embedded themselves in the walls of the residence.

Towards the end of Monday afternoon the attackers stormed the barracks, massacred the defenders and captured the arms they found there.

The Father sent all the residents home, asking them to let him know when they arrived.

He found out by telephone that Juan Jiménez Vargas, Alvaro del Portillo and José María Hernández de Garnica had all arrived safely at Juan's house, and told them of his decision to leave the flat on Ferraz Street. It would have been like signing one's own death warrant to go out in a cassock, so he put on a blue boiler suit they had found for him, which was a bit on the large side. Thus attired, he made his way with Isidoro and José María González Barredo through the crowds seething around the barracks. Such was the excitement that the Father's fairly conspicuous tonsure went unnoticed.

He went straight to his mother's house, where he stayed in hiding for several days with Juan, who joined him a few days later.

Juan Jiménez Vargas had been to the morgue and was able to confirm that the rumours which were going around of mass executions by firing-squad were, unfortunately, only too well-founded.

The quest for a safe place to stay

Having convinced the Father to stay hidden, Juan returned to the Residence on 25 July to see what sort of state it was in. Hardly had he arrived than there was a violent pounding on the door. It was a patrol of the Iberian Federation of Anarchists, who had come to search the building. They were ruthlessly thorough. When they got to the priest's room they found Don Josemaría's cassock, his cilice and his impressive discipline.

"Do you live here?", the militiamen asked.

"No", answered Juan.

"Let's go to your house then", they said.

They escorted him all the way there and searched it thoroughly. Juan could see himself already in prison, but unexpectedly they left him in peace.

Juan and Alvaro del Portillo met that same day in San Bernardo Street to exchange news on the events that had rapidly followed one another. There were alarmist reports going round. The situation had rapidly crystallised. The uprising had been successful in a number of places and had taken control of Navarre and part of the Basque Country, Aragon, Old Castille (with the exception of Santander), León, Galicia, part of Estramadura and several towns in Andalusia (Cadiz, Seville, Córdova and Granada). The Nationalist zone was, therefore, quite extensive and also included the Canary Islands and Spanish Morocco. In all, it was nearly half of Spain. Official Republican Government communiqués spoke of a limited rebellion and hinted that it would soon be put down. Some people, however, predicted a long war. This was the case with the Father, who very quickly understood the seriousness of the situation.

In the days immediately following the rising, many priests, and religious, men and women, had been murdered, dragged out by force from churches and convents. On 25 July the Republican Government had published a decree expropriating all buildings belonging to religious orders or to charitable institutions. A few days later it would close all the churches. All religious acts became clandestine and punishable by yet more severe laws, even by capital punishment.

Juan and Alvaro realised that the future was very grim and that there would be no religious freedom for a long time. Should they leave the country in order to continue the Work? They knew that in any case God wanted it to be carried out and that it would indeed be carried out, even if it were by extraordinary means.

The Father, in the meantime, was worried because he had received no news from Ricardo Fernández Vallespín or Francisco Botella, both of them still in Valencia. Pedro Casciaro was in Torrevieja, near Alicante, and the other members of the Work were scattered around Madrid. José María Hernández de Garnica was imprisoned in the Cárcel Modelo, out of which a number of men were taken and summarily shot each day.

At the beginning of August the Father learned that the militia were going to search his mother's house on Doctor Cárceles Street. At his family's request he got ready to leave immediately. If they discovered that he was a priest he would be arrested at once and shot.

A dramatic search

From his mother's house he went with Juan Jiménez Vargas to a flat on the third floor of a middle-class apartment block at 31 Sagasta Street. It was the home of an old friend, an engineer called Manuel, who was on his own because his family had left Madrid.

The Father arrived in mid-morning, Juan in the afternoon, trying not to attract the caretaker's attention. They were joined a few days later by a cousin of Manuel.

An old servant made meals for them as best she could. (She bought provisions for two only, so as not to arouse any suspicion). They feared a militia search at any moment, for there had been, in fact, two searches in the block forty-eight hours after they arrived. The following night everyone was ordered to leave all their lights on. The refugees could only stay in the rooms facing the courtyard. The same thing happened a few days later, so tension was extremely high.

The Father prayed for the Church, for those around him, for the members of the Work now physically separated from him, for his family, for the persecuted and for their persecutors ... He was deeply concerned.

Madrid was bombarded by the Nationalist Army on 27 and 28 August and the militiamen became much more vigilant. There was a scare early in the morning of the 30th, when they heard knocking on the door. They all feared it might be a search. The servant, as they had agreed beforehand, took some time opening the door, so as to give the refugees a chance to use the tradesmen's entrance and hide in the attic. But it was only a neighbour and they were able to go back to the flat again.

Later that morning there was another knock at the door. The serving-woman again went to open it, without hurrying. And this time it was the militia. So that she could be heard by the others, she shouted:

"There's no-one here ... I am deaf, don't you know? I can't hear well." She spoke very loudly, as had been arranged, to warn them that it was the militia.

At that the refugees hurried back up to the attic. The roof was so low that they had to sit on the floor. It was unbearably hot.

Suddenly they could hear footsteps coming up the stairs. They came closer and closer. It seemed as if the men were on the other side of the wall, although in fact they were in the room beneath. Little by little the the steps receded, but the noise of the search continued.

Don Josemaría revealed to Manuel's cousin, who was terribly afraid, that he was a priest. The militia came back again and were so near that it seemed as if they were going to enter the attic. The Father then gave absolution to him and Juan, without hearing their confession, but reminding them that they would have to confess their sins as soon as they were able. Juan felt so much at peace at the words of the Father that he soon fell sound asleep.

Around half past nine they heard no more noises. They waited for another half an hour before going down to the fourth floor. All covered in dust and with their tongues completely dry, they called at the door of the flat of a family they knew.

I had no idea just what a glass of water was worth![130] the Father commented to those who had sheltered them.

They then found out that they had not been able to warn Manuel, who had gone out, and that he had been arrested on his return.

The militia came back the following day and searched the flat to the right, on the fourth floor. On the left-hand side, which is where the three had found a refuge, they did not go at all. They only asked for some tools to break open the adjoining flat.[131]

Don Josemaría tried to make light of the situation with amusing remarks, helping those with him to relax. But the conversation kept coming back to the war. They then said the Rosary, led by the Father.

A day and a half later he told them that it was neither good nor reasonable for them to stay there any longer. They slipped out in the morning while one of the family distracted the caretaker's attention, and the refugees were taken to another flat where a widow lived with two of her children. One of the children was very young, however, and as they could not take any risks they had to move to another house.

Don Josemaría was always in danger of being recognised as a priest. One day he learned of a rumour being circulated in Madrid to the effect that he was dead. A man who looked like him had been hanged from the tree in front of the house of Doña Dolores. His blood froze when he heard the news; he imagined how his mother must have felt. He thought, too, of the unfortunate man who had died in his place: from then on he prayed for him every day in his Mass.

Such were the circumstances that his friends did not want to have them in their homes, knowing as they did the enormous risk they ran sheltering a priest. Those who did so were terrified, and the Father tried to leave as soon as possible so as to minimise the risk for them. They slept in a different house each night; during the day they wandered around the streets, for they had no official papers.

The Father suffered very much from not being able to say Mass; instead he would recite from memory all the liturgical prayers with the exception of the formula of consecration. The Collect, the Prayer over the Offerings and the Postcommunion were always the same: a plea to Our Lord to send labourers into His harvest. The Gospel was invariably the calling of the apostles by Jesus. A spiritual communion took the place of Holy Communion. Don Josemaría called them *dry masses* .[132]

The Father with Alvaro and Juan

Alvaro del Portillo had stayed in hiding with one of his brothers in a house on Serrano Street which belonged to some friends of his family. A board painted in the colours of Argentina fixed to the facade made it moderately safe. The house next door, which was one of the centres of the Service of General Security, was guarded round the clock by militiamen, so it was better not to attract any attention ...

After about a month, however, Alvaro, only half-aware of the dangers he was running, went out to go to the Ministry of Public Works. He wanted to see if he had been crossed off the list of engineering staff in the Hydrographic Confederation of the Tagus, where he had been working in previous months. When he went out he sat down at a café table in the street. Suddenly, a man came up to him: it was the father of José María González Barredo. He whispered in his ear:

"Do you know who I've got at home? The Father! He asked me if he could rest there a little while because he can't keep on his feet any longer. But the caretaker can't be trusted. If he realises what's going on, we're all in trouble ..."

"He must come and stay with me!"

"I'll go and get him at once."

The Father and Alvaro had the joy of being united again. Later Juan Jiménez Vargas joined them.

Their days were very busy. They studied and wrote and prayed ... But there were also periods of relaxation to help them better support the confinement they were subjected to. The Father directed their daily meditation out aloud.

On 1 October another of Alvaro's brothers came to warn them that they were searching the houses of the owner's family. They had to move, *so as not to tempt God*. [133] The Father was thinking first and foremost of the future of the Work. As for himself, he feared nothing.

Besides, on this eve of the anniversary of the foundation of Opus Dei, he was convinced – and talked about it to Alvaro del Portillo – that Our Lord was reserving a special favour for him, as he often did on that date, and always in an unexpected fashion.

That is what he thought. But suddenly he felt afraid, as if the anguishes accumulated over the last few months now weighed heavily on his shoulders. He was happy to be a martyr, but felt a physical fear. For several seconds his legs shook as if they did not want to carry him any further. When he got a grip on himself again, he understood that Our Lord wanted to teach him a lesson: it was not on his own strength that he had to count.

This, then, was the awaited "favour".

All our fortitude is on loan. [134]

Juan set off to look for another refuge. The Father, after making several telephone calls, also went out of the house, leaving Alvaro there with his brother Pepe. When he returned, it was to tell them, with tears in his eyes, of the martyrdom of two priests who had just been assassinated.

One of them, Don Lino Vea-Murguía, was one of the priests the Father had been meeting every Monday for a study circle he

organised and who had helped him to hear the confessions of the
first members of the Work and their friends. The other was Padre
Poveda, the founder of the Teresians, who was a great friend of his.
*What a joy after having lost him – shedding many tears – to know
that he continues to love us from Heaven! That was precisely the
theme of one of our last conversations …* They had in fact talked
about the possibility of their being killed and they had come to the
conclusion that there – in Heaven – they would love each other
even more.[135]

The Father also told Alvaro that, thinking he was doing him a
favour, a member of the Work had given him the key to a house
belonging to some friends of his who were away. But learning that
there was still a young woman servant living there who was about
twenty-two or twenty-three years old, he had turned down this offer
and, to avoid temptation, had dropped the key down a drain.

A strange hiding place

They found a strange hiding place for the Father in the first
days of October. It was a small clinic for mentally-ill patients in
Arturo Soria Road, in Madrid, run by a psychiatrist, Doctor Suils,
the son of a doctor the Escrivás had known in Logroño.

Some twenty people made up the total of staff and inmates;
the rest were fugitives. They admitted the Father there, ostensibly
as a patient, taking all sorts of precautions so as not to attract the
attention of the nurses and other staff. That meant that he had to
act as if he were mentally disturbed, especially as some nurses
suspected that there was something odd going on. Indeed, one day
the militia came looking for one of the refugees, who was executed
shortly afterwards.

Happily Don Josemaría's young brother Santiago came to stay
with him. His mother, who had had to move after the bombard-
ments carried out by the Nationalist troops, had sent him to be with
his brother at Doctor Suils' clinic.

Only Doctor Suils, his deputy, one of the nurses and another fugitive knew that Josemaría Escrivá was a priest. Isidoro, thanks to the arm-band proclaiming his Argentinian nationality, was the only one who could go freely around Madrid. Through him the Father received news about his sons, scattered in different parts of Spain, and, also through him, sent words of encouragement and consolation to them.

Alvaro del Portillo was then in hiding in the Finnish Legation, which was stormed on 4 December. Juan Jiménez Vargas had been put in prison and was on the point of being executed, but, unexpectedly, he was released shortly afterwards. There was no news of Vicente Rodríguez Casado; they would know later, in February 1937, that he had taken refuge in the Norwegian Legation. José María Hernández de Garnica had escaped death for an unknown reason after being condemned by a People's Tribunal, and had been transferred to a prison in Valencia.

Taking advantage of his stay at the clinic, Don Josemaría was treated for rheumatism. The effects of this severe treatment were very painful, and every time the medicine was administered to him it left him paralysed. But Don Josemaría continued to trust more than ever in God's help. His serenity astonished everyone. Those who received his letters drew hope and comfort from them. José María González Barredo and Juan Jiménez Vargas had spent some days with him in Doctor Suils' clinic, but they could not stay for long, and had to leave him.

He had suffered above all from not being able to say Mass until, making use of the license published by the Holy See on 22 August, he started to celebrate it in his room, with no altar, no vestments, using a simple glass as a chalice, while the single "safe" nurse kept watch in the corridor ...

9. MADRID: MARCH 1937

José María González Barredo had at last found a less dangerous refuge. It was the house of the Consul of Honduras, on the Paseo de la Castellana, which was covered by an assumed diplomatic immunity. The owners had removed most of the furniture on the ground floor to make room for the many people who had already taken refuge there. They had also hired another flat on the floor above.

Don Josemaría went to the Honduras Legation at the beginning of March with his brother Santiago. A few days later they were joined by Alvaro and by Eduardo Alastrué, a student who before the war used to go to the residence in Ferraz Street. In May, Juan Jiménez Vargas also joined them.

They spent most of the day in a room about ten square yards, lit by a narrow window opening onto an interior courtyard. Their only furniture was some mattresses they spread on the floor at night and used to sit on during the day. To avoid being idle, the Father had made out a timetable which was followed strictly. Early in the morning the Father said Mass in the room on piled up suitcases. On Sundays and feast days he would say it in the hall so that any of the refugees could attend if they wanted to. Without any vestments, using a little glass plate for the paten and a gold cup lent by the Consul's daughter for the chalice, he said the prayers with deliberation. The congregation responded with a faith that put one in mind of the Christians in the catacombs. Our Lord was permanently reserved in two round silver boxes shut up in a writing desk, an oil lamp burning permanently in front of it. Don Josemaría and those accompanying him spent long stretches in front of the desk.

Every day the Father commented on a passage of the Gospel, helping his listeners to follow the actions, gestures and teachings of Jesus step by step. Alvaro and Eduardo made handwritten summaries of these meditations and passed them on to Isidoro when he came to see them. He took them to read to those he could meet in Madrid.

The Father and his companions devoted several hours daily to keeping up with their respective specialities as well as studying foreign languages. The thought of the future growth of the Work was always in their minds.

A weary confinement

The atmosphere at the Legation was often one of anxiety, owing to the number of people practically living on top of each other. They could not go out, nor even go near the windows. Tension frequently mounted among the occupants, exacerbated by alarming reports coming in from outside.

At the beginning of October 1936 the Nationalist army had tried to take the capital, and although they had not succeeded, they controlled all access to it except from the east. The Republican troops, commanded by General Miaja and supported by the International Brigade, repulsed a new offensive launched on 7 November by General Franco, who had become the Commander-in-Chief of the Nationalist army. Fierce fighting went on around the university until 23 November. By that date most Embassy personnel had already left Madrid.

The Government was well aware that many Spaniards were in hiding in diplomatic quarters. On 4 December, 1936, the militia had broken into the Finnish Legation and arrested 525 people (including Alvaro, who then spent nearly three months in prison) and had killed many of them.

The knowledge of this only increased the nervousness of the reluctant hosts of the Honduran Legation. Don Josemaría tried to defuse the inevitable clashes. He was also, noticeably, the only one not to join in the noisy celebrations at the news of victories of the Nationalist troops: probably he was thinking of the wounds that would have to be healed when the time came to reconcile the two Spains that were now at loggerheads.

The Father managed to help those who were with him to be an element of peace in the charged atmosphere of the consulate. He urged them to be patient, and encouraged them to "grow interiorly": *Outside events have placed you in voluntary confinement, worse perhaps, because of its circumstances, than the confinement of a prison. You have suffered an eclipse of your personality ... The absence of flowers and leaves (external action) does not exclude the growth and activity of the roots (interior life). Work: things will change, and you will yield more fruit than before, and sweeter.* [136]

Isidoro, to be prudent, had to space out his visits. Two children – Alvaro's brother and sister – kept up the links with outside. They carried the written meditations of the Father slipped in between their shoes and their socks.

Don Josemaría was ever confident about the future of the Work: *the waters will pass through the mountains* (Ps 103:10). But he suffered from the close confinement.

Physically, these last few months had been very trying. One day his own mother, who had come to see him, had only recognised him by his voice. He had lost more than forty kilograms in weight because of illness, in addition to the privations he imposed on himself on top of an already insufficient diet.

Risking his life on the streets of Madrid

The thought of all the people in Madrid who had need of him, and whom he could not help, was unbearable. Thus after a first failed attempt at the beginning of the Summer, he made up his mind to leave his hiding-place at the end of August. All he had in the way of papers was a letter signed by the Consul which purported to show him as an employee of the Legation. A lame excuse in the case of any serious interrogation, it could just be enough if he were caught in a routine check.

He went to live with a friend in Ayala Street. A short while later they were joined by Juan Jiménez Vargas, with similar papers obtained from the Panamanian Consulate.

For several weeks, at the risk of his life, the Father again took up his travelling all over Madrid in a pair of overalls or in a suit: here to visit someone on his deathbed, there to celebrate Mass, over in that quarter to bring a sick person the viaticum – he reserved it in a cigarette-case inside a canvas bag in the Honduran colours with the seal of the Consulate of Honduras. He also gave Communion to those who had stayed behind in the consulate. He went back and visited them often, encouraging them to stand fast and deepen their interior lives.

He tried to track down those who had been in contact with the Work, and who were now scattered around Madrid. He was anxious to comfort them and to strengthen their faith. He preached a retreat over three days for those who could attend. Among them was Isidoro, a young teacher in an agricultural school called José María Albareda, (with whom he had talked a number of times in the DYA Academy in 1936), as well as a friend of his, Tomás Alvira. Completing their meditations in hiding, each would leave the house by a different exit and meet again several hours later in another house so as not to attract attention.

The religious persecution continued to rage. The churches remained closed; open-air images and statues were mostly destroyed. The Father, who knew every one of them from his prayer-filled trips in Madrid, discovered one Madonna which had gone unnoticed by the iconoclasts: it was chiselled in the stone base of the monument to Christopher Columbus, in the Plaza de Colón. Every time he passed that way she was the object of his regard and of his prayers for the Church, for the spreading of Opus Dei, for Spain in the convulsions of civil war and for peace in the whole world.

One day soon after leaving the Honduran Consulate he entered a shop where they sold frames, engravings and mirrors, and asked the man if he had a picture of the Blessed Virgin. After he had assured himself that it was not a trap (the Father had shown him his "official papers"), the man brought out a little print, elegantly framed. The Father bought it and took it away with him; a glance at it kept him going in hard times.

10. BARCELONA: 19 NOVEMBER 1937

Around midday Don Josemaría got onto the bus headed for Seo de Urgel, accompanied by Juan Jiménez Vargas, Pedro Casciaro, Francisco Botella, José María Albareda (the young Doctor in Chemistry and Pharmaceutics for whom the Father had preached a few weeks before in Madrid, and who had soon after asked to join Opus Dei) and Miguel, a student and an old boy of the DYA.

The Father wore a pair of flannels fastened at the ankles, a blue polo-necked sweater and a black beret. His companions were also equipped for a long march.

As they approached the mountainous area of the Pyrenees, the checks became stricter; so Pedro, Francisco and Miguel, whose papers were not entirely in order, got off the bus at the village of Sanahuja, about twelve miles from the most dangerous point, and continued on foot.

At Peramola crossroads a man in his forties approached the bus and by signs asked them to follow him. They reached the village about an hour later and came to a farmhouse where they could stay for the night. But the Father could not sleep, thinking of the other three who had not yet arrived ...

The next day they set off regardless, and as they got further up into the mountains they became more worried about those who were still missing.

After a long time they came to a farmhouse and stopped again. The Father made himself known as a priest to those who had joined them, and celebrated Mass there.

The hours went by and Pedro, Francisco and Miguel were still missing ... But at last, next morning, 21 November, they arrived: their guide had lost his way, and had made them go round in circles.

They started off again on their march towards the Pyrenees; they were determined to try to cross the mountains, risking everything. If everything went well they would be able to reach Andorra and then, by way of France, to reach the Nationalist zone.

A difficult decision

It was not without hesitation that the Father had left the capital. His sons, concerned about his safety, had pressed him to take this step. He had let himself be convinced by the thought that he would be able to carry on with Opus Dei in complete freedom in the other zone, and establish contact with so many students who were fighting on the battle fronts. Isidoro remained in Madrid and would be able to keep in touch with those who had stayed behind, and with his family. Vicente Rodriguez Casado, Alvaro del Portillo and José María González Barredo were still in hiding in various diplomatic premises.

He had arrived in Valencia in the afternoon of 8 October, and waited for a favourable moment to go on to Barcelona and, from there, to the frontier. In Valencia he had met Francisco Botella and Pedro Casciaro, who were delighted to see him again after more than a year's separation. The next day he had taken the train for the Catalan capital ...

He could still see them waving to him on the platform, getting smaller and smaller with the distance ... At the moment the train moved off, he had slipped his hand discreetly into his jacket and blessed them, saying mentally the formula for the blessing for the journey which he had composed from the words of Tobias in the

Bible: *Through the intercession of Holy Mary may you have a safe journey; may God be on your path and may His angels go with you.* [137]

During the couple of days he spent in Barcelona he had been gnawed by anxiety for those he had left behind ...

A few days later Juan left Madrid for Valencia to pick up Francisco and Pedro. At Daimiel, a town in the province of Ciudad Real, they had met Miguel, who had been hiding there since the outbreak of the civil war.

Don Josemaría had taken advantage of his short stay in Barcelona to give the Sacraments to those people who had heard that he was there.

The crossing of the Pyrenees presented many dangers. A judge who was a friend of his – he knew him from the Law faculty in Saragossa – had tried to dissuade the Father from setting off on this adventure: "When they catch fugitives, the border patrols don't usually take them prisoner. They shoot them. And if by chance they are caught, they'll certainly be condemned to death." To convince him he took him into a courtroom where some such people were being tried. But despite this, and despite the bouts of rheumatism which struck him from time to time, the Father persevered in his plan.

A mother's answer

The man serving as their guide on 21 November advised them not to spend the night where they were. They would spend the night in an old brick bread oven, in a nearby house.

Everyone slept, overcome with exhaustion. But the Father could not get to sleep. Had he been right to throw himself into this escapade, leaving those he loved behind him? To go on was to abandon them. But, on the other hand, how could he continue to work in what God wanted ...? Again and again he begged Our Lord ceaselessly to show him where His Will lay: should he go on, or should he go back?

In the end he invoked the Blessed Virgin once again, asking her to show him which way to go by means of a precise sign that he himself suggested to Our Lady.

In the small hours of the morning he got up and left the place where they had passed the night. Some time later, when he returned, he held a rose of gilded wood in his hand and his face was radiant with joy.

He immediately asked his companions to get ready everything necessary to say Mass.

Seeing his change of mood – the night before they had heard him weeping – they realised that something important had happened; they refrained, however, from asking any questions.

After Mass, the march towards the Pyrenees continued. The Father, carrying the gilded rose, marched with a firm step.

They travelled for an hour through the Rialp forest, and stayed hidden there, waiting for the right moment to start the climb proper. They were joined by two more young men, Tomás Alvira and Manuel Sainz de los Terreros.

The next morning the Father said Mass on an improvised altar made with large stones, and addressed a few words to them.

Over the next five days they trained, in preparation for the physical endurance test they were about to undergo. They walked in the woods and did exercises. And so as not to lose sight of their professional concerns, they each took turns to give the others talks on their own particular speciality.

The crossing of the Pyrenees

On Saturday 27 November the time came to get under way. The previous night they had slept in a cave used for cattle, while they waited for daylight.

A young man, energetic and determined-looking, arrived before dawn; he told them to call him Antonio and asked them to follow him.

The next day, a Sunday, they stopped in a ravine where they

spent the day in hiding before continuing the march. They were joined by several people. Don Josemaría announced that he was going to celebrate Mass. He said most of it on his knees, using the flattest stone he could find as an altar. The atmosphere of devotion and recollection was extraordinary. Many of the people there had not been able to enter a church since July 1936. That same day a Catalan student noted in his diary: "I have never been to a Mass like today's. I do not know if it is because of the circumstances, or because the priest is a saint."[138]

After distributing Communion, Don Josemaría placed several consecrated hosts in the cigarette-case he had already used for the same purpose in Madrid.

The expedition started off again in mid-afternoon. Now they were going to have to get up a mountain. They went forward in single file. Juan walked behind the Father, to support him in case he fell; but it was Tomás who weakened first, and Don Josemaría had to intervene to convince the guide not to press on and leave him behind. By the end of the ascent it was already the middle of the night. Some of the travellers who joined them had cursed and sworn when they stumbled, and the Father suffered greatly and decided to consume the hosts out of respect for the Blessed Sacrament.

They spent the next day in an isolated mountain farmhouse and left in the evening with some food, the last they would be able to get and take with them. More climbing, and then the path flattened out again. Finally, after crossing a stream, they started to climb Mount Ares, almost five thousand feet high. At moments the Father had to be supported and almost carried by two of the others.

After a halt they started off again, until the guide told them to stop. There was someone missing: he was afraid that the one who had disappeared might have been an informant for the border patrols. In fact it was only someone lagging behind and the guide brought him up with the others by force, threatening to use his pistol.

But now it was far more difficult to get going again. José María Albareda, in his turn, had to lie down ... Hoisted to his feet by his companions, he stumbled on, half-dazed.

When it was still dark, they arrived at a farmyard, where they would take refuge during daylight. At first light they could see that they were on flat land with meadows and two farmhouses nearby. The cold was intense ... In the evening – of Tuesday, 30 November – they set off once more on the fourth night-stage since they had left the woods of Rialp. They were joined from time to time by mysterious individuals, weighed down with packages ... Smugglers, no doubt ...

The terrain was flatter now. The Father discreetly encouraged his companions not to interrupt their dialogue with Our Lord, despite their fatigue.

With great care they crossed the road that leads to Noves de Segre, and a little later went under the country road that goes from Seo de Urgel to Sort, at the point where there is a bridge over the river Arabell. They followed the course of the river for a while, then spent the day lying low, hiding between the stones and bushes so as not to be spotted. After they had slept for a while they picked themselves up for the last leg. A few flakes of snow began to fall.

It was the evening of 1 December. They were setting off on the final night trek, which would lead them to the frontier. But this was by far the most dangerous zone, for it was constantly patrolled by the border guards.

After more climbing they came down the slopes of the Sierra del Burbre. Their feet loosened some rocks, some of which rolled and bounced down the slope: the guide reminded them in no uncertain terms that they had to be totally silent.

There were still several more danger spots: they had to cross a road, then a river.

At one moment the guide told them all to lie flat on the ground, behind trees and bushes, while he went cautiously on ahead to see where the border guard look-outs were scanning the frontier. When he had to get up again, the Father started to shudder with the cold; Juan had to rub his arms and legs briskly until he could stand up and stagger on. They only had to climb one steep hillside to reach the frontier with Andorra. To be on the safe side they had to wait for what seemed like ages before starting the ascent.

At last they passed the frontier, but the guide told them to keep silent until they were out of the range of fire of the border patrol ... Suddenly, just as they began to go down a hill they heard the crack of several shots. But they were already out of danger. A few minutes later the guide pointed out the path they would have to take to get to the first Andorran village.

The expedition's joy burst out exuberantly. The Father and those who were with him started to say the Rosary. Further on, the guide and his helpers lit a fire while they waited for dawn to break. When they had finished the Rosary, they came up and warmed themselves at the fire.

A good while passed before daybreak revealed the little village of Sant Julia de Loria. Don Josemaría said the first words of the *Salve Regina* out loud, and everyone joined in. It was the morning of 2 December 1937.

On reaching the village they went first to the church. It was the first unprofaned church they had seen since the beginning of the war. Then, after taking some refreshment in a café, they took the road to Andorra la Vella.

There Don Josemaría saw a priest in the road, and went forward to greet him with arms outstretched. The next day, in a small chapel set up by some Benedictine nuns from Montserrat near the hotel where they had stayed, the Father would be able to celebrate Mass in normal conditions for the first time in many months. His hands were, however, so swollen from the thorns which had stuck in them when he had been sheltering among the bushes that Juan had to extract them one by one in the hostel where they were resting. The snow which had been threatening during the last stage of the journey now fell heavily.

In the Mass, the Father had given thanks to God with his whole heart for having delivered them from so many dangers. He made an intense petition for those who had stayed behind in Madrid, and for those scattered throughout both the zones of Spain, some of whom he would have the joy of seeing again. He prayed for the growth of Opus Dei which Our Lord had wished to slow down in its advance for a time. But that did not matter: the water also swirls and slows down as it dashes against the rocks before rushing forward again with renewed energy ... [139]

IV

TREADING OUT THE PATH

You will stop where the world reaches its limits.
Paul Claudel

1. LOURDES: 11 DECEMBER 1937

Don Josemaría Escrivá was celebrating Mass at a side altar in the crypt of the Basilica at Lourdes, a couple of yards from the grotto where Mary Immaculate had appeared to a young girl of fourteen some eighty years earlier. He renewed the intentions of all the Masses he had said in perilous or dramatic circumstances over the last few months: for the Church, the Pope, peace for Spain and the world, the expansion of the Work ... He had been on French soil for a few hours, a few hundred miles from Paris, where he was still planning to put down the roots of Opus Dei as soon as possible.

The weather had been cold. The mountain peaks were white with snow and heavy blizzards had delayed the crossing of the frontier. In the end José María Albareda had managed to phone his brother at Saint Jean de Luz for a car to take the Father and his companions from the border to Saint Gaudens, where they spent the night.

Then Lourdes. A few hours after the Mass here they found themselves back in Spain again, but this time in the Nationalist zone. The Father immediately telephoned two bishops, friends of his, at Vitoria and Pamplona.

Juan, Francisco and Pedro reported to the military authorities at San Sebastian. Juan was assigned to the Teruel front, the other two being sent to Pamplona. The Father was left on his own.

On 17 December he went to Pamplona, invited by Bishop Olaechea, who offered him a room in his episcopal palace and provided him with some clerical clothes. He took advantage of the occasion to spend a few days in silent recollection, something he had not been able to do for a long time. Pedro and Francisco seized every opportunity they could to get leave from the barracks and come and spend some time with him.

After Christmas he went to Burgos, then the capital of the Nationalist zone. He thought that as the Bishop of Madrid was there, he would find it easier to get in touch with people.

Life in Burgos

In a boarding-house on Santa Clara Road the Father met up with José María Albareda, who had just obtained a post which entailed assessing certain matters appertaining to the General Office of Secondary Education. They were soon joined by Francisco, at the end of January, and by Pedro at the beginning of March.

On 29 March all four moved into the Hotel Sabadell, where they occupied a single large room. They divided it into three: a living area where Pedro, Francisco and José María slept, an alcove separated from the rest by a curtain, where the Father slept, and a bay-windowed *belvedere*, which was used to receive visitors.

This extremely modest 'suite' very quickly became the scene of a flurry of activity. Don Josemaría received a great number of people, who came to talk with him and for Confession. His activity was as intense as usual, without his taking any notice of a bad attack of pharyngitis which he had caught just after his arrival in Burgos.

One day he realised he was spitting blood. He thought it might be tuberculosis and decided to consult a doctor: if it was, he would have had to go into isolation, to avoid the risk of infecting his sons. Fortunately, after having suffered the illness without the doctors being able to find out what was wrong with him, or its cause, it ceased. But really the Father was but a shadow of his former self after all the trials he had been through. Added to his great physical exhaustion there had also been the very difficult crossing of the Pyrenees. On top of that, he had begun again with his self-imposed fasts ...

When Pedro and Francisco returned to the hotel after work, the Father helped them to establish a warm family atmosphere, and they remembered those who were absent.

All told, they had very little money, even taking José María Albareda's earnings into account. They went without even the barest essentials. Besides, precisely at that point, the Father decided to put into practice a heroic decision he had made in 1930: not to take a stipend – neither he nor any future priests of the Work – for preaching, saying Mass or any other religious task. It was hard, very hard, but Don Josemaría would repeat over and over again a verse from the Psalms: "Place your worries in the hands of the Lord and He will feed you" (Ps 54:23).

This lack of material means did not stop him from looking up the addresses of all the students he had known before the war, and arranging to go and see them as soon as possible. Which is what he did.

One day he went as far as Cordoba, in very difficult conditions because the railway lines into Andalusia were cut, and one had to go there in a very roundabout way. To return to Burgos, all he had in his pocket was small change, which he put down on the ticket counter at the station:

How far can I go with this? he asked.

The man gave the name of a village near Salamanca.

All right, to there then. After that, God will provide. [1]

And he was left without anything to eat.

He sent letters everywhere, spurring on the people he knew and encouraging them not to abandon their interior life, and to live in a spirit of fraternity with everyone. The letters managed to get delivered, with difficulties and delays. He was overjoyed at the replies he received. They invariably showed the effect his letter apostolate had had in boosting the morale of his correspondents.

Your letter arrived at a moment when, for no reason at all, I was feeling depressed, and I have drawn great encouragement from seeing how hard the others are working ...

Your letters, and the news about my brothers, help me like a marvellous dream in the midst of this down-to-earth reality ...

What joy to get word from you all and to know myself a friend of such friends!

And another: *I received a letter from X, and I am ashamed at my lack of spirit compared to theirs.*

Now don't you agree that the 'letter apostolate' is effective? [2]

To help with this effort the Father again took up his old idea of sending a couple of sheets reproduced on a stencil duplicator. As in the DYA days, he used this method to recreate the family atmosphere and Christian charity with which he had imbued the first centres of Opus Dei. He would add a few personal words in his own hand on a separate sheet of paper which he affixed to the others.

He asked each one of them, especially those who were fighting in the front line, not to let things slide, and to seize every opportunity they could find to bring those around them towards God.

'And in a paganised or pagan environment when my life clashes with its surroundings, won't my naturalness seem artificial?' you ask me. And I reply: Undoubtedly your life will clash with theirs; and that contrast – faith confirmed by works! – is exactly the naturalness I ask of you. [3]

The replies came flooding in. Those who wrote to him thanked him for having comforted them in circumstances when they had tended rather to see the dark side of things, and for his encouragement not to forget to struggle in the little details of each day, when the temptation was to think only in terms of "great" heroism.

He would take those who came to see him up to the roofs and towers of the gothic cathedral in Burgos. There he would get them to look closely at the the beautifully carved gargoyles and pinnacles, whose details cannot be appreciated from below. *This is God's work*, he would say, *this is working for God! To finish your personal work perfectly, with all the beauty and excellent refinement of this tracery stonework ... The men who spent their energies there were quite aware that no one at street level could appreciate their efforts. Their work was done for God alone.* [4]

He would also teach them how to profit from the particularly hard times they were going through. *War! 'War', you tell me, 'has a supernatural end that the world is unaware of: war has been for us ...' War is the greatest obstacle to the easy way. But in the end we will have to love it, as a religious should love his disciplines.* [5]

The apostolic work moves forward

The tragic events Spain was experiencing had not diminished the apostolic zeal of the members of the Work.

On several occasions during these months of the war the Father had found new vocations arising from both men and women. But he was, nonetheless, impatient for peace to return, so that the growth of the apostolates could continue with a greater impetus. He was generous in offering his prayer and mortifications to that end.

From the moment he arrived in Burgos he had tried to get in touch with those he had known at the DYA Academy and who were in that zone. He also looked around, constantly, for possible openings for the apostolate. He contacted families he knew, made new acquaintances and spoke to several bishops about Opus Dei and the new spirituality it was bringing into the Church. He also offered and gave his assistance to nuns, trying to adapt this to their particular spirituality, as well as to the Teresians, whose founder, his friend Padre Poveda, had been assassinated.

Not content with the already exhausting amount of work he had taken on, he spent a certain amount of time writing his Canon Law doctoral thesis. All his papers, which had reached quite an advanced stage, on *"Ordination to the priesthood among half-castes and quadroons in the sixteenth century"*, had been left in Madrid, and would probably have been lost by then. But the nearby abbey of *Santa María de las Huelgas* provided him with a new subject for research: the theological and canonical problems posed by the

jurisdiction of an abbess there in that monastery in the Middle
Ages.

The Father was also working on a new, augmented version of
Spiritual Considerations. Even before the book came out with its
new title of *The Way*, he was using the typewritten manuscript
pages in his preaching. He also let some of his friends read them,
among them Monsignor Lauzurica, the Apostolic Administrator of
Vitoria, who was so impressed by the book that he offered to write
the foreword. As a considerate gesture towards Don Josemaría he
dated it on his feastday – 19 March 1939.

" ... In these pages breathes the spirit of God. The sentences
are left unfinished, so that you may complete them by your conduct.
If you transform these maxims into your own life, you will be a perfect imitator of Jesus Christ."

Unfortunately, the Father could not afford to have the book
published. That would have to wait for better days.

For the founder of Opus Dei, the hazards of the war constituted so many calls to pray more and to push his spirit of self-
sacrifice still further. Very often he managed to go without eating,
drinking water or sleeping, offering these sacrifices for the Church
and for the Work, which had to grow at whatever the cost and
despite all obstacles.

These concerns brought him to Our Lady of *El Pilar*, in Saragossa, on 1 June 1938, and on 17 July to Santiago de Compostella.
These and other pilgrimages nurtured his prayer, as also did his
retreat at the monastery of *Santo Domingo de Silos*, near Burgos,
between 25 September and 1 October.

The Father prayed intensely that those sons of his who were
engaged in combat might be spared, for some of them had already
fallen in battle. On 7 June 1938, one of them, Ricardo Fernández
Vallespín, had been wounded by a bomb that went off while it was
being defused by an explosives expert on the Madrid front. The
Father went to see him in hospital as soon as he could.

News of those who were still in the Republican zone reached
him more or less regularly via Isidoro, who sent it by way of France.
The Father transmitted his replies by the same route.

On 12 October 1938 three members of the Work, among them

Alvaro del Portillo, managed to cross the battle lines near Guadalajara. The Father had received a presentiment of this happening in his prayer, and was overjoyed on meeting them. Soon, each of the three was given a military posting to different sectors by the Nationalist army.

Those who had been called up and found themselves in the vicinity would come and join the Father as often as they could. He would encourage them, speaking about the future of the Work and confiding his plans to them.

In the autumn the Nationalists, having won the battle of the Ebro, prepared to march on Catalonia. Troop movements in January 1939 took Pedro Casciaro to the front in Aragon, and Alvaro to the vicinity of Valladolid. The Father remained in Burgos, alone except for the company of Francisco Botella. To economise even further they had moved, just before Christmas, from the Hotel Sabadell into an even more modest boarding-house.

On 26 January 1939 the Nationalist troops entered Barcelona. There was no further resistance in Catalonia. The next objective was Madrid. Everyone felt that the end of the war was near. The refugees in Burgos made their preparations to leave and return to the capital.

On 27 March the Father decided to go too. He left word for Francisco Botella at the barracks.

As he headed for Madrid he thought of what he had seen in June the year before, through a pair of field-glasses borrowed from a Nationalist officer, when he had come to the front to visit Ricardo. Don Josemaría had burst out laughing and the officer had asked him why he laughed.

It's because I am seeing my house in ruins,[6] he had answered.

The officer had not dared to ask any more questions.

2. MADRID: MAY 1939

The DYA Academy at 16 Ferraz Street had indeed been destroyed, even more completely than the Father had realised. He had visited it as soon as he could, accompanied by Juan Jiménez Vargas. The Father had decided, there and then, that they would have to find another flat at once if they wanted to set up the residence for October. For the time being, until they had actually found the flat, the Father continued to use the lodgings attached to the post he still held as rector of the Foundation of Saint Elizabeth.

The Convent of Saint Elizabeth had been converted into a barracks and used during the whole of the war as the headquarters of a Revolutionary Committee. The church had been burned down and, for the moment, the only habitable rooms were the flats of the rector and the chaplains – after they had been suitably cleaned, of course ...

He had an emotional reunion with his own family, meeting them again after long months of separation and only receiving news of them intermittently, amidst so many dangers. Now he had to take up again, as quickly as he could, the apostolic work in Madrid and in the other cities of Spain.

He wrote in June to one of the young men who had taken part in the formative activities before the war: *Soon we will have a house ... if you can help us with your prayer and your desire to take up your*

*books again. In the meantime, do not lose your blessed sense of fra-
ternity: love it more each day, and show it in your collaboration in
this concern we all have to set up home again. May we soon be
reunited, close to Jesus in our own tabernacle.* [7]

The Father resumes his journeys

Don Antonio Rodilla, a priest friend of his in Valencia, invited
Don Josemaría to preach a retreat starting on 5 June for the students of a residence (*Colegio Mayor Beato Juan de Ribera*) of which
he was Rector. Don Josemaría arrived on the day the retreat was
due to begin.

The students were impressed by the Father's way of capturing
their attention in order to make them face up to their responsibilities. On the wall of one room a large poster, stuck up there several
months before by the Republicans, proclaimed: "Let each traveller
follow his own path".

He asked them to leave it where it was, because he liked the
motto and also because it gave him the opportunity to refer to it: *If
you see your way clearly, follow it. Why don't you shake off the cowar-
dice that holds you back?* [8]

*Your perfection consists in living perfectly in the place, occupa-
tion and position that God, through those in authority, has assigned
you.* [9]

*'There are so many ways' ... Make your choice once and for
all: and the bewilderment will turn into certainty.* [10]

Two young men who had met the founder of Opus Dei for the
first time on that occasion very soon pledged themselves to follow
the way he had indicated to them. They were Amadeo de Fuenmayor, then reading Law at the University; and José Manuel Casas
Torres, who was studying in the Faculty of Arts.

Recreating a family atmosphere

In Madrid, the search for a house continued. At last they found one that would do, at 6 Jenner Street, near la Castellana. They got three flats, two on the fourth floor and one on the second.

In August they started to set up the main part of the residence on the fourth floor. On the second floor, they would have the dining-room, kitchen and domestic area, as well as a bedroom for the Father, another for his mother and sister Carmen and a third one for his brother Santiago.

How could they give this residence the family atmosphere it should have?

In the future, members of the Women's Section of Opus Dei would be able to attend to this; but for the moment they were too few. The Father solved the problem by asking his mother and Carmen to help. He remembered that it was, after all, in his parents' home that he had learned that attention to the material details which makes a house pleasant and attractive.

He gave his mother a life of Saint John Bosco to read. But it seemed as if Doña Dolores didn't realise what was intended. However, after a long time, she said to her son:

"What do you want me to do? To do what Don Bosco's mother did? No, thank you!"

But you are already doing it! the Father answered.

In fact, quietly, she was already in charge of the domestic administration of the house, helped by her daughter Carmen.[11]

Organising the work of the domestics and making sure a residence of forty beds ran smoothly was no light task; but she set to, with a generosity that she concealed with her good humour and discretion.

The residence was a new "folly". Once again it proved necessary to ask for money right and left. Special care, as ever, went on the oratory, for which they had chosen the best room in the apartment. Everyone helped according to his talents, laying carpets, painting, wallpapering or just hammering.

Everything was ready for the new term in October; but they were so short of money that several times they had to ask a prospective resident for his fees in advance, without telling him, of course, that the money was needed to buy his bed.

A new start for the Women's Section

The Father had recommenced his apostolate with women from where he had had to leave it at the beginning of the war. He had to begin almost afresh, for, although he had stayed in contact with several of the young women he had been directing, he now doubted that they could really form the kernel of the Women's Section of Opus Dei. His conversations with those he had managed to find again, coupled with a discreet word from his mother, had finally made up his mind.

Shortly after his return to Madrid, after thinking things over at length in his prayer, he let them know of his decision. It had nothing to do with the depth of their piety or their Christian life. It was only that they had not grasped that essential aspect of the Work, its secularity. After gently explaining this to each of them, he assured them of his affection and of his prayers and offered to recommend them, if they wished, to any religious order or institution of their own choice.

At the same time, the founder was trying to foster other female vocations. One young woman was already willing to respond to his call. She was Dolores, the sister of Miguel, the architectural student who had accompanied him on the crossing of the Pyrenees. When Miguel was in hiding in his parents' village of Daimiel, it was to Dolores (or Lola, as she was called) that the Father had addressed his letters, so that she could pass them on to her brother. Miguel had spoken to her about all that he had lived and heard at the DYA Academy; above all, he had told her about the Father, the attractiveness of his personality and the spirit he had taught them to live. Lola began to consider the possibility of joining the Work, and confided this to Miguel, who, in turn told Don Josemaría. In May 1937 the Father added a few lines to her directly, at the end of a letter addressed to her brother. She replied at once that she was ready to commit herself to the path of which he had spoken.

The Father went to Daimiel on 19 April 1939, shortly after his return to Madrid, and Lola confirmed her decision. To help the workings of grace in her soul, in which he could indeed see the possibility of a vocation to Opus Dei, Don Josemaría wrote to give her some advice. In fact it was a whole programme of interior life, adapted to her situation, that he had drawn up for her: half an hour of prayer, at a fixed time in the morning; an effort to keep in the presence of God throughout the day, concentrating, for instance, on a specific devotion for each day of the week; some minutes of spiritual reading; saying the Rosary; and making a daily examination of conscience ... He does not mention Mass and Confession, which had not been available to her during those three war years without any priest or any worship in church, and while she was still in those circumstances in which, only just after the war, life had not yet got back to normal ... [12]

Lola began to travel regularly to Madrid to complete her formation. She met with the Father, along with his mother, Doña Dolores, and his sister, Carmen, in the Jenner Road flat during September and December.

Spiritual help for priests

While Don Josemaría put the finishing touches to his doctoral thesis, which he wanted to defend in December, the Jenner residence became very busy with study circles, meditations, retreats and cultural activities looked after by the first members of the Work.

In response to an increasing number of requests from different bishops, the Father preached retreats to groups of priests in various towns and cities in Spain. They had gone through a great deal of suffering, often endured heroically: this would be the opportunity for giving their spirituality a fresh impetus.

The Father was well aware that he was addressing men used

to teaching and preaching. That is why he would disarm them by telling them first of all that when speaking to them he felt rather as if he were *selling honey to the beekeeper*.[13] He urged them with all his powers of persuasion not to be content with carrying out their ministry conscientiously, but to aim at sanctity, at heroism in their daily lives: the spread of God's kingdom in the world depended on the measure of their availability.

A priest from Avila who attended one of his retreats took down the following notes from a meditation:

The priest is the leader. He has to march in front, as Jesus did. This leader always wins, but he must stake everything, everything that souls demand (their conversion), all his health, all his money and all his time ... The priesthood is not a career: it is an apostolate ... Jesus is my brother. We have to do the same as He did. To suffer like him. We have to be like him: to be interested in the same things. We have the same Father ... We must be the same. He is our elder brother. We have the same Mother, the same business, we lead the same life, have the same goal, the same reward ... The two of us are identified in everything ... A priest without heroic sanctity? He would be the strangest, most disproportioned, most dangerous, most harmful creature ... [14]

This was demanding preaching, but eminently positive. It comforted those who heard it, and gave them a stimulus to pray more and to do apostolate.

Don Josemaría always accepted invitations to preach when asked by the bishops of the different dioceses. Faithful to the resolution he had taken, he posed only one condition: he asked not to be paid, and to pay for his journeys himself.

Everything centred on Christ

There was no great difference between what he said to the priests and what he said to the students who lived in Jenner, or other young men. What the Father asked of laymen was that, while keeping their lay outlook, they should also have a *priestly soul*,[15] open to the deepest needs of those around them and trying to bring them towards Jesus Christ.

The founder of Opus Dei encouraged his listeners to take up again the studies that had been broken off by the Spanish civil war, and reminded them that they had to sanctify themselves in their work and shoulder their responsibilities in society.

The students in this post-war era, many of them influenced by the ideas then in vogue, felt a great need to be up and doing. In reaction to the recent religious persecution, the dominant political ideology was eager to identify itself with "Catholic values". Enormous public demonstrations of the faith, inaugurating religious schools and other buildings, and fiery (and often revanchist) speeches were the fashion of the day.

Don Josemaría put the students on their guard against too human a conception of political actions, which, he admitted, could be noble and patriotic. *But don't forget*, he went on, *that there is a much greater reality: the kingdom of Jesus Christ, which has no end. And if Christ is to reign in the world, he must reign first in your heart. Does He really? Is your heart given wholly to Christ?* [16]

He said this one last Sunday in October, the feast of Christ the King.

As had happened earlier, in the troubled days of the Republic, some students left him, more attracted by a formation oriented directly towards politics. Others, however, felt moved by his words, which echoed those of Our Lord in the Gospel and which also call them to do practical things, but in a different way.

Several dozen new members thus joined the Work during the academic year of 1939-40 and the following one. The Father forewarned them about the false interpretations that could be put on their attitude, and reassured them in the same way as he had written in 1932:

We do not go to the apostolate to receive applause, but to defend the Church in the front line when is is hard going to be a Catholic, and to pass unnoticed when Catholicism is in fashion. [17]

You will have to live, he added, *you'll have to work at your job, whatever it may be, with all the uprightness and noble self-giving of those who, in their manner of conducting themselves, make their citizenship really count and their professional preparation noticeably thorough, not just their "Catholicity" ... with all the supernatural joy and human optimism of people deeply convinced that Christianity is a religion with nothing negative or private about it, but rather one to be joyfully affirmed and made to resound in all the different environments of the world.* [18]

In the cities of Spain

The world, in the meantime, was going through one of the most dramatic stages in its entire history. On 3 September 1939 Britain and France went to war against Nazi Germany. All the indications were that this second World War would involve more countries than the previous one, with far greater means of destruction. For many observers, the war in Spain had been a testing-ground for this wider conflict.

In the hall of the Jenner Road Residence, the Father had a map of the world put up to serve as a reminder of the universal dimension Opus Dei's apostolate. It's growth had once more been checked by the course of history. The founder would sometimes with his hand turn the globe that was in his study, looking at the different continents where they would have to carry the divine seed as soon as possible. Owing to the war, it was now impossible to start the Work in Paris. The first expansion, then, would have to take place within the borders of Spain.

The journeys had started again, more of them than ever. The Father was soon worn out. In Valencia, where he was preaching another retreat in September 1939, he had had to stop in the middle of Mass in the Cathedral after a sudden attack of fever. He had to be carried to the sacristy, then to the little flat in Samaniego Street which had been set up by several members of the Work. The furnishings were of the most rudimentary sort imaginable, and there were no blankets, so they had to use folded curtains to cover the Father while he lay on a couch until the bout was over.

More of these "exploratory" journeys followed, in appalling

trains with no heating, or along patched-up railway lines that had often been cut during the civil war: Saragossa, Valladolid, Barcelona, Salamanca ...

The car journeys were livelier. The Father liked to sing popular songs, and he applied the lyrics which talked of human love to the divine love, so that they brought him closer to God.

When they arrived they would go to an inexpensive hotel, and then the Father and those who had gone with him would set off in search of friends and acquaintances.

He received people incessantly, in the hotel itself, or in some quiet corner of a café, or on a park bench. Untiringly, he proposed to those he judged capable of responding. the ideal of holiness in the middle of ordinary occupations, which had been his very life's work since 1928.

Vocations began to spring up in the different cities, fruit of the prayer, mortifications and apostolic daring of the Father and his sons. And they, lacking everything, felt no doubt in some way the same as the disciples sent out on their mission with "no purse and no haversack" (Luke 10:4), their only provisions being their faith in the power of the Master's word: "It is I who have chosen you, and I have appointed you to go out and bear fruit, fruit that will last." (John 15:16)

By March 1940 the members of the Men's Section of the Work already numbered about forty. It was indispensable to arrange a period of more intense formation for them. Coming from several different places in Spain, they gathered around the founder. These were happy and unforgettable days.

On 19 March, the feast of Saint Joseph and the Father's feast-day, the Vicar-General of the diocese of Madrid, Don Casimiro Morcillo, passed on to him the affectionate greetings of the Bishop, Monsignor Eijo y Garay.

To the four corners of the world

The Father spoke to them about faithfulness, and of the need to persevere, whatever happened. To help them understand better, he reminded them of the heroism of the forty martyrs of the Armenian town of Sebaste, in the fourth century: they had been thrown into an icy lake for refusing to sacrifice to idols. "Forty of us," they exclaimed, "have entered the fight; we ask You, Lord, for forty crowns; grant that not one be lacking from that number." In the middle of the night, however, one of them abandoned the struggle, overcome by the agonising cold. But one of the guards, moved by the scene, declared himself a Christian in his turn and descended into the freezing waters to take the place of the deserter.

Your effectiveness, my sons, will be a consequence of your personal sanctity, that will yield responsible works which will not become hidden anonymously. Jesus Christ, the Good Sower, holds us tight – like wheat – in his wounded hand, he soaks us in his Blood, we are cleansed and purified, inebriated! And then, he scatters us, generously, far and wide over the whole world, one by one, which is how my sons in Opus Dei must go, spread out: for the wheat is not sown in sacks but one grain at a time. [19]

A large book, bound in white, had been edited and published the year before. It was the text of *Spiritual Considerations*, slightly modified and enriched with 566 new points, bringing the total to 999 (a symbolic homage to the Blessed Trinity). The new title, *The Way*, was a reference to Christ, who had spoken of Himself as the Way, the Truth and the Life.

The Father had written there: *Get rid of that small-town outlook. Enlarge your heart till it becomes universal, 'catholic'.* [20]

The closer an apostle is to God, the more universal his desires. His heart expands and takes in everybody and everything in its longing to lay the universe at the feet of Jesus. [21]

Or again: *To be 'Catholic' means to love your country and to be second to none in that love. And at the same time, to hold as your own the noble aspirations of other lands. So many glories of France are glories of mine! And in the same way, much that makes Germans proud, and the peoples of Italy and England . . ., and Americans and*

Asians and Africans, is a source of pride to me also. Catholic: big heart, broad mind! [22]

Thoughts return to the map of the world in the hall of the Jenner Residence.

When would the divine dream become reality?

3. MADRID: 1940

The apostolic work of Opus Dei was by now sufficiently developed for the Father to have to rent two small flats, one in Valladolid and the other in Barcelona, in addition to the one in Valencia.

In Madrid, where the house in Jenner Street continued to be used as a residence, a flat was rented for the older members of the Work to move into. It was in the same street of Martinez Campos, near the house where Don Josemaría's mother had lived before the war.

The Father, with his mother, sister and brother and some members of the Work, went to live in a three-storey house with a tiny garden at one end of the borough of Salamanca, at the corner of the streets called Diego de León and Lagasca.

It was a generously-proportioned building, and its reception rooms looked attractive. But the scant furniture was rather out of keeping with the setting. They did not have enough money to have the boiler of the heating system mended, or even to buy coal.

The Father slept on the third floor, in a little bedroom under a terrace. It was bitterly cold in winter and stifling hot in summer. His mother and sister occupied another bedroom on the second floor, and his brother another. They really did not have much room to spare, because the rest of the house was occupied little by little by the members of the Work who went there to receive intensive formation close to the Father.

Don Josemaría was as active as ever, spurring on the apostolic work, forming the new vocations and looking after the students in the Jenner Residence, giving spiritual guidance to a growing number of people, preaching days of recollection and giving retreats ... to say nothing of his continuing post as Rector of Saint Elizabeth's, and going on journeys to preach to priests in many dioceses.

Between the 1st and the 7th September 1940 he preached a retreat for young women in Madrid. From among those attending were to come some of the first vocations of women to Opus Dei.

Rumours and slander

Now that the tree of Opus Dei was beginning to spread its branches, the apostolic work of the members could no longer pass unnoticed. The founder's preaching, also, was now spreading beyond the already wide circle of men and women of all conditions that surrounded him.

At the beginning of the Work, before the civil war, some less-than-complimentary remarks had already come to the ears of Don Josemaría. These same criticisms, more or less veiled, started up again.

What was the origin of his influence over souls? Was not the rapid success of this new form of apostolate something suspect? Was it not dangerous to lead ordinary lay men and women to think they could sanctify themselves in their state in life, staying in the world, without entering a convent or becoming priests? Was it not shocking to speak to the ordinary faithful of a "vocation"?

At first it was only "hearsay", perhaps a little inaccurate, but not necessarily ill-intentioned. The Father paid little heed to it. He was sure that in the end the empty chatter would die down when people discovered, beneath what seemed to them the unfamiliar newness of the Work, the profound Gospel roots of its spirituality.

But the rumours swelled and, contrary to all expectations, they seemed to find credit in some quarters where the Father might have expected more sense. There was curiosity and a taste for tittle-tattle mixed in with it, as well as (though he could hardly believe it) a certain ill-will on the part of some people. Soon he had to admit that it was no longer a matter of simple gossip spread by those who knew no better. Two centuries after Beaumarchais, *sotto voce, a mezza voce*, Basile was muttering again words of slander ...

The founder's first reaction was to draw a lesson of humility from these troubles. *Tongues have been wagging and you have suffered rebuffs that hurt you all the more because you were not expecting them. Your supernatural reaction should be to pardon – and even to ask pardon – and to take advantage of the experience to detach yourself from creatures.* [23]

But he also had to admit that the accusations were not aimed only against him personally, and that Opus Dei, still so young, was threatened in its very existence.

Don Josemaría knew that he could count on the support of the Bishop of Madrid, who was utterly convinced that the Work came from God and did not hesitate to cut short the slightest suggestion of criticism against it. Someone recalls that one day, during the Corpus Christi procession, Monsignor Eijo y Garay had spoken to the President of Catholic Action, who was one of the men carrying the canopy:

"Listen: by all that is greatest in the world, by all that I most esteem – that is, Jesus in the Blessed Sacrament – do not say anything that may tarnish that Work: it is the apple of my eye!"[24]

Despite these clear statements by the Bishop, the slander and criticism went on unabated. They were, on the contrary, enriched with added details. Then one day the unthinkable happened: Opus Dei was formally denounced to the Special Tribunal for the Suppression of Freemasonry (just set up, on 1 March 1940). The accusation was a serious one, and could have had very grave consequences in Spain at that time; the Work was described as "the Jewish branch of the Freemasons", or else as "a Jewish sect in league with the Freemasons".

When the case came up before the court, the prosecution

went in with all guns firing. One of the lawyers, carried away by his own eloquence, attested in his indictment that the members of Opus Dei, so as to fool their companions the more easily, tried not to distinguish themselves from their fellow-countrymen in any way: they were honest, hard-working and clean-living ...

The president of the Tribunal, General Saliquet, pricked up his ears:

"They're clean-living, you say?"

"Yes, they live chaste lives."

"Oh well, no need to go any further: if they're chaste, they're certainly not freemasons. I've never met one who was!"

At that peremptory statement by the president, the case against Opus Dei was dismissed and the judges moved on to the next one.

Later, the Tribunal decided to send the two counsel for the prosecution to see Don Josemaría and let him know the verdict. The founder of Opus Dei received them in the Jenner Residence, quite unperturbed. As they were about to take their leave, one of the two "prosecutors" could not contain his curiosity:

"Father, could you show us the oratory where the people who accused you of being a freemason said you performed miracles?"

Certainly I'll show you; but what miracles?

Rather embarrassed, they repeated the rumours that others had been spreading: that he had arranged some complicated lighting trick to make it seem as if he was levitated off the ground during Mass ...

Well, with the weight I am at the moment, lifting me off the floor would certainly be a first-class miracle! [25] said the Father with a smile as he showed them the way to the oratory.

It was true: for some time now he had been putting on a good deal of weight ...

Peace in prayer

That incident was closed, but the slander showed no signs of stopping. On the contrary. Don Josemaría tried not to pay much attention to it and to forget it altogether. *God has forgiven you much more.* [26] He advised his sons not to allow themselves to get a persecution complex, and not to speak to one another about what was going on, but simply to carry on praying and working.

Despite everything, he could not avoid suffering at the thought that even when some day justice would be done to the Work, the enemies of the Church would go on using those same accusations against the Work, and that people would repeat them in good faith without realising that what they were putting about was straightforward slander.

For this reason the Father prayed very hard that these troubles might end. He never lost his serenity: but at the beginning of each day's work with Alvaro del Portillo (the one he worked with the most) he would wonder out loud where the attack would come from that day.

This went on until one day, very early in the morning, after a sleepless night, he went into the oratory and kneeling before the tabernacle put everything in God's hands: *Lord, if You don't need my honour, what do I want it for?* [27]

He was then filled with an immense peace.

Until he finds this peace, a son of God doesn't know what it is to be happy – until he is reduced to that nakedness, that self-giving, which is a gift of love, but founded on mortification and pain. [28]

For a Christian, joy is not *physiological good spirits, the happiness of a healthy animal;* [29] it comes from supernatural causes – it has *its roots in the shape of a cross* . [30]

The Father was still worried: but never for a moment did he dream of cutting back his activity, or slowing down the apostolate of his sons.

One night the telephone rang in the house at Diego de León. It was past midnight. When Don Josemaría answered, a familiar voice that seemed slightly changed called him by his Christian name and then pronounced in Latin the words of Jesus to Simon Peter.

Ecce Satanas expetivit vos ut cribaret sicut triticum – Simon, Simon, Satan has claimed you, to sift you like wheat; but I have prayed for you, that your faith might not fail you. (Luke 22:30-31). After a moment or two's silence, the voice added: *et tu confirma filios tuos* . With that the phone call was broken off.

The Bishop of Madrid, who used to work very late at night, had called to tell him, through these simple words, that the persecution was not going to let up. To encourage him to hold firm and to sustain the faith of the first members of the Work, he had slightly changed the second part of the verse of Saint Luke: "et tu confirma *filios tuos* " – and you, confirm *your sons* (instead of "your brothers").[31]

The members of the Work remained unshaken, though they suffered at the thought of how much the Father must be suffering. But he explained to them that *God Our Lord has blessed us with the Cross to make us be more effective* .[32] In his region of Spain, he told them, *they prick the skins of the early figs to make them sweeter and so that they will ripen more quickly.* [33]

Everything that happens, so long as we live it with faith, humility and a Christian spirit, will help us to improve and make the apostolate yield more fruit.

A trip to Barcelona

The Father could personally, by his very presence, comfort those who lived by his side in Madrid or in nearby Valencia, but this was not the case for those in Barcelona, where half a dozen students, in a small flat which they jokingly called *El Palau* (the palace), were trying to weather the storm. He was quite aware that the Governor of Barcelona had every intention of putting him in detention if he caught him there. In spite of this, he was determined to go. In 1941, after taking the advice of the Papal Nuncio, Monsignor Cicognani, he bought a plane ticket to Barcelona in the name of Jose María E. de Balaguer (the name Balaguer came from the Catalan town where his father's family originated). He went for just one day.

His sons were overjoyed to see him when he arrived. He encouraged them to cultivate their optimism: *From the very fact of being children of God, we should always be happy. Even if they break our skulls? Yes, even if we have to go around with a broken head, for it will be a sign that our Father God wants it to be broken.* [34]

The storm of persecution is good. What is the loss? What is already lost cannot be lost. When the tree is not torn up by the roots – and there is no wind or hurricane that can uproot the tree of the Church – only the dry branches fall. And they ... are well fallen. [35]

As long as you are making straight for your goal, head and heart intoxicated with God, why worry about the voice of the wind, or the chirp of the cricket, or the mooing, or the grunting or the braying? Besides, it's inevitable: don't waste time answering back. [36]

One of the crazier rumours going round Barcelona at the time, thanks to the "well-intentioned", was that the young members of the Work practised human sacrifice and nailed themselves to a wooden cross ... The origin of that one was a plain wooden cross which the Father had hung in a room next to the study. The wooden cross, *alone and uncared-for* of which he had spoken in *The Way* : *When you see a poor wooden Cross, alone, uncared-for, and of no value ... and without its Crucified, don't forget that that Cross is your Cross: the Cross of each day, the hidden Cross, without splendour or consolation ..., the Cross which is awaiting the Crucified it lacks: and that Crucified must be you.* [37]

The accusation was absurd. Nevertheless the Father asked them to replace the large cross with another much smaller one. Nobody could then say that they were crucified on it, there just wouldn't be enough room ... [38]

Several months later the director of *El Palau* was able to reassure the Father that despite the contradictions and the slander, not a single one of his sons in Barcelona had borne the slightest grudge against those who had attacked them.

The wind of persecution

In Madrid, certain people who wanted to harm the Work had asked some students who were under their influence to infiltrate the meetings of formation offered by Opus Dei. These "false brethren" had taken particular note of some details in the decoration of the oratory at the Jenner Residence: around the top of the wall, quite near the ceiling, the Father had had a frieze painted with the words from a liturgical hymn (*Congregavit nos in unum Christi amor*, the love of Christ has brought us together) followed by a sentence from the Acts of the Apostles: *Erant autem perseverantes in doctrina Apostolorum, in communicatione fractionis panis et orationibus* (Acts 2:42). They remained faithful to the teaching of the Apostles, the breaking of the bread and the prayers. The Latin words were separated by traditional Eucharistic and other Christian symbols: loaves, ears of wheat, the vine, light, the dove, the cross ... Those poor misguided lads, in their ignorance, started the rumour that these were secret cabalistic signs ... [39]

Something similar happened in Barcelona. Things had got to such a state that Padre Escarré, the new Abbot Coadjutor of the Monastery of Montserrat, thought it wise to write to the Bishop of Madrid, on 19 May 1941, to ask for proper information on Opus Dei, so that he could answer those who questioned him on the subject. Monsignor Eijo y Garay replied as follows:

"I know that a storm has been unleashed against Opus Dei in Barcelona. The sad thing is that persons who have given themselves very much to God should be instruments of evil; of course it is *putantes se obsequium praestare Deo:* thinking they are rendering a service to God. I do indeed know everything about the matter, for Opus Dei has been so much in the hands of the Church since its foundation in 1928 that the Ordinary of the diocese – either my Vicar-General or myself – knows and, if necessary, can direct each step it takes; so that its first whimpers of infancy, right up to its present groans of pain, echo in our ears and in our heart. Believe me, most reverend Father Abbot, this *Opus* is truly *Dei*, from its very conception, in every step and every action it has taken. Doctor Escrivá is a model priest, chosen by God for the sanctification of many souls; he is humble, prudent, full of a spirit of self-sacrifice, extremely obedient to his prelate and possessed of a rare intelligence, a very solid doctrinal and spiritual formation and an ardent zeal ... I am aware of all the accusations that are being bandied about, and I know that they are false; I know that some persons are being persecuted, and even the things they are interested in are attacked, in the belief that they are in Opus Dei, whereas they are not! I know, too, that some are causing distress to the mothers and fathers of the students, and that they seek the support of the public authorities ... From all this Our Lord will draw only good for Opus Dei. But it is sad to see 'good people' discredit themselves in persecuting this good work."[40]

The persecution, indeed, did not content itself with attacking the members of Opus Dei, it was also directed at their families. The mother of a student who had just recently asked to join the Work in Valencia was visited, on one of her trips to Barcelona, by a religious priest she did not know. He had felt it to be his duty "in all charity", to inform her that her son would go to hell if he continued to follow Father Escrivá, because he taught that it was possible to become a saint in the middle of the world. He entreated her to turn her son from this path, without taking any account of the fact that he was of age. The poor woman was so overcome that she was taken ill and was in bed for a number of days. Finally, although the religious had warned her against it, she consulted the Vicar of the Diocese of Valencia, Don Antonio Rodilla. He more than reassured her. He affirmed, in no uncertain terms, that her son had found in Opus Dei a true path of holiness in the world.

Don Antonio had in fact to dispel other similar lies for prelates, national Catholic Action councillors and religious men and women. For it was no longer a matter of isolated criticisms, but a real hurricane of moral persecution fuelled by utterly treacherous accusations.

The Father changes his spiritual director

On returning to Madrid, the Father had gone back to his old confessor, Father Sánchez, again. Although he had only talked about his interior life, and not about Opus Dei as such, he had told him of his distress as soon as the first slanderous rumours came to his ears.

But strangely enough he did not find the expected sympathy. One day Padre Sánchez, who seemed very nervous, suddenly let the cat out of the bag: in his opinion, the Holy See would never approve Opus Dei. To back up his argument he mentioned an article of the Code of Canon Law – not a very convincing one, as it happened.

Don Josemaría was dumbfounded by this about-turn. His spiritual director had always seemed certain that what had happened in his soul on 2 October 1928 had been of divine origin. Not only that, but when he had gone to consult him on 14 February 1930 after having seen, during Mass, that he had to found a Women's Section in Opus Dei, Padre Sánchez had assured him that "this has come from God, like all the rest".

The only possible explanation for this abrupt change of attitude was that his spiritual director was under very heavy pressure to persuade him not to carry on with the founding of Opus Dei.

Spiritual direction, for Don Josemaría, was inconceivable outside an atmosphere of complete openness. Before leaving Padre Sánchez, then, he explained very carefully that, owing to what he had just heard, he would not be able to come to him any more for Confession. From that day on, in 1940, he went to Confession with a priest friend of his, Don José María García Lahiguera, who was the spiritual director of the Madrid seminary.[41]

First official approval

Bishop Eijo y Garay was worried. Around 1940-41 the Lord had allowed Opus Dei to encounter terrible contradictions, and as Bishop of Madrid, having followed every step in the development of the Work, he resolved to give the first diocesan approval in order to put an end to the persecution.

This proposal rather perplexed the founder of Opus Dei. He knew that he could always count on the support and encouragement of his bishop; besides, he had always tried to keep him informed on what he was doing. As a good canon lawyer he realised that the Work would have to grow and mature before it was able to find its own juridical framework, for the legislation then in force would certainly have to be adapted to the novelty of its approach.

While these contradictions continued, on 22 August 1940 the Archbishop of Toledo died, and the Father knew that the most likely candidate to succeed him was precisely the Bishop of Madrid.

That is why, very loyally, in a conversation he had with him, he told Don Leopoldo: *Your Lordship, let it be. Don't help us. Don't you realise that the mitre of Toledo may be at stake?* And Don Leopoldo answered: "Josemaría, it's my soul that is at stake!"[42]

Several months later, the Father realised that he still had not sent Monsignor Eijo y Garay the necessary papers.

My Lord, he wrote, *I always want to be very obedient to Your Lordship, and yet in spite of the fact that you asked me for the documents so that you can proceed with the approval of the Work, I have not yet sent them; it is only now that I have realised this, that I have not done what Your Lordship has told me to do. But when I realised this I felt a great joy, for any other cleric would have hurried to the Bishop's Palace to bring you the documents his Bishop had asked for. I thus have another proof that the Work is not mine, but God's. If it is not Your Lordship who approves it, it is your successor who will!* [43]

On 14 February 1941 the founder presented the petition for the approval, along with the necessary documentation. On 24 March the Bishop of Madrid signed a decree, by virtue of Article 708 of the Code of Canon Law (which permitted the faithful to join an association for a work of piety and charity), approving Opus Dei as a Pious Union, but following what Don Josemaría had asked for, not erecting it canonically. As a gesture towards the founder, Don Leopoldo dated the document the 19th of March, the feast of Saint Joseph, the Patron chosen by the founder. He also added a few words to the traditional formula, showing his affection and encouragement for Opus Dei: "And we ask God Our Lord, through

the intercession of Saint Joseph, on whose feastday we have the
pleasure of canonically approving so important a Work of zeal, that
He grant this Work that none of the many fruits we expect of it be
lost."[44]

When he heard the news from Monsignor Eijo y Garay, Don
Josemaría was in the house in Diego de León. He went immediately to look for his mother and the various members of the Work
who were there. They entered the oratory and knelt before the
tabernacle, giving thanks.[45]

4. MADRID: 14 FEBRUARY 1943

On this Sunday, the thirteenth anniversary of the foundation of the Women's Section of Opus Dei, Don Josemaría Escrivá celebrated Mass for his daughters at a Centre in Jorge Manrique Street.

In the few words he addressed to them, he recalled that other Mass, on 14 February 1930, when he had felt in his soul, after his Communion, the feeling that a father must have when God sends him a child he has not been expecting:

Since then, I feel that I must have more affection for you: I see you as a mother does her youngest child. I assure you that it has been by an express command of the Lord, transmitted on this date in 1930, that the Women's Section of Opus Dei exists today. God has wanted it! [46]

An influx of new vocations in July 1942 had made it possible to open this house. It was rather small, but with three floors and a basement, with "room for improvement". Dolores Fisac, Nisa González Guzmán and Encarnación Ortega – who had met the Father on a retreat in 1941 – had gone to live there. The Father had given careful instructions about setting up the oratory, in which he often said Mass and addressed a few words to those present.

A new light

At that time, and on this day in particular, Don Josemaría was preoccupied. He had a problem to which he had been searching for a solution in his prayer – so far without success – and for which he had offered, as usual, many penances. The problem was how to incardinate priests into the Work. From the beginning, he had in this way wanted to complete the structure of Opus Dei, which was indeed eminently secular. But it could not reach its goals without priests who would be totally identified with its spirit and capable of helping its apostolic growth, ensuring the formation of its members and providing them with the Sacraments.

The priests who had helped him before the Spanish Civil War had not really understood the spirit of the Work, even though he had done his best to explain it to them. Nor had they grasped the necessity of being very united with the founder in order to ensure that the apostolate both grew and stayed united.

He had already come to the conclusion several years previously that the only possible solution would be the ordination of laymen of Opus Dei, who would already have been formed by the spirit of the Work. Only thus would the unity of the Work be solidly guaranteed.

He had placed this call to the priesthood before those sons of his whom he thought able to receive it – Alvaro del Portillo and José María Hernández de Garnica. They had both answered yes.

Now that the apostolic work was getting under way again, the Father's thoughts came back to this same idea, although there were difficult problems, both practical and legal, to be dealt with. A priest must be called to the priesthood and ordained by a bishop (this would have been the easiest condition to fulfil: there was no shortage of bishops who understood the Work and encouraged it). He must also have received, prior to ordination, a sufficient philosophical, theological and canon law training: this was normally provided by the diocesan seminary. Finally, he must be attached to a bishop, or at least be "incardinated", that is to say, be canonically linked with the Church.

The Bishop of Madrid, Monsignor Eijo y Garay, was,

naturally, perfectly happy to call to the priesthood, and to ordain, those members of the Work whom Don Josemaría might suggest to him. Alvaro and José María had in fact already begun their courses of philosophy and theology, outside the seminary. José Luis Múzquiz, a civil engineer who had met the Work before the War in 1935, joined them.

All three of them took their examinations regularly at the seminary of Madrid with great success. For the Father had insisted that their training be provided by the best teachers who could be found, giving convincing reasons to those who had asked why he had done this: *The second (reason), was to please God; the third, because many were looking at us with affection, and we could not defraud those souls; because there were people who did not love us, and sought excuses to attack us; then, as in their professional life I have always demanded the best formation of my sons, I was not going to demand less in their religious formation*. But to all these reasons the founder added another, which he judged to be the most important: *The first reason is – because I could die at any moment – that I must render an account to God of what I have done and I ardently desire to save my soul.* [47]

The condition for ordaining priests – the "title of ordination" – posed a more serious problem, which was practically insoluble. The Father had asked advice from several important people in the Church, including Bishop Eijo y Garay. But none of the solutions thus far advanced seemed really feasible.

In these last few days he seemed to have come up against a brick wall; though he was still quite sure that a solution *must* exist, because priests too were present when Our Lord had made him see Opus Dei on 2 October 1928.

Once more the light came during Mass. When he had finished Mass on 14 February 1943, he had the solution: a priestly society oriented towards the apostolate. Without wasting any time, he drew in his diary a Latin cross inscribed within a circle, which would be from then on the seal of Opus Dei.

All that remained to be done was to submit the project that he had just conceived to the appropriate authorities. With the help of God, it would be put into effect. It would, no doubt, be a long haul finding the precise legal framework, but at least the goal was now clear: and it had the advantage of avoiding those forms so far suggested by friends, which were incompatible with the spirit of Opus Dei or, in fact, impracticable.

Legal studies and steps to be taken

The next day the Father went to the Escorial, to visit his three sons who had gone there to prepare more intensely for their ordination. As soon as he arrived, he talked to Alvaro del Portillo. They strolled around the monastery built by Philip II. The Father explained briefly what he had seen the day before, with the legal steps it would be necessary to take because of this new development in the Work. He asked Alvaro to accompany him back to Madrid. The Father wanted to work on a specific, detailed proposal which the Bishop of Madrid could pass on to the Holy See.

Two members of the Work had been living in Rome since November 1942, following specialised courses in Canon Law at a pontifical university. The Father had asked them to take advantage of their stay and get the Work known among some members of the Roman Curia. But what had been happening in his soul made him inclined to think that a further step forward was needed. Alvaro del Portillo, as Secretary-General of the Work, should go to Rome as soon as possible and present the Holy See with a definite, specifically-detailed project to be approved.

Alvaro touched down in the Eternal City on 25 May 1943 after a lively and eventful flight, for the War was still being fought. On 14 June he was received by Pope Pius XII and presented the documents prepared by the founder of Opus Dei, together with an official letter from Bishop Eijo y Garay. He answered the questions the Pope put to him about the Work. Later on, he met various Church figures, among them the Papal Secretary of State, Cardinal Maglione, and his Substitute, Monsignor Giovanni Battista Montini.

The first papal approval

When he returned to Spain on 21 June, Alvaro announced to the Father that they could expect a first pontifical approval known as the *appositio manuum* .

Don Josemaría was overjoyed. He had been praying for this intention for months. He had prayed even more before Alvaro's journey, and asked those around him to help too.

His first spiritual son, Isidoro, was offering the sufferings he was enduring. For just under two years now he had been suffering from an illness that they realised now was incurable. The doctor, diagnosing Hodgkin's Disease (cancer of the lymphatic glands), gave him only a few months more to live. In January Isidoro had to give up his job and go into hospital, where he was always accompanied by one of his brothers.

New trials and intentions

This first papal approval was very timely, for the smear campaign had not died down. On the contrary, it had increased.

For Opus Dei the gestation period was over. The house in Diego de León Street was full of young members of the Work, still students, who came there to receive an intense ascetic and doctrinal formation. As for their elders, they had already started to work in their professions in the footsteps of Alvaro del Portillo, Isidoro Zorzano, José María Hernández Garnica and José Luis Múzquiz, all of them engineers, and Ricardo Fernández Vallespín, who had just opened an architect's office. Others had applied to sit the competitive examinations set up by the Ministry of Education, which opened the way to posts in higher education. This, for no apparent reason, was enough to provoke the most absurd comments. Before any member of the Work had actually obtained a post, a rumour spread, apparently from what was recognisably the same source as before: "Opus Dei is trying to take over the university!"

The rumour made Don Josemaría's sons laugh – and suffer. Very few members of the Work applied for university posts in any case. Between 1940 and 1943 only seven obtained posts out of a total of one hundred and forty-five places offered. What was more, several of those who applied for posts had the distinct impression that they had been turned down precisely because they were in Opus Dei.

During a retreat preached at the house in Diego de León from the 4th to the 9th September 1942 the Father reaffirmed, in no uncertain manner, what was to him the rock solid principle that each member of the Work is entirely autonomous in his professional work. Our aim, he told them in substance, is to sanctify ourselves so as to sanctify others. The only means we use are prayer, the sacraments, self-sacrifice and orderly and persevering work. Occupying important posts, of whatever sort, is not one of our ends. If you are a good Christian, if you carry out your duties towards society and your country, if you study and work with order and perseverance, if you exercise properly your rights and duties as citizens, it will be quite natural and not at all surprising that some of you should have such posts one day. But that is your affair, not the Work's. The Work does not "arrange" jobs for anyone. The Work does not offer places to anyone! All you will find here is a spiritual impetus and a Christian formation, the example of your elder brothers to stimulate you to work in earnest, and a preaching that encourages you to beware of "taking it easy" and urges you to try harder. But to get jobs, or to push someone who does not deserve it into one? Never! Never!

The Father spoke with all the vehemence he usually employed when it was a case of some key point in his preaching. His words were a reminder to his listeners of something they had heard frequently before and were already putting into practice.

When those outside suggested that the members of the Work might at least be helping each other to obtain important posts of responsibility, Don Josemaría stated emphatically that there was absolutely no truth in these allegations, that the members were forbidden to do so and that, besides, it would be contradictory and senseless for someone who had left everything for Christ to put his eternal salvation at risk by practising favouritism, which would be a fault against justice.

Above: Andorra, 3 December 1937. After crossing the Pyrenees.

Below: Getting past the censor – a post-card in faltering English, dated 29 December 1937, sent to Isidoro Zorzano.

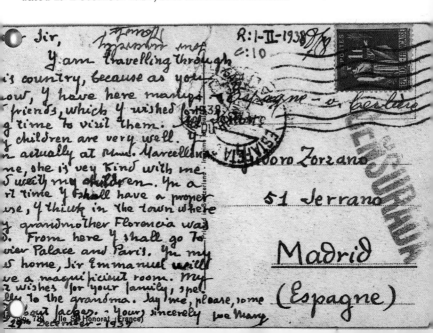

Above: Vergara, Guipúzcoa, June 1937. Don Josemaría with a group of deacons, after preaching a pre-ordination retreat to them. Below: Jorge Manrique Street, Madrid. The first Centre of the Women's Section.

Nothing could be further from the spirit of the Work than to form a ghetto, setting up groups within a university, say, a research centre or a faculty. The members of the Work do not think that way. We never have constituted groups – the founder would affirm – and we never will. It is in our nature to open out like a fan, each member following his own path, working hard where he is and taking the seed of Christ with him.

The Father himself gave the example, accepting the job of teaching professional ethics in the Madrid School of Journalism founded in 1940. It was there, more than on the National Education Board (of which he had been made a member that same year, albeit in a rather honorary capacity), that he found an opportunity to imbue present and future journalists with a Christian spirit and a strict professional ethos.

It was an additional task among the many activities that he already had in hand, taken on in spite of exhaustion caused by the rigours of the civil war and aggravated by his constant sufferings in the face of the appalling lack of understanding he had met with.

The death of his mother

He had on top of all this received a heavy blow in the spring of 1941.

His mother had taken ill around the middle of April. The doctor had said it was pneumonia and Don Josemaría was worried because he had promised the Apostolic Administrator of the diocese of Lérida to preach a retreat for his clergy. The doctor's view of his patient's condition had been quite optimistic, so he decided to go.

Before leaving he went up to his mother's room.

Could you offer your sufferings for this work I'm going to do? [48] he asked her.

As he left the room, he heard her murmur:

"This son of mine ...!"

Arriving at the seminary of Lérida, he had knelt before the

tabernacle, saying:

Lord, look after my mother for I am taking care of your priests. [49]

Two days later, on 22 April, while he was still thinking of his mother, ill in bed back in Madrid, he had devoted one of his talks to the mothers of priests. He told the priests that the mother of a priest was so important that he asked Our Lord to grant all priests that their mothers should not die until the day after they left this world ...

Having finished, he went to kneel before the Blessed Sacrament. Suddenly the door of the chapel opened: Monsignor Moll, the Apostolic Administrator of the diocese, who was also doing the retreat, came up to him and said:

"Alvaro del Portillo is on the phone."

His mother had died.

Deeply moved, he went straight back to the chapel.

Lord, how have you done this to me? This is what you've done while I was looking after your priests? [50]

He had soon realised, however, that the Lord had taken his mother because she was ready for Heaven. Then the tears flowed in abundance; he wept like a child, even while he recited a long prayer he had so often recommended to those who had to accept a decision of Providence that seemed particularly hard:

May the most just and most lovable will of God be done, be fulfilled, be praised and eternally exalted above all things. Amen. Amen. [51]

It was not without reason, surely, that Our Lord had asked this sacrifice of him at the very moment he was preaching to priests. The peace that came to his heart after his slow and sorrowful prayer convinced him that his mother was interceding in Heaven for those diocesan priests to whom he had given of himself so much.

The Governor of Lérida, Juan Antonio Cremades, who had been a friend of his from their student days together at the University of Saragossa, sent a car for him to return to Madrid.

When the Father entered the oratory of the house of Diego de León, he saw his mother's body already laid out, surrounded by members of the Work. Kneeling by the body, he felt his tears welling up again. When they saw him get to his feet and ask for a stole, those who were keeping vigil expected him to intone the *Requiem aeternam* . It was a *Te Deum* instead.

But the Father could not stop himself from complaining, as a son complains to his father:

My God, my God, why have you done this to me? You've taken everything, you take everything away from me. I thought that these daughters of mine needed my mother very badly, and you have left me without anything – anything! [52]

With his sons present, two days later, he spoke very differently:

Lord, I'm happy, because I know you love me and you have shown me this mark of confidence ... We must see to it that all my children can be close to their parents when they come to die, but sometimes it will not be possible . And you have allowed me, Lord, to lead the way in this. [53]

Everything for God

As the campaign of slander which had been unleashed against Opus Dei increased, Don Josemaría became so worn out physically that his sons managed to convince him – not without difficulty – that he should rest for a week.

He spent a few days in September 1941 at La Granja, near Segovia. He said his Mass in the collegiate church of the palace that Philip V had built at the foot of the mountain like some Versailles. The founder's prayers were offered in continual reparation for the unjust accusations he had to bear. He made an act of abandonment into the hands of God and begged insistently for light and help from Our Lord. Suddenly he experienced again the same feeling that had seized him in Madrid one day in the 1930's. The Lord seemed to leave him practically in the dark and the devil seized the chance to whisper in his ear, without articulating any words:

"Nothing of what you are doing comes from God. All this,

taking souls away from their families so that they follow you, is so that they do something which is 'only yours' ... You are deceiving them."

His reaction was exactly the same as it had been before: *Lord, if Opus Dei isn't to serve you, to serve the Church, destroy it right now!* [54]

Immediately there followed that total peace which removed all doubt and bitterness. It was a silent answer that repeated the comforting words of Jesus to the unbelieving apostles when they found themselves sinking among the angry waves of the Sea of Galilee: "Do not fear, it is I" (Matt 14:27).

5. TUY: FEBRUARY 1945

Sor Lucia, with all the things they are saying about you and about me ..., and in addition we end up in hell ...!

"It's true, you are quite right."[55]

The visionary of Fatima had stopped for a moment, sunk in thought, before speaking. The founder of Opus Dei was pleasantly surprised by this proof of Sister Lucia's humility, reinforced by the slight alteration in her voice.

Since the time of the apparitions of the Blessed Virgin to the three shepherd children, large crowds had been drawn to Fatima. The last survivor of the visionaries had entered a religious Congregation and endeavoured to maintain her anonymity. At that time Sister Lucia was in a convent in the neighbouring Spanish diocese of Tuy. The Bishop of Tuy, the Very Reverend José López Ortiz, wished to make an exception for his intimate friend, Don Josemaría, and arranged an appointment on the occasion of a visit by the nun to the Bishop's house.

During the course of the conversation, Sister Lucia dos Santos expressed her desire to the founder of Opus Dei that the Work start in Portugal. Don Josemaría, who had already thought of this but had not considered going there yet, asked her for her prayers to help them break the necessary ground for the success of this supernatural undertaking. *Whenever I see her*, he would say years later, *I remind her that she is largely responsible for the beginning of the Work in Portugal.*

In Portugal

As a result of the war it was very difficult to travel from Spain to Portugal, or to stay there for any length of time, as the Father intended to. Nevertheless, a few days after his meeting with Sister Lucia, thanks to her effective intervention, it was all arranged and the Father was able, to his great delight, to pray in the little chapel at Fatima, and put this first expansion of the Work beyond the borders of Spain under the protection of Our Lady.

On that journey, he was accompanied by Alvaro del Portillo as well as by the Bishop of Tuy and his secretary Don Eliodoro Gil. Don Josemaría visited the Bishop of Oporto, the Bishop of Leiría – the diocese where the shrine of Fatima is situated – and the Cardinal Patriarch of Lisbon, His Eminence Gonsalves Cerejeira. Cardinal Cerejeira was much taken by the apostolic horizons opened by the spirit of Opus Dei, and advised the founder to start work in the university city of Coimbra, where he himself had taught. So Don Josemaría travelled down to Coimbra, where he met the local bishop.[56]

The world was still at war at the beginning of 1945, and the Church began to be persecuted in the countries of the East. Trusting in the *powerful weapon*[57] of the Rosary, the Father dated the Preface to the fourth edition of his *Holy Rosary* in Fatima. He referred to the conflict still going on – "their tongue is as an arrow that inflicts a wound" (Jer 9:8). *May you recognise this and have the desire to heal these wounds by means of this wonderful Marian devotion and through your watchful love.*[58]

This fourth edition was signed Josemaría Escrivá *de Balaguer*. He had adopted this second surname to distinguish his family from the Escrivás de Romaní, a Valencian family which was very well-known in Spain and could have been a source of confusion. He had already used the name de Balaguer – after the town which had been the cradle of his father's family since the twelfth century – for the trip he had made incognito to Barcelona in 1941.

Once the Second World War was over he would at last be able to realise the dream he had symbolised in the 1930's when he drew – to the wonder of his sons – a Greek cross of four arrows, pointing to the four points of the compass.

So must it be with the horizon of your apostolate: the world has to be crossed. But there are no ways made for you. You yourselves will make them through the mountains with the impact of your feet. [59]

The 'nihil obstat' from the Holy See

On the other hand, how much of the path had already been covered since 11 October 1943, when Pope Pius XII had signed the *appositio manuum* of the Holy See! It had been dated the day the Church then celebrated the feast of Mary, Mother of God: for the founder, it was an obvious proof of Our Lady's intercession.

On 8 December, the feast of the Immaculate Conception, the Bishop of Madrid put into effect the diocesan application of the papal decision. It had been the prayer of everyone, united around the Father, with sacrifices offered day after day for this intention, which had gained them this first approval by the Church. Among them was Isidoro, who had offered his sufferings and his life. He died like a saint, at half past five in the afternoon of 15 July. "How lucky I am to be sick at this particular time," he had said shortly before his death, "so that with this illness I have something to offer when there are such important matters to be solved."

The Father had interrupted a day of recollection he was preaching for a group of women of the Work, to go and pray at the feet of the first of his faithful sons, the first who had persevered without doubting for a moment about his vocation, from the time of their decisive conversation in the flat at the Foundation for the Sick in August 1930.

New developments in Spain

Solidly supported by prayer and penance, they were working now in several places in Spain: Valencia, Valladolid, Saragossa ...

The Father travelled more and more, in spite of the difficulties, and in spite of the strain imposed on his health, which was not good at the time, by long hours on the road and incessant meetings and talks from the minute he arrived until he left again for Madrid.

The Work was now better received in Barcelona. On 26 May 1943 the Master of Ceremonies of Barcelona Cathedral blessed the oratory of the centre on Balmes Street which they had always called *El Palau* .

In July, in Madrid, the owner of the Jenner Road property told them that he wished to start using his house again. The Residence was moved to two small houses near the University campus in Madrid, on Moncloa Avenue. There would now be room for about a hundred students.

La Moncloa was to be the first large residence of the Work, without losing the homely atmosphere that the Father had given to all the others from the beginning. It maintained a family air, where people learned to live with each other, to understand and respect each other, with cheerfulness and good humour, in accordance with the spirit of the Work. The residence was open to all, including non-Catholics. It gave the members of the Work many apostolic possibilities, enabling them to get to know the residents personally and carry out an apostolate of friendship and mutual trust which was so characteristic of their spirit. The residence was, for many others also, a meeting place where Christian fraternity was practised, and where they had the opportunity to deepen their formation. In that residence, many students – some who were resident and others who went there to receive the formation offered – would hear the call to a vocation to holiness in their own state in life, in the world. Others, again, thanks to the healthy environment of *La Moncloa* , would discover a vocation of another type – to the priesthood or to the religious life – for it is true that if you *raise the spiritual temperature* ,[60] you can help each soul to discover its own path and give itself fully.

All the students who passed through *La Moncloa*, however, when they later found themselves *at all the crossroads of the world*,[61] would know that it was precisely there that they should sanctify their work by their Christian conduct, and sanctify themselves, whether or not they had received the specific vocation to Opus Dei. And this all the more easily in that the spirituality being placed before them was an essentially lay one, which could be lived by any of them at all during their years at university, and later on in their professional and social life.

As the academic year 1945-46 began, the expansion in Spain continued. In October some members of the Work moved to Seville to carry on their studies or professional work there, whilst developing an intense apostolate.

A fruitful apostolate

The Women's Section of the Work had now developed sufficiently for some of them to be able to take over the domestic administration of the Residence of *La Moncloa* at the Father's request. They would look after the maintenance, decoration, cleaning, catering, laundry and so on. Although they worked in a completely separate section of the buildings, they gave the residence that family atmosphere that Don Josemaría's mother and sister had known how to create in the house on Jenner Street. To carry out this task they had employed a few domestic servants. But the Father, in this point as well, had already foreseen the future. He had asked his daughters to extend their apostolate to women who, like those they had employed, had as their professional job the task of helping housewives in their domestic work. That task should be considered as a real *profession*, open to being sanctified and to sanctifying those who did it, like every other human occupation. For the Father it was not a chore that was useful but inferior, as too many people, even good Christians, were given to thinking regarding those whom they called their "maids". For him, the value of a job had nothing to do with its social standing, but everything to do with the love put into it. *The world admires only spectacular sacrifice, because it does not realise the value of sacrifice that is hidden and silent.* [62]

To the Father it was clear that many vocations would come from this professional area.

The first priests are ordained

With the development of the apostolates and the continuous influx of new members, it was becoming increasingly urgent to be able to count on priests formed in the spirit of Opus Dei.

The arrival of the papal and diocesan permissions allowed Don Josemaría to press ahead with the ordination of those three members of the Work who had now spent several years of preparation.

On 25 June 1944 the Father said Mass in the oratory at Diego de León. Although he was alone with José María Albareda, he united himself closely to the Ordination Mass being celebrated at the same moment by Alvaro del Portillo, José María Hernández de Garnica and José Luis Múzquiz in the chapel of the Bishop's Palace in Madrid. The Father had not wanted to be present, to avoid the risk of being the centre of attraction for the many people there who would have felt themselves obliged to congratulate him personally. Yet it was not he but God who had wanted the Work; it was He who should be at the centre of the ceremony ...

Don Josemaría had, however, been present at the back of the chapel a few weeks earlier, on 20 May, at the ceremony of the tonsure by Bishop Eijo y Garay, who was also ordaining these first three priests. A painful carbuncle had prevented him from being there when they had received the four minor orders.

After the ordination ceremony of the 25th they returned to Diego de León for a family gathering with the Bishop of Madrid. The afternoon finished in the oratory with some words from the Father:

When time has passed ..., and I, by the law of nature, will have disappeared from the scene, your brothers will ask you: What did the Father say on the day when the first three priests were ordained? Tell them quite simply: the Father repeated as always: prayer, prayer, prayer! Mortification, mortification, mortification! Work, work, work! [63]

These first three priests were indeed the fruit of his prayer over many years. It was not, however, without an initial hesitation that he resigned himself to ordaining precisely these three, who had been among the first members of the Work. Great apostolic fruits could have been expected from their professional work and they would have been a valuable financial support by reason of their occupations. But his sorrow turned to joy when he thought of the immense amount of good that would be done by these priests, and by those who would come after them, working shoulder to shoulder, though always a very small minority in comparison with the laymen who were their brothers.

The ordination of three engineers did not pass unnoticed. The Madrid press remarked on the presence of the Papal Nuncio and a number of Church personalities at the ceremony, as well as teachers and past students from the schools and faculties where the new priests had studied. The event raised a lot of interest; but it also gave rise to a number of acerbic remarks on the part of some churchmen who, neglecting to mention that the three young priests had been studying for several years under the best teachers, questioned the quality of their training – exactly as the Father had foreseen.

He was rather more amused by those who said "Now he's ordained them he'll work them to death ..." There was certainly no lack of work, especially for these priests whose arrival had been so timely. The Work immediately set them to the exercise of their ministry, and the souls soaked up their service as dry ground soaks up the first raindrops. Besides administering the Sacraments, they were a great help to the Father in preaching and spiritual direction, both within and outside the Work.

The Father continued to say 'yes' to the requests that came in from every direction, without sparing himself. He had a sudden attack of fever in the middle of a retreat he was preaching to the Augustinians in the Escorial in October 1944. He had also developed a bad infection in his neck. The doctor he consulted, noting other symptoms, thought it could indicate diabetes. The Father continued his preaching, despite the fever. But later analysis confirmed the original diagnosis: he was suffering from diabetes. From then on he received daily injections of insulin in increasing dosages.

The three newly-ordained priests could now help him in his work. They took on some of the journeys to the different towns in Spain, and helped his daughters to direct the Women's Section and to form their members. The Women's Section, in November 1944, had set up a house called *Los Rosales*, in Villaviciosa de Odón, near Madrid.

Travelling, preaching ...

During the year 1945, before going to Portugal, the Work continued to spread throughout the different regions of Spain.

On 27 March the Father left for Andalusia, to visit his sons in Seville and to find out how best to start the apostolate in Granada. In both towns he went to see houses with gardens that might be possible future student residences.

When he returned to Madrid, after meeting several bishops in the south and south-east of the peninsula, he had travelled over fifteen hundred miles in nine days.

A month later Pedro Casciaro and three other members of the Work moved to Bilbao, with the idea of opening a Residence there too.

The Father devoted more and more of his time to directing and forming the members of the Work, although he carried on his apostolate with all sorts of people outside it.

Churchmen and associations would very often ask him to preach retreats: he accepted whenever he could, knowing that much good could come from them, for souls in particular and for society in general. Many important dignitaries, some of them very well known, thus benefited from the preaching of the founder of Opus Dei. It mattered little to him, in fact, what sort of audience he had. His message was the same for everyone: they must sanctify themselves wherever they had been placed, be it in the humblest of jobs or the highest positions in the State. They must try with all their might to sanctify their work, their ordinary occupation, making of it a work worthy to offer to God and of use to men; finally, they must sanctify those around them with their work, looking for an opportunity in their professional life to help them find the ultimate meaning of their lives.

Let no one think it is necessary to withdraw from the world in order to fulfil your obligations towards God. Nor is it necessary *to lead a double life: on the one hand, the interior life, the life of your dealings with God; on the other, a distinct, separate life, your family life, professional life, social life, full of small earthly realities.* [64]

Unity of life, responsibility towards other men, trying to direct souls, and the whole of society, towards God: this language was addressed to every person who lived immersed in the different activities of the world, not only to the members of Opus Dei. The only difference was that the members responded in a specific, "vocational" manner to the universal call to holiness, and found support and encouragement in the Work.

During Lent 1945, the Father was invited to preach one of the retreats organised for university lecturers in a chapel in the centre of Madrid. The other preachers were well-known Jesuits and Dominicans.

He managed to keep up all his activities in spite of his diabetes, which had become chronic: he suffered from continual headaches and thirst, had become much heavier and tired easily.

During the summer months he spent some days near Segovia, at *Molinoviejo*, a rented house, which is like *an emerald ring on the brown hand of Castille.* [65] Groups of members of the Work took turns to go there to rest a little, though in rather cramped conditions. At the same time they continued their intensive formation in special courses, which were like a halt to gather energy and launch out again into the apostolate with renewed life and agility.

In September the Father visited Portugal for the third time to prepare the beginnings of the apostolic work in that country. On his way back, he stopped off in Santiago de Compostella, where a number of his sons were already living, and passing through Oviedo reached Bilbao. Here, thanks to help from friends − among them the family of a nobleman the Father had met in Burgos during the Spanish Civil War − the members of the Work in Bilbao had been able to find a house and begin to set it up as a students' Residence. As always, the idea was that this formative activity, which would be of benefit to the whole area, would also complement the personal apostolate carried out by each member of the Work in his professional surroundings. The Residence was called *Abando*.

Several months later, in February 1946, a member of the Work went to Coimbra in Portugal. There were soon others.

Thus very naturally, thanks to the impetus given by the founder, Opus Dei had begun to spread both within Spain and outwith its borders.

The Father, seeing what had become of this Work of God which had been placed in his hands on 2 October 1928, repeated to his sons the words of an old song from his native Aragón:

> *Rosebud, rosebud,*
> *Soon to be a rose:*
> *The time has come for somebody*
> *To tell you what he knows.* [66]

Dream, and you will see how your dreams fall short of reality,[67] he had said to those around him in 1942.

But for the founder that was only the beginning. For if he was to be faithful to the mission he had received, he had to take Opus Dei along new paths and quicken still more the pace of events.

6. ROME: 23 JUNE 1946

On the covered terrace of a small flat on the top floor of a house on the Piazza della Cittá Leonina, to the right of Saint Peter's Square, Don Josemaría Escrivá de Balaguer prayed intensely, his eyes fixed on the windows of the papal apartments at the top of the Vatican Palace.

On several occasions during the night, Don Alvaro del Portillo, José Orlandis and Salvador Canals had in vain tried to persuade him to rest. The journey from Genoa, where they had been that same morning, had been a very long one. And the crossing of the Mediterranean on board the J.J. Sister − an ancient steamer dating from the late nineteenth century − had been very trying. The doctor in Madrid had formally advised him against the journey, and when he learned that Don Josemaría was determined to go anyway, had disclaimed all responsibility for the possible consequences.

The founder of Opus Dei continued praying the whole night, sometimes contemplating the dome of Saint Peter's Basilica which rises over the tomb of the first Pope, sometimes the lighted window behind which lived and worked his successor, Christ's vicar on earth. *Thank you, my God, for that love for the Pope you have placed in my heart*,[68] he had written one day to express his feelings in some way. So many years of waiting and hoping *to see Peter*[69] had now reached their fulfilment. Besides, the supernatural business that brought him to Rome demanded a sacrifice on the same scale.

When he had first caught sight of the dome of Saint Peter's, several hours earlier, the Father had invited those who were with him to say the Creed with him, pronouncing with deep emotion those words, "I believe in One, Holy, Catholic and Apostolic Church ..."

First steps in Rome

It was a letter from Father del Portillo, about mid-June, that had made up his mind to undertake this trip to Rome, where the Secretary-General of Opus Dei had been since 26 February.

The other two members of the Work in Rome, Salvador Canals and José Orlandis, lived in a small flat near the Piazza Navona.

Don Alvaro had spent several weeks taking the necessary steps for the approval of Opus Dei as an Institution of Pontifical Right. In the founder's mind the 1943 approval had only been a first necessary stage to solve the problem of the incardination of the priests of the Work. But it was quite clear that the apostolates of the Work would not be limited to one or two dioceses, for they were universal and concerned all countries and all human beings. Under the ecclesiastical law of the time, only religious orders or congregations could be approved as institutions of universal right and regime. Extending this possibility to an institution made up of laity and secular priests was unthinkable.

"You have arrived a century too soon!" On hearing this comment from one prelate, Don Alvaro realised that without the founder's presence in Rome all his efforts would be useless. But knowing the state of the Father's health, it was not without hesitation and careful consideration of the matter in his prayer that he had written and asked for him to come.

A decisive voyage

Don Josemaría, as a good lawyer, knew that it would be no easy task to have all the consequences – canonical as well – of a pastoral phenomenon as new as Opus Dei accepted. But they could wait no longer: there was a good chance that the slander and the intriguing manoeuvres that had tried to nip the Work in the bud would flare up again with renewed vigour. Papal approval would be the only way to silence them.

He also remembered what the auxiliary Bishop of Madrid had let slip one day: it was that Don Josemaría had been denounced as a heretic in Rome! *That makes me very happy!* he had said to Don Casimiro Morcillo at once. *They've accused me before the Holy Office! But what can come to me from Holy Mother Church, except good?* [70]

He had written to his sons several months earlier, to put them on their guard against the slightest shadow of discouragement. *Our spirit demands a close union with the Sovereign Pontiff, the visible head of the Universal Church. I have so much faith and so much confidence in the Church and in the Pope!* [71]

When he received Don Alvaro's letter in Madrid, the Father called a meeting of the members of the General Council that directed Opus Dei with him, always in a collegiate way. Their opinion was exactly the same as his: he should go to Rome. He then told them: *Thank you for your advice. I would have gone in any case. What must be done, must be done.* [72]

But as on every important occasion, it was to the Blessed Virgin that he turned for the success of his undertaking. The day after he left Madrid, 19 June, he prayed before the statue of the Virgin of *El Pilar* in Saragossa. It was she who, after years of filial pleas, had shown him, on 2 October 1928, what the divine Will, so long obscure, really was. It was she to whom he had come once he had reached the Nationalist zone in 1938, to thank her for saving him. He repeated now, with his former fervour, *Domina, ut sit!* Our Lady, may this Will of God, may this Work of God which has already borne so many fruits of holiness, be carried through to the end!

Before going aboard ship he had addressed another prayer to Our Lady, climbing up to the Monastery of Montserrat which sits perched on the top of the Holy Mountain, a few miles from Barcelona.

The following day, 21 June 1946, in the tiny oratory of a flat on Muntaner Street in Barcelona, the Father wanted to share his worries and his hopes with the members of the Work who had gathered there. To explain his feelings he turned to those simple words of Peter to Jesus: *Ecce nos reliquimus omnia.* (Matt 19:27) We have left everything to follow you; what is going to happen to us?

Lord, could you have allowed me to deceive so many souls in good faith? When I've done it all for your glory, knowing that it was your Will, is it possible that the Holy See will say that we've arrived a century too soon? ... I never wanted to deceive anybody. I never wanted to do anything other than serve you. Is there any possibility that I can be a fraud!? [73]

But God cannot go back on His word. He will remove the obstacles.

Near the port of Barcelona, not far from the wonderful gothic church of Our Lady of the Sea, rises the dome of the Basilica of Our Lady of Ransom, Patroness of the City. Before the niche that enshrines the wooden statue of the Blessed Virgin there, he once more placed his intention in the hands of the Mother of God.

Only then did he take ship for Rome.

At Saint Peter's Chair in Rome

When the founder arrived in the Eternal City, the flat in the Piazza della Città Leonina had only just been set up. The Blessed Sacrament was still absent, but soon they were able to keep Our Lord in a tabernacle of painted and gilded wood. It was all they were able to find in those difficult times after the war.

They started the busy round of meetings with the relevant people in the Curia. The Father was only concerned with one thing: that the law of the Church had to uphold and protect the spirit of

Opus Dei, not hamper it. But he was confident that, despite the difficulties, the Church could not be wrong and would not fail to recognise the voice of the Holy Spirit, even if for the moment it would have to choose the least inadequate way offered by ecclesiastical law.

On the feast of the Sacred Heart, 28 June, a few days after the Father had arrived in Rome, Pope Pius XII sent him a photograph with the dedication: "To our dear son José María Escrivá de Balaguer, founder of the Priestly Society of the Holy Cross and of Opus Dei, with a special blessing. 28 June 1946. Pius P.P. XII" At the same time he received a document of the Holy See praising the aims of Opus Dei together with the Apostolic brief *Cum Societatis*, in which, among other things, the Holy Father granted various indulgences to the members of the Work.

In the explanation of the reasons for the brief, this last document mentions the steps already covered by the Work: "The apostolic work of its members has extended not only within the boundaries of Spain but also into other regions, carrying the light and truth of Christ especially to the minds of intellectuals, so that each transmits to the others, by word and by example, the light and truth of Christ that he has received."

The indulgences granted to all those who carry out their work, accompanying it with a pious invocation, were in accordance with a fundamental trait of the spirit of Opus Dei: the value given to work as a sanctifying and sanctifiable reality. This Indulgence was confirmed and extended in the following year by another Apostolic Brief, *Mirifice Ecclesia*.

On 16 July, the feast of Our Lady of Mount Carmel, Don Josemaría was able to express his thanks to the Pope when Pius XII received him in a private audience which was very cordial.

He returned to Madrid on 31 August with a document of "approval of aims" of Opus Dei, and the firm conviction that the Roman Dicasteries would find a legal formula for it which would guarantee and recognise the universal nature of the Work, even if it was not foreseen in the Canon Law legislation then in force. The founder anticipated that this would only be a first stage on the way to achieving a definitive juridical framework. A new phase in the history of the Work was beginning.

Before the end of the summer, bringing forward a decision that he had wanted to make sooner or later, the founder decided to move to Rome permanently. This was for him a clear way of showing the universality, the *catholicity*, of Opus Dei.

Apostolic work in Europe

Before returning to the Eternal City, however, he wanted to settle a few questions – such as how, for example, to begin spreading the Work in new countries: some of his sons were already in Portugal and Italy.

In *Molinoviejo*, near Segovia, he spoke of the countries where they would have to go, starting that year.

Travelling and residing outside Spain was not easy at the time, owing to the country's political and diplomatic isolation. Therefore those who were ready to go and could do so would have to start applying for visas as soon as they could, for the administrative procedures were long and complicated.

They had decided on three countries, Great Britain, France and Ireland; the first two were just beginning to recover from the scars left by the Second World War.

At the end of 1946 Juan Antonio Galarraga, who had a doctorate in pharmacy, left for London to continue his research in biochemistry. In early October 1947 José Ramón Madurga, an engineer, went to Dublin with a grant to study for an MSc at the University there.

Finally there was Paris, where the founder had thought of sending some of his sons as early as 1936. The Spanish Civil War, and then the Second World War, had prevented him from carrying out his plans, but now he took them up again. A young lawyer, a specialist in International Law, Fernando Maycas, had obtained a place for the academic year 1947-48 at the Spanish College in Cité Universitaire. He arrived towards the middle of October, not without difficulty, for Spain was under blockade from various countries and the Franco-Spanish border was closed.

In Madrid, six more members of the Work were ordained on 29 September 1946. The founder was not at the ceremony, for the same reasons that had led him to be absent from the ordination of the first three priests in 1944. As then, he prayed during the ceremony for his sons and for the enormous amount of work awaiting them.

On 19 October 1946 he visited Barcelona again, passing through Saragossa, where he knelt once more at the feet of the Virgin of *El Pilar*. He did the same in the Catalan capital, at the Basilica of Our Lady of Ransom, where he had sought strength and consolation on 21 June of that same year. But this time his prayer was an act of thanksgiving to Our Lord and to the Blessed Virgin who, in reply to the trusting and passionate plea that he had been making to them for months, had enabled him to open up the legal pathway of the Work.

As a detail to show his gratitude, he had an image of Our Lady of Ransom painted on the altarpiece of the house in Muntaner Street, along with the phrase he had taken as the theme of his prayer out loud on that 21 June: *Ecce nos reliquimus omnia et secuti sumus te, quid ergo erit nobis?* (Matt 19:27) Underneath were two dates, those of his two visits to the Basilica of Our Lady of Ransom: 21 June – 21 October 1946.

Opus Dei, a Secular Institute

The Father returned to Rome on 8 November. He continued his activities in the various Curial departments of the Holy See. In between times he spent long hours in front of the Blessed Sacrament in the oratory at the Piazza della Città Leonina, and recited many *Credo's* at the tomb of the Prince of Apostles in Saint Peter's.

His relations with some prelates – those more involved in his business – quickly extended beyond his official dealings with them. Among them was Monsignor Sebastiano Baggio and two who worked directly for Pope Pius XII, Monsignor Domenico Tardini

(Papal Secretary for Extraordinary Affairs) and Monsignor Giovanni-Battisti Montini (then in charge of Ordinary Affairs), a man whose courteous tact and sincerity the Father greatly appreciated.

The Holy Father himself received him a second time in private audience on 8 December.

At last, the Apostolic Constitution *Provida Mater Ecclesia* of 2 February 1947 created a new legal structure under the General Chapter of Associations for the Faithful – the Secular Institute.

On the 24th of the same month, after a plenary meeting of the competent Congregation which had taken place on the 14th, The Pope approved Opus Dei in conformity with the new legislation, granting a Decree of Praise (the *Decretum Laudis*), and thus making it the first Secular Institute of Pontifical Right.

On 22 April Don Josemaría Escrivá was made Domestic Prelate to the Pope. He had hesitated before accepting the title, which made him a *Monsignor*, as he wanted nothing for himself. If he accepted in the end, it was so as not to give offence to those who had put his name forward and also because the title could only be given to members of the secular clergy, and not to those in religious orders or congregations. Opus Dei's fundamental difference from them would thus be emphasised.

Before the Constitution *Provida Mater Ecclesia* was made public – the text appeared in the *L'Osservatore Romano* on 14 March and was commented on by Vatican Radio together with the news of the approval of Opus Dei – the Father wrote to his children on 7 March: *The approval of our Work is being made public, and furthermore ... I've practically been given an order ... not to keep quiet about it. That is why you can tell everyone this piece of good news, without boasting of course, but without hiding your joy.* [74]

7. ROME: 28 JANUARY 1949

Pope Pius XII looked up; the founder of Opus Dei could read surprise in the keen gaze behind the fine metal-rimmed glasses.

Yes, Holy Father, he confirmed, *the books and pamphlets you have in your hands are the work of some of my sons and daughters* ...[75]

For his third audience, in which he was accompanied by Don Alvaro, the Father had decided to give the Pope an example of what the highly diversified apostolate of the Work could imply, with a selection of scientific books and articles published by some of his sons and daughters.

The Work obviously does not attribute to itself the merits of professional activities carried out by its members at their own initiative. Nevertheless the Father wanted to choose this eloquent example to show that his children's apostolate was carried out with an entirely lay mentality, in all the realities of the world – from the most humdrum to the most glamorous.

From the beginning of the Work he had never stopped trying to ensure that this specific call to holiness reached people from all walks of life. He had, then, been particularly happy in 1946 when vocations began to arise among women whose professional work was to "serve". It was these women who now – without being at all involved with the activities of the men – helped to make agreeable and inviting the houses where some members of the Work lived. For the Father this was one of the many signs of the Work's vitality, which had also been shown by the expansion that had taken place since the last papal approval.

London, Dublin, Paris, Mexico, the United States ...

Indeed, the three years that had gone by since the approval was granted had seen Opus Dei put down roots in a number of very different situations and different countries, and the fruits were very encouraging.

On 17 December 1946 the Blessed Sacrament was reserved for the first time in the tabernacle of the oratory of the Residence in Coimbra, which was the first in Portugal. On 24 June 1947 some of the Father's sons moved into a flat in Rutland Court, their first centre in London. In October of that same year the Father gave his blessing to José Ramón Madurga, who was leaving for Dublin; and then, about a fortnight later, to two young postgraduates headed for Paris, Fernando Maycas and Alvaro Calleja. To these two he gave a piece of the shroud of the first member of the Work, Isidoro, whose process of beatification opened in Madrid the following year.

On 25 July 1947 a Mexican, Guillermo Porras, asked to join Opus Dei. When the Father returned to Rome, he met the first Italian member of the Work, Francesco Angelicchio. Francesco was soon followed by others in early 1948.

That same year, those sons of his who were starting the apostolate of Opus Dei in these countries sent him a continuous stream of good news. On 9 January a telegram to Rome announced the first Irish vocation. In April Don Pedro Casciaro and some other members of the Work undertook a long tour of the different countries in the New World, working from north to south. The Father had entrusted him with the job of studying the particular features of each country, and making the initial contacts prior to establishing the first centres of the Work in America. In the United States Don Pedro met up with Professor José María González Barredo, who had been there for a while doing some research. Together they visited a number of important cities in the United States and Canada.

In May, Don Pedro arrived in Mexico and stayed there for about two months. Shortly after Don Pedro's return, the Father decided that they would start in Mexico and the United States.

In Molinoviejo, at the end of 1948, the Father gave his blessing to Don Pedro Casciaro, who was going to Mexico at the beginning of the following year with three other members of the Work. Don José Luis Múzquiz left for the United States in February.

Wherever they went, in whatever situation they found themselves, the first members of the Work sent by the Father into a new country set about starting the apostolic work in the same way, for in the spirit of Opus Dei apostolic work is inseparable from plain work, from ordinary occupations. Each of them would thus awaken vocations quite naturally among their colleagues at work, through that apostolate founded on *friendship and trust* ,[76] which the founder had always recommended, and which was nothing more than the consequence, the *overflow* [77] of their own interior life: recourse to the Sacraments, prayer, mortification (especially in accepting in good part the many sacrifices, large and small, which were the inevitable consequence of the problems at the beginning) and constant mastery of one's character and senses. This was the treasure they sought to spread around them and share with others whose human qualities of generosity, loyalty, sincerity and so on, would make them more likely to give themselves to God.

The priests of the Work, always a very small proportion of the whole (and therefore entirely occupied by their priestly tasks), were ready to help those friends who came to them and expressed the wish to follow the path of sanctifying themselves in the midst of the world – which Opus Dei offered them, whether they received a vocation to the Work or not.

The material surroundings, too, were always broadly speaking the same. From the beginning they would look for a house, as the Father had done in the 1930s, and would set up an oratory there as soon as possible, after having obtained the *venia* from the local bishop. A few members of the Work would live there, giving an impetus to all the apostolates carried out from the house and providing formation for the new members. But as most of the members – especially if they are married – live with their families, it is in these surroundings, and in their professional milieu, that they carry out their apostolate.

In the meantime the Father would continue from Rome to give renewed impetus to the development of the Work. He encouraged them with his prayers, his letters, and his ideas. When possible, he would go and give a good push to the apostolic work wherever it was needed.

On 11 October 1948 he took advantage of a trip to Spain to go on into Portugal and visit his sons in Coimbra, and in Oporto, where they had just opened the Residence *Boavista* . The visit was a great source of joy both for him and for those he already knew – and for those he met for the first time – and whom he encouraged to accept, with a smile, the consequences of the heroic poverty that inevitably accompanied the first beginnings of apostolic work.

Every time he saw his sons leave for a new country, it was as if he saw himself again, at the age of twenty-six, when, without any means, he had to open up *all the divine paths of the earth.* [78]

He had considered this idea aloud with the two preparing to join Fernando Maycas in Paris. *We have always begun with means which were out of all proportion to what was required.* [79]

The vocation to holiness in marriage

His stay in Spain had allowed the founder to put into practice a very old project of his that would represent a decisive step in the growth of the Work.

What he had seen on 2 October 1928 included, among those who would respond to the divine call to holiness in the middle of the world, a majority of married men and women who could serve the Church and all souls in every possible human situation, sanctifying their family lives and making their homes *bright and cheerful* .[80]

Their vocation could only be identical with that of the celibate members, even if the circumstances in which they lived were, naturally, very different. The spirit of the Work was like *a single cooking pot* [81] into which everyone could dip his spoon, according to his needs and his availability.

From the 25th to the 30th of September the Father preached a retreat in Molinoviejo to fifteen men who had recently asked to join the Work. Among them was Tomás Alvira and several others he had met before or during the civil war.

The Father commented on some pages which he had started writing in 1935 and was now completing. The document was an instruction, a blueprint of the enormous apostolic task destined to penetrate every level of society throughout the centuries. This was the ever-expanding apostolate that he had once, in nearby Segovia, placed under the protection of the Archangel Gabriel: *I see that great band in action: men and women, office workers and manual labourers, eminent university figures, important research scientists, miners, peasants ... all of them knowing that they have been chosen by God to aim for personal holiness in the middle of the world, exactly where they are in the world, each of them, with a solid and enlightened piety, taking up their duty to be fulfilled in each moment with joy – even at the cost of considerable sacrifice.* [82]

The call, to which some of his listeners had responded, had been maturing in their souls for months or years. Others retained in their memory what the Father had told them a long time ago – that they had a vocation to marriage: *You laugh because I tell you that you have a 'vocation for marriage'? Well, you have just that: a real vocation.* [83]

This statement, which the Father had put in *The Way*, came as a shock to some people and it had been one of the reasons for the lack of understanding that he had come up against in some church circles. But the Holy See would soon, in 1950, come down in favour of Monsignor Escrivá, in admitting that married people could form part of Opus Dei in response to a specific vocation to holiness in their own state.

The battle of formation

Now he would have to give the *common denominator*[84] of Christian doctrine and the spirit of the Work to all these people, men and women, married and celibate, so varied in origin, profession, social status and education. The very diversity and spontaneity of their apostolates demanded this effort, for it was this that would guarantee the unity and the apostolic results of Opus Dei down the centuries. In the words of the founder, it was time for *the great battle of formation* of the members of the Work.

This formation would normally be given "on the job", wherever the members of the Work might be, going with them, as it were, wherever their professional or family life might take them. For the members who remained celibate, however, it could also be given in a more intensive way, in longer periods, given their greater availability.

The Father's idea was that some of them should also spend some time in the capital city of the Christian world, in order to acquire a universal, catholic spirit, while at the same time, in the very heart of Opus Dei, close to the founder, they could imbibe the spirit of the Work. This meant that it would be necessary to acquire a building in Rome large enough to accommodate them.

At that time, Monsignor Escrivá was preparing a central house for Opus Dei in Rome, for the Work was becoming day by day more and more universal in extension. The provisional solution for that Centre of formation which was seen to be necessary in 1948, was found in that central house, a part of which would be used as an international Centre – the Roman College of the Holy Cross – until suitable definitive premises were found.

In February 1947, after several months of searching, they discovered a Roman villa in the Parioli district, north of the Villa Borghese. The house, which had been the residence of the Hungarian ambassador to the Vatican, was quite large, and the gardens attached would allow them to put up more buildings. Unfortunately, an embassy official was still living there with his family, although he had no legal right to do so, for diplomatic relations between Hungary and the Holy See had been broken off when the Communists took over in Budapest. Hence the quite modest price asked by the owner. It was still far more than Don Josemaría could afford. And they had to pay in Swiss francs ...

When Don Alvaro had told this to the Father, he had answered, amusingly: *That doesn't worry us, because we don't have either lira or francs and, anyway, as far as Our Lord is concerned one currency is as good as another.* [85]

They had to be sure that they could persuade the occupants of the Villa to leave. According to the lawyers this could be done, but one had to be patient ...

That prospect, coupled with Monsignor Montini's encouragement, had made up the Father's mind.

"Do buy it," the Substitute Secretary of State had said; "it's a good house and the financial conditions are very favourable. The Holy Father knows the building, because he visited it when he was Secretary of State, and he'll be very happy to know that you've bought it."

Indeed, it was in that very house that, before the Second World War, the then Cardinal Pacelli had met Count Horthy, the Hungarian Regent.

At Villa Tevere

Although they had not managed to get the occupants of the Villa to vacate the premises right away, the Father left the Piazza della Città Leonina and set up house provisionally in the porter's lodge, on the corner of the two streets, Bruno Buozzi and Villa Sacchetti.

The arrangement was extremely uncomfortable. The Father had to sleep several nights on the floor, on a wooden board, with a book for a pillow. The cold very quickly gave him a paralysis of the face which made it very difficult for him to move his left side. But the little house made it possible for them to accommodate, in addition to those who had been in the Piazza della Città Leonina, the first Italian members of the Work. Each of them brought his friends, and Don Alvaro preached for them and looked after them spiritually.

But the Father was already thinking of those who would come for formation in Rome before returning to their own countries. Without waiting for the Hungarians to go, he had drawn up, and signed on 29 June 1948, a document by which he established, provisionally at Villa Tevere until they could find a permanent location, the international centre designed to give that formation. He named it the Roman College of the Holy Cross.

"College", he had explained, *because there will be many hearts coming together to form – "consummati in unum" – a single heart, living in a single love; "Roman", because we are in our soul, in our spirit, very Roman. Because at Rome lives the Holy Father, the Vice-Christ, the sweet Christ on earth. Of the "Holy Cross", because Our Lord wanted to crown the Work with a Cross, as one crowns a building, one 14 February ... And because the Cross of Christ has been inscribed into the life of Opus Dei from its very beginnings, as it is in the life of every one of my children. And also because the Cross is Our Lord's royal throne, and we must place it high, at the summit of all human activities.* [86]

On 5 February 1949 the Hungarian occupants left the Villa and the Father and his companions moved in. The major alterations could begin. It was obvious that they were going to take a long time, considering the size of the project and the effort it would require to raise sufficient money.

In his two and a half months in Spain and Portugal, from 11 February onwards, the founder asked his sons and daughters to pray hard for the success of this new project, which was far beyond the means they could then count upon, but which was essential for the future of the Work and for the unity and the permanence of its spirit in every country.

As is the tradition in Opus Dei, priority was given to the oratories, then to the completely separate building required for the women members of the Work, who would look after the upkeep of the house.

Apostolic work in Italy

The Work in Italy itself was beginning to spread at that time. The founder had travelled to Milan in 1948, as well as to the south, passing through Naples and going as far as Catania in Sicily.

The first few months of 1949 were to see his sons travelling in their turn to the major Italian cities, in order to establish the first contacts and build the foundations of a stable apostolic work: Bari, Genoa, Turin, Milan, Bologna, Pisa, Padua, Naples, Palermo, Catania. The ground, already well prepared by prayer and sacrifice, seemed favourable and some vocations sprang up.

In mid-August some thirty young men who had asked to join the Work found themselves in a villa at Castelgandolfo, overlooking Lake Albano and next to the papal territory there, for a period of intense formation. The house, which had been rather neglected, belonged to the Holy See. Later on, Pope Pius XII granted the use of the property to Opus Dei.

The Father spoke a great deal to his sons about prayer, work, humility, perseverance and the need to imitate Christ, "obedient unto death, death on the Cross". It meant a new impulse for everyone, helping them all to advance in their interior lives and to take up their professional work and their apostolic activities with even more enthusiasm in the new academic year.

On 28 October, in Rome, the Father spoke again to Italian members of the Work, urging them to be *sowers of peace and joy*,[87] *quasi fluvium pacis* (Is 56:12): like a great river of peace in a society troubled by sin. *The Lord wants you to be present*, he told them, *on all the divine paths of the earth, sowing the seed of understanding, of forgiveness, of overlooking faults, of the good will among people that comes from charity and peace, "in hoc pulcherrimo caritatis bello".*[88] And his sons must fight in this "peaceful war" in every country in the world, without giving up despite the inevitable misunderstandings and criticism – that have always been present on the paths of those Christians who have lived in conformity with their faith – but with many joys as well.

Preparing the ground for cultivation

The founder followed the development of the apostolate in other countries step by step. In the letters he sent to his sons, now scattered practically throughout the world, he advised them to clear the ground and prepare it with their prayers, their self-sacrifice and the effort they put into bringing the divine calling to souls.

The first vocations, soon followed by others, started to spring up everywhere.

In the Spring an Irishman and a Portuguese asked to join the Work. In August a French girl, Catherine Bardinet, met Opus Dei through a Spanish friend whom she had invited home to Bordeaux. She started to translate *Camino* into French. On 15 August she decided to put everything into God's hands and asked to join Opus Dei. Hers was the first vocation in France.

Of course the Work met with obstacles in the various countries where it was starting. But as the founder liked to say, what would a painting be like if it were all light and there were no shadows? *There would be no painting!* [89] When such incidents occurred he advised his daughters or sons to keep to the rule of behaviour he had always followed himself: pray, keep silent, work and smile.

The Father liked to contribute by his prayers to the preparation of the ground while he travelled through countries and regions where his sons were already spreading the spirit of Opus Dei or would soon be doing so. Thus, on 22 November 1949 with Don Alvaro and another member of the Work he visited Genoa, Como and Milan. In Milan two or three of his sons were living in a boarding-house while they looked for a permanent home. He advised them to invoke often the *Madonnina* on the top of Milan Cathedral. He spoke of the interior life and of the holiness that they had to seek unceasingly in their daily lives, such as in their present circumstances, for instance. If they had faith the rest would come, thanks to their efforts.

After Milan he carried on to Turin and the north of the Italian peninsula, as far as Bolzano on the upper reaches of the River Adige. From there, on 29 November, they crossed into Austria.

Pray hard for all this, he had written from Milan to his sons in

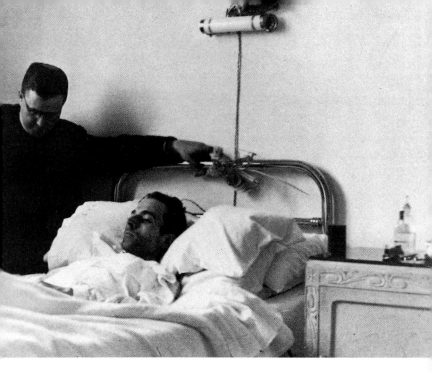

Above: Madrid, 21 April 1943. With Isidoro Zorzano, an Argentinian and one of the first members of Opus Dei, who died on 15 July 1943.

Below: The founder of Opus Dei with the first three members to be ordained priests: (from the left) José Luis Múzquiz, José María Hernandez de Garnica and Alvaro del Portillo.

Above: Madrid, 16 September 1944. The Bishop of Madrid, Monsignor Leopoldo Eijo y Garay with Don Josemaría, outside the Moncloa hall of residence.

Right: Rome, Christmas 1956. Carmen Escrivá, the founder's sister, at home with Chato, her bulldog.

Portugal, *so that Our Lord will not look at our wretchedness but at our faith, and we can definitively begin the work in Central Europe.* [90]

They went through Innsbruck, reaching Munich – the capital of Bavaria – in the South of Germany; they passed Innsbruck again and returned to Italy through the province of Venice.

During the last stage of the trip, all the Father did was pray, invoking Our Lady in those churches with white-and-gold walls, reciting the Rosary in the car: *We have sown the roads of Europe with Ave Maria's and songs*,[91] he said on his return.

It was as if he were living a novel, *a wonderful tale of love and adventure*.[92]

Thinking of the marvels that Our Lord had revealed to him, those that had already become a reality, and those that were to come, he sometimes felt as if it all went beyond his powers of imagination and that his heart and his head were going to burst.

Earlier, more, better: "Prima, piu, meglio!" These three words became a motto he would use, in his trusting conversations with God, asking him to make His Work grow even faster. He wished to express with them that, with the faithfulness of everyone, things would be accomplished earlier, there would be more results and things would be done better than could be thought of with a purely human expectation.[93]

A heart beats in Rome

Christmas Day, 1949. Pope Pius XII knocked three times with a silver hammer on the Holy Door, on the right of the façade of Saint Peter's, to inaugurate the Holy Year. Thousands of pilgrims had already arrived in Rome.

On 1 January 1950 Monsignor Escrivá, accompanied by Don Alvaro and two other sons of his, visited Saint Peter's to gain the Holy Year indulgence, in conformity with age-old Christian tradition.

This year would be, for Opus Dei, a year of greater effort and – God willing – of more grace. The founder also had two things to ask for: the spreading of the Work into many other countries, and to receive soon the definitive approval from the Holy See, although he knew that this would only be a further step towards provision of the proper juridical framework for Opus Dei.

In the meantime, the works in Villa Tevere went on. The main construction work of the part of the complex facing Villa Sacchetti Street was finished. They were now studying plans for two additional floors to the building of the Villa.

The usable part of the porter's lodge was more or less completely furnished. It was filled with people coming to receive spiritual direction, to study, to chat to a friend or to pray. At Castelgandolfo, on the other hand, conferences and retreats were organised regularly.

Members of the Work passing through Rome would come and see the Father. It always made him very happy to see them. He offered his fatigue, his thirst (due to his diabetes), his acute hunger (caused by his medical diet) and also the many hours of work that made up the greater part of his day, for the visitors and for his children all over the world and the apostolate they were carrying out with such generosity.

Persevere in the exact fulfilment of the obligations of the moment. That work – humble, monotonous, small – is prayer expressed in action that prepares you to receive the grace for that other work – great and wide and deep – of which you dream[94] – to put Christ on the peak of all human activities. [95]

For months at a time the Father would not leave Rome, except for short visits in the Summer, usually during the afternoon, to his sons who were in Castelgandolfo.

He had been working with the help of Don Alvaro since the end of 1949 on the preparation for the definitive papal approval which would complete the *Decretum Laudis* of 1947. Documentation to be presented to the Holy See is important, and there were times when the papers covered three tables in the study. They often worked until late at night.

The Father continued to follow the progress of the different apostolates of the Work throughout the world.

A small group of women in Opus Dei left for Mexico on

4 March 1950 to work in their various professional fields. Others intended to go to the United States once they had solved the administrative problems.

On 12 March two university teachers, Francisco Ponz Piedrafita and Ismael Sánchez Bella, arrived in Buenos Aires with Don Ricardo Fernández Vallespín, who had been ordained priest. They had gone to give a series of conferences in Argentina on their respective specialities: animal physiology, history of law and modern architecture. They were so well received that after writing to Rome asking for advice, the Father decided that they should stay.

On 13 March 1950 the Father wrote to Don Alfonso Rodriguez Vidal, who had arrived in Chile a few days earlier, in the following terms: *The first letter written from Santiago arrived a few minutes ago. You cannot imagine how affectionately, and how enthusiastically, I read it. God bless you, my son! God bless you and make your heart grow greater and greater, your mind more and more keen, so that you know how to love and understand that wonderful country where Our Lord has placed you to work on His vine of Opus Dei ... My son: be happy! Once in a while, pay a visit for me to our Heavenly Mother, in her shrine of Carmel; be certain that everything will work out, even if you meet the odd difficulty ... Receive the blessing and an affectionate embrace from your Father.*

8. ROME: 28 MARCH 1950

Surrounded by his sons in Rome, and following his custom of disappearing and passing unnoticed, the Father was celebrating the twenty-fifth anniversary of his ordination as a priest.

Many memories would have come to his mind: the first presentiments of the Work, in 1917 and 1918; the seminaries of Logroño and Saragossa; the ordination itself, the first years of his priestly ministry and, at last, that 2 October 1928 in Madrid, when he had seen fully what God wanted him to do. He would then have recalled the first years of the Work, the souls sought one by one so that he could pass on the divine call to them; the irresolution of some, the generous response of others, the faithfulness of the first vocations ...

And now the corn was rising tall in many places, on three continents, with other countries to come soon. How could he do other than give thanks fervently to God?

As in all families – and the Work is a family with supernatural ties – his sons and daughters knew only a small part of what they had cost him. But he did not like to refer to this:

Sacrifice, sacrifice! Indeed, in order to follow Christ – as He said himself – you have to carry his Cross. But I do not like so much talk about the cross and sacrifice among those souls who love Our Lord, for where there is Love, the sacrifice is joyful – even if it is costly – and the Cross is the Holy Cross. The soul that knows how to love, how to give itself in this way, is filled with joy and peace. Why talk about sacrifice, then, as if you were looking for consolation, when it is the Cross of Christ, which is your Life, that makes you happy? [96]

His sons, especially Don Alvaro, had expressed the desire to have a plaque engraved – following Roman custom – to commemorate his priestly silver jubilee. In the end he gave way, but on one condition: at the top of the inscription there must be a little donkey ... the little donkey at the water wheel or the mangy donkey to which he likened himself when he spoke to Our Lord.

Two important legal steps

The procedure leading to the definitive papal approval followed its course. The documents presented by the founder of Opus Dei were studied several times by groups of experts in the Roman Curia: first by a commission of "consultors", then by the "Plenary Congress". Monsignor Escrivá insisted that the decree had to take note of Opus Dei's own characteristic spirit and apostolates. He was particularly firm about admitting non-Catholics, and even non-Christians, not as members but as Co-operators, taking part in the apostolic work.

"Monsignor, you're always asking for new things!" they had replied the first time. The Holy See had never, in fact, allowed a Catholic institution to admit within its ranks any person who was not part of the Church. In the end, after a non-committal but obviously procrastinatory answer that he had seen as an implicit recognition that his request had been accepted, the approval was given.

Another of his concerns was how to allow diocesan priests, who had been trained in their own seminaries and incardinated into their own dioceses, to join the Priestly Society of the Holy Cross.

What have I done for my brother priests?, he often asked himself. His concern for the spiritual lives of priests went back a long way. *A priest*, he would say, *does not lose or save himself alone ...* [97] From his days at the seminary in Saragossa, he knew the generosity and love of God characteristic of so many of his brothers in the priesthood, and he had a burning desire to help them in a mission that they often carried out with silent heroism.

He was urged on by the very great respect in which he held the ministry of the priesthood: it had been no idle gesture that, when preaching to priests in the 1940s, he had remained on his knees at the foot of the altar for the whole time he spoke about this theme.

The founder was convinced that the spirituality of the Work could be a great help for these priests to sanctify themselves in their state in life. But how could he bind them to the Work without taking them away from the dioceses where they worked, without in any way upsetting their relations and the link with their own bishops? The suggestions given to him by some experts in Canon Law, and by various dignitaries in the Curia, had not satisfied him. He continued to search for a solution, as he had looked for the way to ordain priests for Opus Dei until he found the answer on 14 February 1943.

This apostolate seemed more and more urgent to him every day. He felt that God was asking him to do something about this, and soon ... That is why, in 1949, after careful consideration of the matter in his prayer, and in spite of the interior wrench this would mean for him, he came to the conclusion that it would be necessary to create a new foundation specifically for priests. To do so would perhaps mean that he would have to leave Opus Dei. The Holy See, when consulted, authorised him to make a new foundation.

He immediately informed the members of the General Council of the Work of his decision. Though they were very moved and overawed when they heard what he intended to do, they decided to respect the wishes of the Father.

Even while preparing to take the step, he continued to consider other possibilities. Thus it was that he suddenly discovered, one day, how he could bring diocesan priests into the Priestly Society of the Holy Cross without having to found anything new at all.

The solution that no one had been able to suggest, and which he had long searched for, turned out to be very simple. After all, if

the vocation to Opus Dei consists in seeking holiness in one's ordinary occupation – professional work and family duties for most
Christians – it was obvious that priests could do the same; in their
case, they would try to fulfil their ministry as perfectly as possible,
and the Work would only give them all the help they needed to do
so.

Thus diocesan priests, who are incardinated in their own
dioceses, could become members of the Priestly Society of the Holy
Cross while continuing to serve and depend entirely on their own
bishops. These priests would have no "superiors" in the Priestly
Society of the Holy Cross: their only superior would be the bishop
of the diocese they belonged to. The Work would be there to give
them spiritual help, so that they could sanctify themselves in their
priestly ministry. In the ministry itself, they would depend on the
bishop alone. Besides, the spirit of the Work, and the ascetic struggle and the strong interior life that it presupposes, could only reinforce the link between these priests and the hierarchy. And the fraternity and friendship that they would find and live in the Work
would avoid any risk there might be of their feeling alone at some
moment or other in their lives. Finally, by this new calling they
would try to make their ministry and their lives as priests more
fruitful. They would do so by living the spirit of Opus Dei, which
means, for everyone, to carry out one's ordinary work as perfectly
as possible, both humanly and supernaturally.

The Father knew that this solution, which he had not looked
for in vain and yet was apparently so simple, could have great consequences for the priests who responded to the call, as well as for
those priests around them who could benefit from their influence
and example. And so too it would have for the faithful in contact
with them. There was no doubt that society could not but be more
quickly and more effectively re-Christianised.

The Father had been greatly relieved when he realised that he
did not have to leave Opus Dei to begin another foundation. The
Lord, no doubt, had for a while let him think that He was asking
this terrible sacrifice of him, rather as He had asked Abraham to
sacrifice his only son, in order to test his obedience.

Ludens in orbe terrarum ... (Prov 8:30) God had been playing with him, as He plays with the children of men on the face of the earth ... As a father plays with his children: *The child has wooden blocks of different shapes and colours ... And his father tells him: put this one here, and that other one there, and that red one further along ... And in the end, the castle is built!* [98]

A decisive approval

1950 was a year of great joy for the founder of Opus Dei. After all the necessary steps had been taken, and after letters of recommendation to the Holy See had been received from a hundred and ten prelates from seventeen countries – among them twelve cardinals, a patriarch and twenty-six archbishops – the Pope signed the decree of definitive and solemn approval of Opus Dei on 16 June, the feast of the Sacred Heart.

The document, rather longer than normal, spoke of the rapid growth of the Work which, as in the Gospel parable, "has so multiplied that the small mustard-seed has been transformed, in an admirable way, into a tree with spreading branches."

The decree also remarked on the special characteristics of the spirit of Opus Dei: its secularity, which distinguished it from religious institutions, the Christian and human virtues that its members undertake to practise, the liberty these members enjoy in the fields of professional work and politics, the divine filiation which is the foundation of their spiritual life, and so on.

Three days after the decree had been published, it was explained on Vatican Radio in each of its thirty foreign broadcasts. The Father listened to one of the commentaries in silence, his head bowed as if it had nothing to do with him ...

When he heard the news of the approval, he had recited a *Te Deum* with some of his sons. He asked those who were far away to join with them in this act of thanksgiving, and to respond to God's mercy with renewed desires for holiness and apostolate.

At Villa Tevere and throughout the world

The first fruits were now appearing wherever the seed had been sown. On 16 June, the same day as the publication of the definitive papal approval, Father Vidal said Mass for the first time in the oratory of the first Opus Dei Centre in Santiago, Chile.

On 15 July an American – Richard Rieman – asked to join the Work. He had just finished his university studies and had served in the U.S. Navy during the Second World War. The Father wrote to him personally a few days later, speaking of the *blessed responsibility* that his vocation implied and which applied to him in a special way, as he was the first member of the Work in the United States.

During the Summer there were more courses of formation. They were held in Spain, particularly in Molinoviejo; at Coimbra (Portugal); in the west of Ireland, near Toormakeady; and also in Italy, at Castelgandolfo.

The work of Opus Dei in Italy was beginning to mature, as had happened in Spain some years before. The young people in Castelgandolfo came from Milan, from Palermo in Sicily and several other cities. One of them wrote to another : "The Father comes almost every afternoon and the family feels complete. He stays with us for quite a while; and when he goes, the day is more intensely meaningful, because the Father passes on his supernatural joy to us, spurs us on with his example and makes us feel closer to everyone else in the Work."

The founder took advantage of his visits to show them how concerned he was that they should take off on their own wings. The buildings of Villa Tevere, which had made it possible for the apostolic work to start in Italy, would soon be used only for the direction of the Work, and provisionally (for a few years at least) used also by the Roman College of the Holy Cross. His Italian sons would, therefore, have to look for a new house, *or else*, he told them with a smile, *you'll have to go and shelter under the bridges of the Tiber* ...

The construction works in the central offices went ahead as quickly as possible. By mid-September, members of the Women's Section were able to move into an independent building, which they could use as the base for their own apostolates. As well as that, they could take charge of a great variety of domestic matters – always, again, with the desired separation – such as the cooking, cleaning, laundry and decoration in the buildings occupied by the Father and the members of the Men's Section, as others were doing already in the residences of the Work in Spain and other countries.

Under the mantle of Our Lady

On 1 November 1950 the first Argentinian asked to join the Work. On the same day, the Father was indescribably happy: In Saint Peter's Square, Pope Pius XII had proclaimed the dogma of Our Lady's Assumption into Heaven. It was a day of rejoicing for Catholics all over the world, seeing as they did another of the Virgin Mary's privileges solemnly defined. It was a day of special thanksgiving for Josemaría Escrivá, who had always put everything under Our Lady's protection – his vocation as a priest, and this Work of God, both before he had seen it clearly and subsequently all the way along its path. He had been more than repaid. Many of the decisive steps in the history of the Work had been taken on a feast of Our Lady.

Many years previously, during his act of thanksgiving after Mass in the church of Saint Elizabeth, he had written the words which now help thousands of Christians to contemplate the Assumption as they recite the five decades of the Glorious Mysteries, as well as the other mysteries: ... *God has taken Mary, body and soul, to Heaven: and the angels rejoice! So sings the Church ... Jesus wants to have His mother, body and soul, in Heaven. And the heavenly Court, arrayed in all its splendour, greets Our Lady ... The Most Blessed Trinity receives and showers honours on the Daughter, Mother and Spouse of God ... And so great is the Lady's majesty that the Angels exclaim: who is she?* [99]

The Holy Father's voice had rung out more strongly at the moment when he recited the words of the solemn formula by which he defined this truth of the faith: "By the authority of Our Lord Jesus Christ and of the Blessed Apostles Peter and Paul, and by our own authority, we proclaim, declare and define as a dogma revealed by God that the Ever-Virgin Mary, the Immaculate Mother of God, having accomplished the course of her life on earth, was assumed body and soul into the glory of Heaven."[100]

Facing the little statue of polychromed wood presiding over the sitting-room, the founder of Opus Dei, surrounded by his sons, listened to these words on his knees ...

9. MOLINOVIEJO: MAY 1951

Monsignor Escrivá left Rome on 28 April 1951 to spend a few days in Spain, near Segovia, in that house, Molinoviejo, which brought back so many memories for him.

The reason for the journey was to hold a General Congress of the Men's Section of Opus Dei there. The Holy See, through its solemn approval, just one year earlier, had confirmed the organisation and government of the Work. The founder's apostolic dynamism and his profound juridical mind was apparent both in his style of government and in the Work's internal structure, which he was one day to describe to a French journalist as that of *an unorganised organisation*.[101]

The structure was reduced to the bare minimum. At the head of each Section – one for men and one for women – each functioning independently, but always with the same spirit, there would be a Council made up of priests and lay people advising and assisting the President-General* – at the foundational stage it was the

---

* Since 28 November 1982 it is the Prelate who provides and assures the fundamental unity of spirit and jurisdiction between the two Sections. Cf footnote on page 299.

founder himself – in the government of each of the Sections. Similar structures in each country are presided over by a Counsellor.*

From top to bottom, each level of government is solely concerned with giving an impetus to the apostolate of each member and ensuring that the inherent spirit of Opus Dei is always kept. The essential activity of the Work – the reason for its very existence – is simply to assure the formation of its members and to help them persevere on the path to which Our Lord has called them. Their apostolic initiatives can take the most varied forms, following the enormous variety of situations in which they find themselves. Thus the autonomy of each member of the Work does not concern only his professional, family or political opinions and activities, but also the particular way he chooses to try and bring others to God. The Work is only interested in making sure that the supernatural spirit with which it is imbued should be transmitted in its entirety.

Thus the way of governing is essentially decentralised, (delegating responsibilities and initiatives), and collegiate, which, after all, fits in perfectly with the secular character of the spirit of Opus Dei. The Father had complete confidence in the ability of each member to take on his own job, and taught his daughters and sons to have the same attitude. He would willingly say that he had *more confidence in the word of one of his sons than in that of a thousand unanimous solicitors.* [102]

One of the norms approved by the Holy See establishes that each Section will organise a separate General Congress regularly, with a certain number of members of the Work participating. These meetings provide an opportunity to look at the situation of the apostolate in each country, to formulate proposals and to name the members of the General Council of the Men's Section and the Central Advisory of the Women's Section.

The founder was now about to preside over the first of these

---

* now, Regional Vicar

Congresses.

Consummati in unum

When he arrived at Molinoviejo the Father was delighted to find some of his eldest sons there.

He told them about life in Rome, and about how the reconstruction of the Villa Tevere complex was getting on ... With characteristic faith, he also sketched out the future growth of the Work. He spoke as vibrantly as ever.

During his preaching and the conversations he had with the members of the Congress, the Father commented on the words of Our Lord, *consummati in unum* : "So that they be perfectly one, and that the world may know that it is You who have sent me and that I have loved them as You have loved me." (John 17:23) The unity he meant was the unity of all the members of the Work, now spread out over more and more countries. It was a deep union of hearts, a profound unity of doctrine, the guarantee of spontaneous apostolic initiatives: it signified union with the visible head of the Church, the Pope.

In reply to the affection shown him by the founder of Opus Dei, Pope Pius XII sent a telegram via Monsignor Montini: "The Sovereign Pontiff, deeply touched by the faithful adherence shown him by the General Congress of Opus Dei, begs light and grace from God for its work and for its sure and telling service to the Church, granting with all his heart his Apostolic Blessing to Your Excellency and to all those taking part in the Congress."[103]

A new smear campaign

Disagreeable news awaited the founder, however, on his return to Rome on 12 May 1951. For some time now, despite the approvals of the Holy See, the old slanders against the Work had again raised their ugly head. As had happened in Spain in the

1940s, someone had taken it upon himself to cause confusion among the families of the first Italian members of the Work. Taken in by false information, a few people had got together to write a letter to the Pope accusing Opus Dei of having turned their children away from the right path. Such an accusation could have had grave consequences at a moment when the Work had only recently received the definitive approval by the Holy See.

It was all the more painful for the Father as he had always been concerned to teach his sons to be as kind and affectionate as possible in their relations with their parents. When speaking of the Fourth Commandment, which demands that one honour one's father and mother, he called it *that most sweet precept of the Decalogue.* [104]

Before doing anything to counteract these calumnies, he made the following note: *Rome, 14 May 1951. Under the patronage of the Holy Family, Jesus, Mary and Joseph, we shall place the families of our people so that they too can receive the "gaudium cum pace" of the Work, and obtain from Our Lord a true affection for Opus Dei.* [105]

When he visited the construction site at Villa Tevere a few hours later, the Father kept his promise. Stopping inside the unfinished rectangular-shaped room that would later be an oratory, surrounded by those concrete walls which were still shuttered, he solemnly entrusted the solution of the particular problem facing him, and, in a more general manner, the families of all the members of the Work, now and in the future, to the Holy Family of Nazareth.

In the days that followed, all the people who had signed the petition to the Pope withdrew their signatures, one by one. They had acted in good faith: it had been enough to explain the ends of the Work clearly to them, and to refute the lies they had been told.[106]

When the construction of the oratory dedicated to the Holy Family was finished, the Father had asked for a painting of the Holy Family of Nazareth by an Italian artist to be placed over the altar, and on a side wall a marble tablet engraved with the words of the consecration composed by the founder. This consecration, which is said every year on the Feast of the Holy Family, in all the centres of the Work, reads:

... O Jesus, our most lovable Redeemer, Who in coming to enlighten the world with Your example and doctrine, chose to spend the greater part of Your life subject to Mary and Joseph in the humble house in Nazareth, sanctifying the Family that all Christian homes were to imitate; graciously accept the consecration of the families of Your children in Opus Dei, which we now make to You. Take them under Your protection and care, and fashion them after the divine model of Your holy Family. [107]

A pilgrimage of reparation

Once things had calmed down, the founder continued to devote all his energies to forming his sons and daughters, and to his responsibilities as President-General. Among other things he had in mind was the journey of those who would soon be going to Colombia, as well as the setting up of a large students' residence in London, from which a Christian spirit could spread out over the whole of England and all the other countries in the British sphere of influence. He was also considering other projects such as beginning a university in Spain ...

And yet, although there was no obvious reason, the Father had a feeling of foreboding, deep down. It was almost like the premonition of mothers who have a sixth sense which tells them of the needs of their children, even when they are far away ... *Something's going on; I don't know what it is, but there's something in the wind ...* [108]

The Father's uneasiness did not diminish despite the absence of anything definite to go on, or of facts he could confront anybody with. There was no way he could either demand an explanation or say anything in his defence.

In this sort of situation, his only possibility was to go to the Mother of God. So, a few days before 15 August 1951, at Castelgandolfo where he often went, he told his sons that he was going to make a pilgrimage to Loreto on the Feast of the Assumption, to honour Our Lady and to put the whole Work in the hands of the Blessed Virgin.

On the 15th I will place the whole of the Work in the hands of Mary; I am going to put all your hearts on a paten to offer to Our Lord. I will also offer Him all men and every country in the world, through the intercession of Our Lady, for where Our Lord is concerned I am very ambitious. It will be a short trip, as a mortification. [109]

On the afternoon of the 14th he left by car for Loreto, accompanied by Don Alvaro del Portillo and two other members of the Work. The heat was stifling as usual at that time of year the Italians call the *ferragosto* . Unlike his usual self on journeys, the Father did not talk or sing. His companions respected his recollection, and united themselves mentally with his prayer, for they realised that they were experiencing a moment of exceptional importance.

When they arrived near Loreto, around sunset, there were big crowds of pilgrims making their way on foot to the shrine. The moment the car stopped the Father was out and on his way into the basilica, walking so quickly that the others lost sight of him. He prayed fervently in the little House of Nazareth, enshrined within the church. (Tradition tells that it was miraculously transported to Loreto from Palestine). He read again and again, and meditated with emotion, the inscription engraved over the altar of the chapel: *Hic Verbum caro factum est. Here, in a house built by human hands, on a piece of the earth where men live, God became Man.* [110]

He said Mass at the same altar at nine o'clock the next morning. But the to-ing and fro-ing of the crowds of pilgrims on this day of the Assumption made it very difficult to be recollected. Each time he kissed the altar according to the rubrics of the Mass, three or four peasant women kissed it at the same time as he did!

At the thanksgiving after Mass there was still the same amount of jostling going on. To avoid being distracted he sought refuge in a little passageway behind the altar. But the pilgrims went there too, pushing him to one side ...

He offered up these inconveniences, which were a sign of the piety of those people, and concentrated intensely on the reason for his being there – to place his worry in the hands of Our Lady, consecrating to her Immaculate Heart Opus Dei and all its members: *our bodies, our hearts, and our souls are for you; we and our apostolates are yours*.[111] He was there to ask her to keep the path of the Work firm and sure.

His heart was soon filled with such a deep peace that when he left the Shrine of Our Lady of Loreto he was quite sure that, if the Work was threatened – as he vaguely suspected – he had nothing to fear. The Mother of God, to whom he had just consecrated Opus Dei in the Holy House, would watch over it.

Cor Mariae dulcissimum, iter para tutum![112] – Most sweet Heart of Mary, make a safe path for us ... Cut down the obstacles, trace out the path for us!

In Italy, Spain and Portugal

During the following weeks the Father continued to visit different Marian shrines: Our Lady of Pompeii, near Naples; Lourdes, on 6 October 1951, on the way to Spain where he was going to take part in the first General Congress of the Women's Section of the Work; the Virgin of El Pilar in Saragossa. In all these places he renewed the consecration he had made on 15 August at Loreto, always concluding with the aspiration *Cor Mariae dulcissimum, iter para tutum!*

He spoke to his daughters, gathered together near Madrid in the villa of Los Rosales, about the growth of the Work in the world, and about the wonderful adventure they would live if they were faithful to the supernatural means they had always used: prayer, mortification, the Sacraments ...

Just a few days before this, an engineer, Bartolomé Roig, had set out for Venezuela, and on 11 October, during his stay in Spain, the Father gave his blessing for the journey to Don Teodoro Ruiz, who was to leave shortly for Colombia. Then, on a sudden impulse of heart-felt emotion, he took down a marble crucifix from the head of his bed and gave it to Don Teodoro, along with two leather-bound volumes of the works of Saint Augustine and a small image of Our Lady painted on copper which was a present from his sister Carmen. These were the only "treasures" he could give him.

On 19 October he went to Fatima once more, on his way from Coimbra to Lisbon. He prayed intensely in the chapel of the apparitions, and renewed again the consecration of the Work to the Heart of Mary.

The threat is over

He arrived back in Rome on 24 October, and almost immediately had to dispense with the services of the building firm. They had let him down, being badly in default of their contract. On the other hand, the Father and those who lived around him were in such dire financial straits that they had to cut down on even the most ordinary expenses. The Roman College students practically gave up smoking and walked to university or to work.

Don Alvaro had great difficulty in meeting the bills, asking help from everyone he could find. On the other hand, there was never any question of stopping, or even reducing in size, the central offices of the Work, for that is not the spirit the Father had transmitted to his sons: *The works of God never fail through a lack of material means. If they fail, it is through lack of good spirit.* [113]

And indeed the works at Villa Tevere were not interrupted. At the end of the year the founder was able to bless an oratory in Villa Sacchetti, and consecrate the altar. It was this separate building that was reserved for the women of the Work. He dedicated the oratory to the Immaculate Heart of Mary, in memory of the consecration of the Work that he had made in Loreto on 15 August. He still had the same forebodings. He still could not pinpoint the danger ...

But then a letter from his sons in Milan gave him some light. On 18 February 1952, a priest and a lay member of the Work went to visit the Archbishop of Milan, as they were in the habit of doing from time to time to keep him informed of their activities. As soon as they arrived, Cardinal Schuster asked them how the Father was:

"Doesn't he have a particular trouble at the moment, a very

heavy cross?"

The two members of the Work said that they did not know anything about it, but that if it was so, they were sure the Father would be very happy for he had always taught his sons that when you are close to the Cross you are close to Jesus.

"No, no," the Cardinal had insisted. "Tell him to think of Saint Joseph of Calasanz who came from his home country, and tell him to do something about it."[114]

As soon as he received the letter from his sons, the Father understood everything. He was well acquainted with the story of the founder of the Piarists; after all, he had studied at a grammar school run by that congregation in Barbastro. Besides, Saint Joseph Calasanz was also Aragonese, and a distant relative of his ...

After founding a religious congregation in Rome to instruct and educate children from working-class backgrounds, the saint had been the victim of all sorts of intrigues put in motion by one of his own spiritual family, a Father Mario. This priest, deceiving the Pope, had denounced his superior to the Holy Office, taken his place and succeeded in expelling the saint, at the age of more than eighty, from the congregation he had himself founded!

Shortly afterwards the Father received more precise information. There was indeed a project to dismember the Work, although this time, unlike the case of Saint Joseph of Calasanz, the attack was from outside. But it was a diabolical plan: the intention was to separate the two Sections of Opus Dei, the one for men and the one for women, and to force the founder not only to resign as President-General, but to leave the Work altogether.

As far as he could tell, the plans were already in the hands of high officials in the Vatican. If they were approved it would amount to the same thing as totally destroying the Work, for the unity of spirit of the two Sections, as well as their unity of government in the person of the President-General, formed an essential part of the Work: it was part of the foundational charisma.

The second objective – the expulsion of the founder – made him cry out in pain: *If they throw me out it'll kill me; if they throw me out they'll be murdering me.*[115] He felt as if he were being crushed between two heavy plates of iron. The only thing that stopped his heart from bursting was his boundless trust in God and the confidence he had gained during his recent visits to the shrines of Our Lady.

He realised that he had to move quickly; he had to "do something about it", as Cardinal Schuster had affectionately advised him through those sons of his who had visited him.

Officially, however, the President-General of Opus Dei knew nothing. Besides, he could hardly present a complaint against a decision which had not yet been taken. The only recourse left to him was to write directly to the Pope, making him realise that they had some idea of what was going on ...

The letter was straightforward and sorrowful, the letter of a son to his father. Monsignor Escrivá was not asking for anything for himself. The only thing he was asking was that, out of justice, he should be told of the accusations being levelled against him. The founder displayed the conscience of a priest in love with the Church: he did not fear the truth. The Father knew full well that it was a campaign of slander and of false accusations. Once again it had been an unbelievable jealousy that had spread falsehoods with the purpose of creating a climate of suspicion and distrust about the Work. He did not care about himself; what he could not tolerate was the offence against God, and the injustice it implied towards all his daughters and sons, who were serving the Church with a complete faithfulness to the spirit and to the norms expressly approved by the Holy See.

When the founder showed the letter to Don Alvaro, he asked the Father to let him sign it too.

A few days later, on 18 March 1952, Cardinal Tedeschini, who was in charge of presenting affairs concerning Opus Dei to the Holy See, read the letter to Pope Pius XII. Although the procedure had really been most unusual, moved no doubt by its extraordinary directness and obvious sincerity, the Pope replied at once that there was no question about such proposals being accepted.

Once more an attempt to destroy Opus Dei had been averted.

For Don Josemaría and the few members of the Work who knew about the matter, it was the Mother of God, ardently implored in her house in Loreto and other places of pilgrimage, who had gained for them this special grace.

In June the founder decided to crown the act of submission to the Virgin Mary with a new consecration, this time with a consecration of the Work to the Sacred Heart of Jesus.

On 26 October 1952, the feast of Christ the King, the Father went to a little oratory in the central house, still under construction, to ask Our Lord for peace for the Work and for all men of good will, for the whole world. *O most sweet ... Jesus, in consecrating to You our Work, with all its apostolic activities, we also consecrate to You our souls with all their faculties; our senses, our thoughts, words and actions; our works and our joys. We especially consecrate to You our poor hearts, so that we may have no other freedom than that of loving You, O Lord.* [116]

It is God who does everything

These dangers, grave though they may have been, did not slow down at all the apostolates of the Work.

More and more undergraduates and young graduates were coming to Rome to deepen their formation. Early in the summer of 1952 the Father asked his sister Carmen to come to Salto di Fondi, a village between Rome and Naples, to look after a country house, which was by the sea, where the students of the Roman College of the Holy Cross would spend some time, taking it in turns.

In July, eight members of the Work were ordained priests in Madrid. A little while earlier, a law school was opened in Pamplona, the first seed sown for a future university. It was an old dream of the Father, who had prayed and worked over many years for it to come about. He saw clearly that while the apostolate of the members of the Work was essentially personal, a matter of *friendship and trust*, wherever they might happen to be, it would also be necessary to set up a few works oriented towards education and social progress in every country. The initiatives would be undertaken by a few of his sons and daughters, working together with many other people. The Work would only provide its spirit to these centres, and their object would be to help resolve specific problems in a district, country or section of society. They would thus be at the same time a means of spreading Christian doctrine, and a way providing an opportunity for the personal apostolate of the members of the Work who would be working there professionally.

That had been the object of the DYA Academy, which the founder had set up in Madrid in 1933, and of all the other student residences opened since then. But at Pamplona it was a matter of a much larger project: a University worthy of the name, which would spread its influence inside and outside Spain. The Father was expecting a lot from it.

At this time good news started to flow into Rome from the countries and cities where people had gone in previous years.

At the beginning of July 1952, some members of the Work who had begun working in Argentina and were living in Rosario, moved to Buenos Aires. In August the Father was told the news of the first vocation to the Women's Section in that same country. On the 30th of the same month a priest left for Venezuela, and an Ecuadorian, who had finished his studies in Rome, went back to his own land. Two other members of the Work settled in Bonn, the capital of the German Federal Republic.

The apostolate continued to grow in 1953: a students' residence opened in Dublin, while two members of the Work went to work in Peru and Guatemala. In Paris, two of the Men's Section moved into a tiny flat in Rue Docteur Blanche. They were joined that summer by Fernando Maycas, the young jurist who had studied at the Sorbonne from 1947 to 1949 and who had since been ordained in Spain. His having now settled down definitively in Paris marked the beginnings of a stable and uninterrupted apostolate in France.

* * *

The Father made another journey to Spain to spend 2 October 1953, the twenty-fifth anniversary of the foundation of Opus Dei, in Molinoviejo. On his way, he stopped at Lourdes to pray to Our Lady, in the very same place where he had invoked her on 11 December 1937, after the long and arduous crossing of the Pyrenees during the Spanish Civil War.

Before leaving Rome the Father had received the blessing of the Holy Father in the form of a letter from Cardinal Tedeschini, confirmed a few days later by a telegram from Monsignor Montini, Pro-Secretary of State for Ordinary Affairs.

His sons were waiting for him in Madrid to celebrate the anniversary. A quarter of a century had gone by since the day Don Josemaría had *seen* Opus Dei for the first time, while the bells of Our Lady of the Angels rang out. Now he contemplated it as Our Lord had wished it to be, and also saw it *projected in time – over the centuries! – opening a straight furrow, deep and wide, full of light and fruitfulness, in the history of mankind.* [117]

As the anniversary drew near, he recommended to his sons and daughters that they carry out their work on that day with even more concentration, and pray even harder: *You must be sowers of peace and joy on this earth so full of hatred: for the silent heroism of your ordinary lives should be the obvious way to celebrate solemnly the silver jubilee of our Mother the Work in conformity with our spirit.* [118]

Before returning to Rome the Father went as far as Portugal, travelling on to Bilbao and Paris, where in that city he took his sons by surprise on the morning of 24 October. He went back through Italy via Milan and Loreto.

The growth of the Work, which was only just beginning, showed him yet again that it was God who had wanted it. *I am worth nothing, I know nothing, I have nothing, I am nothing,* [119] he never gave up repeating, during the time before and after this anniversary, just as when he was only beginning. And he added the natural complement to this act of faith: *But You are everything.* [120]

This 2 October would surely be a new point of departure for his sons, an opportunity to widen the horizons of their apostolate to cover the whole planet.

Your charity should be wide, universal; you should live in the sight of all mankind, thinking of all the souls in the world. This attitude will help you to pray for everyone and, so far as is possible, help everyone. [121]

Who among the older members of the Work, on hearing these words, did not think of the little globe of the world in the Residence on Jenner Road, or of the four arms of the cross that the Father had drawn like arrows stretching out towards the four points of the compass?

•

10. PARIS: 1 MAY 1960

·

The Father was surrounded by his sons in the sitting-room of an apartment on the Boulevard Saint Germain where some of them were now living. He told the first three French members of the Work – two of whom he had met for the first time that day – about his love for France, amusingly explaining his love of freedom by his one-eighth part French blood.

He also asked them to tell those who came after them how he had long been determined to love France very much: he had wanted to make up for some of his teachers in Barbastro who had attempted to provoke anti-French prejudice among their pupils. Feelings going right back to the Napoleonic Wars still ran high in Aragon!

The Father laughed at the surprise this last observation raised on the part of one of his sons, and passed on to other topics, tempering his seriousness with a good dose of humour as always. He was expecting much from France because of the world-wide influence of its culture. He had offered much prayer and many mortifications – including those of this journey – so that the Work in France might set down its roots as quickly as possible.

Work and prayer

Before planting the Work in a particular country, he explained, you have to turn over the ground. The apostolate *of action is the sweet fruit of prayer and sacrifice.* [122]

This spiritual task, of preparing the ground, was the reason for the short trips which took the founder out of Rome.

In some of the countries he visited there were as yet no members of the Work. That did not matter. He would stop to pray, with those who were travelling with him, at shrines of Our Lady, entrusting the intentions of the Church and the future growth of the Work in the country in question to her intercession. Sometimes he visited the bishops, to explain the spirit and apostolates of Opus Dei to them.

When the work had already begun in a city or a town – as was the case, at that time, in France, Germany, Switzerland, Ireland and England – he would try to spend many hours, or even a few days if possible, with his children, encouraging them with his good spirits and cheerfulness.

When he was in Rome he replied to their letters in his own affectionate words, in his round and firm hand. His letters were always optimistic, even if the Father was well aware of the tough problems those who were starting the apostolate in a new country would necessarily come up against. The letters he wrote to his sons in Paris give a very clear idea of how the founder stamped the growth of the Work at its inception, in all the countries concerned, with his dynamism. In the very first years he insisted on the necessity of their primary task, that of preparing the ground with prayer and mortification, *so that a wide, deep and fruitful furrow may soon open in the fair land of France.* [123]

In 1954 he urged his sons there to remain faithful to the moments of prayer that marked out their day: for this would be how, in the end, *this great nation will bear its fruit.* [124] He urged them to have faith and trust during this period when there were as yet no apparent results: *Clear the ground joyfully, for the soil of France is rich.* [125] *May Mary, the Queen of Heaven, bless the work in the dear land of France that its harvest may be plentiful.* [126]

He asked for news about everyone individually; he did not forget to wish each one a happy birthday or feastday, and spoke of faithfulness and generosity in the apostolate. *I am very much looking forward to the blessings that the Lord and his Holy Mother are going to bestow on France as a result of your work,* [127] he wrote, *because God Our Lord always rewards with interest our fidelity and the efforts we make to serve the Church and all souls.* [128]

He asked them to "cut their moorings" and become French with the French. *I'd make myself a Turk to save a single soul!* [129]

He also made them aware of the help that was being given them through the Communion of Saints. *I pray for you especially every day and I am full of hope for the work that awaits you.* [130]

One by one the vocations came, as the Father had promised, as he had foreseen, putting all his energy into helping from afar the blossoming that he had worked for since 1935.

On his short visits to France he always relied on Our Lady for support – at Lourdes, where he prayed at the grotto as often as he could; in the great Gothic cathedral at Chartres; in Paris, in the quiet of the south transept of the Cathedral of Notre-Dame.

In Ars he prayed to Saint John Vianney; he had chosen him as an intercessor of Opus Dei, along with the great English Chancellor Thomas More, the Italian Pope Pius X and the eastern Saint Nicholas of Bari. At Lisieux he prayed to little Thérèse, whose writings he had read many times.

In Paris again, in 1958, he had prayed intensely at Montmartre at the Basilica of the Sacré-Coeur.

Encouraging the apostolates

When he returned to Rome he offered the long succession of identical days for all the countries where the Work was or would be taking root: the hours that made up the "duties of his state", governing the Work and receiving those who wanted to meet him, even for a few minutes, when they were passing through Rome.

He preached as often as he could to those who were with him.

He also wrote letters, as he had done in the 1930s, during the Spanish Civil War and immediately after, tracing out in broad lines for his children the apostolic horizons opened up by the spirit of the Work.

The Lord wishes us to raise him to the summit of all human activities. [131]

Using practical examples, the founder suggested how to live this spirituality in every situation in which a Christian living immersed in the world might find himself.

In past years he had often given news in his letters about the progress being made on the extensions to Villa Tevere. In Paris, in May 1960, he spoke of the completed buildings. The construction work had been carried out as fast as possible since 1955, taking the size of the new structures and their meagre financial resources into account. The money required had been far more than could be provided by the members of the Work alone, even if they generously devoted a large part of their professional earnings to it, which they did. Each member, whatever country he was in, had also had to look for money wherever possible, taking on extra jobs or working overtime. They had asked many people to help, often people who knew nothing about the Work.

Thanks to all these efforts, the central offices of Opus Dei could now accommodate the students of the Roman College more easily. On 31 December 1959 the Father said Mass for the first time in the chapel dedicated to Our Lady of Peace, where the most important ceremonies would be celebrated. Beneath the chapel was a crypt, where, when they died, some members of the Work would be buried. It was there that the founder of Opus Dei hoped one day to rest, in the heart of Rome where he had already "buried" himself since 1946.

Not far away, in another small crypt, his sister Carmen lay buried. She had not wanted to return to Spain after working to set up the villa in Salto di Fondi. On 20 June 1957, she died peacefully in her home on the other side of the Tiber. It was a very hard blow for the Father: yet again he saw a member of his family – and one to whom the Work owed so much – pass away.

When he heard the doctor's diagnosis, he had turned to Our

Lord as a son turns to his father, repeating, as if to implore a miracle, *if You want to, You can ...*

Aunt Carmen, which is how the members of the Work called her, had rendered up her soul to God at twenty-five past three in the morning and the Father, kneeling at the foot of the bed, had repeated the prayer that he used to say in the ear of the dying in the hospitals of Madrid. *May the most just and most lovable Will of God be done, be fulfilled, be praised and eternally exalted above all things. Amen. Amen.* [132]

At the end of the Mass that he said immediately, he was filled with a strange peace: *The tears are over ... Now I am happy, my sons; and grateful to the Lord for having taken her to Heaven, in the joy of the Holy Spirit.* [133]

The Father was then completely certain that his sister was in Heaven. *A touch of honey* [134] in his bitter sadness, as he sometimes said ...

Now Carmen rested there in the crypt, forming part of the foundations of those buildings *which look as if they are made of stone and are really made of love* [135] because of their cost in prayers and sacrifices from those who helped in their construction. Among them was the Secretary-General of the Work, Don Alvaro, who had in some miraculous fashion managed to pay the bills, working very hard in spite of the illnesses he suffered at that time.

An audience with the new Pope

In Paris the Father also spoke of the audience granted him by Pope John XXIII on 5 March.

It was the first time the founder of Opus Dei had met the successor of Pope Pius XII, who had died on 9 October 1958.

Pope John XXIII knew the Work already, for he had visited some of its establishments: *La Estila* , a students' residence in Santiago de Compostela, and *Miraflores* , another in Saragossa. Both of these he had visited during his trip to Spain for the Jubilee Year in 1954.

The Pope retained a very vivid memory of the friendly atmosphere of these Opus Dei centres. People had described the Work to him before as "impressive" and as "doing a lot of good". He had told this to the founder and added, amusingly, that now, when he heard people talking about the Work, they had said that it was "extremely impressive and doing a tremendous amount of good."[136]

The Cardinal Secretary of State's letter to Monsignor Escrivá the day after the audience, which was accompanied by a photograph of it, also made allusion to those descriptions.

Pope John had laughed heartily at a remark made by the founder of Opus Dei, when Don Josemaría had observed with his disarming smile and directness, that he had not learned from the Pope how to practise his ecumenism – for he had made several fruitless attempts before the Holy See would admit, in 1950, that Opus Dei could have non-Catholics and even non-Christians as Co-operators.

Monsignor Escrivá was no longer, in any way, the young and unknown priest coming to Rome to ask for approval for a foundation that would break the moulds of Canon Law, but in the presence of the Pope, the *Vice-Christ*, "the sweet Christ on earth" as he liked to call him with Saint Catherine of Siena, he always felt overcome. *After Jesus and Mary comes the Pope, whoever he may be*,[137] he used to tell his children.

Don Josemaría, whose speech had always been sincere and simple, and who had always acted as a son who loved the Holy Father, had learned that some people smiled on hearing that he had passed his first night in the capital city of Christianity praying for the Pope and watching his apartment windows. It had hurt him to think that they could pronounce so lightly on what was really a profession of faith. From then on his affection for the visible Head of the Church *had become more theological*. He had his own way of expressing this when he came to recite the Creed in front of Saint Peter's, as he did each time he visited the Vatican. When he would get as far as the words, "I believe in the Holy Spirit ... and in the Holy, Catholic, Apostolic Church ..." he would repeat three times: *I believe in my Mother the Roman Church* – sometimes adding *in spite of everything*.[138]

What do you mean by that "in spite of everything"? Cardinal Tardini asked him one day, when he heard this.

Your own personal errors and mine,[139] replied Monsignor Escrivá, accompanying his *holy shamelessness*[140] with a disarming smile.

It was in that same spirit of faithfulness to the Church that he prayed, and asked his children to pray, for the Holy Father's "great intention" – the ecumenical Council that Pope John XXIII had just convoked.

Right: Canterbury, September 1958. Monsignor Escrivá with Don Alvaro del Portillo and Don Javier Echevarría outside St Dunstan's Church, where the head of St Thomas More is buried.

Below: London, August 1961. The founder with some members of Opus Dei, when plans were being drawn up for new buildings at Netherhall House.

Left: Lourdes, July 1960. O: pilgrimage to this Shrine c Our Lady, which he firs visited in 1937.

Below: Pope John XXIII wit Monsignor Escrivá and Mon signor Alvaro del Portillc then Secretary-General c Opus Dei.

11. MADRID: 17 OCTOBER 1960

The baroque Church of San Miguel, in the heart of old Madrid, was absolutely packed. When Monsignor Escrivá entered, vested to say Mass, he was deeply moved to see this congregation, made up for the most part of members of the Work, as varied in age and condition as society itself.

It was in this church, one day in the spring of 1927, that he had said his first Mass in the Spanish capital since leaving Saragossa.

In his homily after the Gospel he spoke of those far-off years when he had been completely alone. Though imbued with the divine presentiments that would one day see the foundation of Opus Dei, he had been far from imagining *that he would one day see this church filled with souls who have such love for Jesus Christ.* [141]

The emotion in his voice found an echo in the hearts of those who were listening to him.

A growing family

The groups received by the Father the day before had felt equally moved by the same atmosphere. Among them there were workers and office clerks who had been living their vocation to

Opus Dei in their daily work for months or years, carrying out an active apostolate by their presence and witness in their own surroundings.

A voice was heard in this family get-together when the Father had started speaking, as always, about the necessity of sanctifying one's ordinary occupations: "And what about us, we who stole wallets?"

The speaker, who had once been a pick-pocket, produced delighted laughter from the audience. He had met a member of Opus Dei who had helped him to "go straight". The Father was deeply touched and would not let him finish: *You can't steal my wallet, my son, because I haven't got one; but you've just stolen my heart!* [142]

In his homily in San Miguel, the Father referred discreetly to this incident.

He spoke about the same things as always, raising his voice because of the size of the church: faithfulness to one's vocation, renewed each day; sanctification of one's work; continuous conversation with our Father God; acting with responsibility in the world, in the "freedom of the children of God", as Saint Paul says; the will to live all the demands of the Christian life, building an active and continuous apostolate on this quiet but effective witness. *Your family, your colleagues, your neighbours and friends will understand. Don't do anything odd, because that isn't in keeping with our way of life: live like everyone else, but supernaturalise every moment of your day. They should see your joy in the world.* [143]

Widening out the apostolic horizons of those who listened to him, the Father asked them to offer their prayers, their small sacrifices of each day, and their work, for the fruitfulness of the apostolate in the countries where the Work was just beginning. No doubt he was thinking particularly of Colombia, Venezuela and Chile, where members of the Women's Section had recently gone to carry out their professional work and do apostolate. And then there was Uruguay, where they had begun in 1956, and Switzerland, where Father Torelló, a former psychiatrist ordained a few years earlier, and Pedro Turull, an architect, had settled in Zurich. He thought of Brazil, where the first members of the Work had arrived in March 1957. And Austria. And Canada. Then there was Peru, where Don Ignacio Orbegozo, another doctor, ordained in 1951, had been made prelate *nullius* of a territory five thousand square miles in extent, lost in the middle of the Andes over fifteen thousand feet up. And then there were Kenya and Japan, where some sons of his had gone in 1958 ...

As for Spain, the cradle of the Work, so much had it developed there that in order to see all his sons and daughters, and tell them what he wanted to tell them, he had received, untiringly, large groups of people.

In Madrid itself, where the Father was now greeting so many of his sons, a group of them had founded a sports club some five years previously in Vallecas, one of the working-class suburbs he had often visited to carry out his pastoral work before the Spanish civil war. The club soon became the beginnings of a secondary school and technical college, installed for the time being in an old farm building in the middle of a piece of waste ground. The centre's influence in the district was already considerable, and it would later become much greater still.

In Saragossa and Pamplona

The reason for Monsignor Escrivá's journey to Spain had been to take part in the ceremony in which the *Studium Generale* of Navarre was to be raised to the status of a university. But first he had to go to Saragossa where he was to receive, on 21 October, a Doctorate *honoris causa* awarded to him by the University of that city.

The enormous amphitheatre of the Faculty of Medicine could not hold all those who wanted to be present. They had come not only from Saragossa and the surrounding district but also from other provinces of Spain.

In his speech of thanks, the Father spoke of the time when he was at the seminary of Saragossa and studied Law at the University at the same time. Then he mentioned those Aragonese who had played an important part in the history of their country and the world.

After the ceremony, it took him half an hour to make his way through the exuberant crowds from the amphitheatre to the lounge beyond.

The next day he celebrated Mass in the chapel of the Seminary of San Carlos, returning with great emotion to the place where he had been ordained deacon and where he had given Holy Communion to his mother for the first time.[144]

At last he came to Pamplona, where lay the main reason for his journey. It was in this town that the University of Navarre had been born in 1952, very modest in its beginnings, but with the aim of becoming a very fruitful seat of learning.

The Law school, which had now become a Faculty, came first. It had soon been followed by the Faculty of Medicine, the Faculty of Arts and Philosophy, the Science Faculty and the Faculty of Canon Law ... Then there was the School of Journalism and a Nursing School. A business school – IESE (the Institute of Advanced Business Studies) in Barcelona, and an Engineering School in San Sebastian were also attached to the university.

As the State had the monopoly of higher education in Spain, it was the Holy See which erected the *Studium Generale* of Navarre as a University, making use for the first time of one of its rights in the Concordat signed with Spain in 1953. The founder of Opus Dei, who was going to be the Chancellor of the University, would have preferred another solution, one which kept the civil character of the University of Navarre. But he accepted this one for the time being, for he had been asked to do so expressly by the Holy See.

The decree of creation of the University, signed by Cardinal Pizzardo in the name of Pope John XXIII on 6 August 1960, was read out on 25 October during a short ceremony in a gothic room off the cloister of Pamplona Cathedral. As at Saragossa, the procession had to make its way through a very large crowd. Monsignor Escrivá bowed to the demands of protocol with good spirit. Then he took part in the blessing of the first stone of the University, in the new campus, on land put at the disposal of the university authorities by the Navarre Local Council.

But he was not finished yet: the same evening, in the Town Hall, he was made an honorary citizen of Pamplona.

Another speech. After sketching in broad strokes the variety of the different "lands" of Spain, he admitted to his hosts that he had a certain weakness for Navarre. This last ceremony was very friendly, almost intimate.

The noise of the crowd who had gathered to greet the Father, and the sound of folk-tunes could be heard from the square in front of the Town Hall. Monsignor Escrivá had to come out onto the balcony with the city dignitaries. In silence he contemplated the mass of people as wave upon wave of warm applause greeted him. People waved their handkerchiefs and regional dances were performed in the square.

But it was not the usual popular homage – a mixture of kind reception and curiosity – given to celebrities. There was a strong current of affection linking the Father and these men and women of all ages, who had come, sometimes from very far away, to show him how happy and grateful they were to see him.

The founder of Opus Dei stood gazing at them for a long time, deeply touched and struck by all those cheers as if they could not possibly be meant for him. But as soon as people started to call "Long live the Father!", he cut them short and suggested that they shout "Long live the Pope!" and "Long live Navarre!" instead.

The Papal Nuncio, Monsignor Antoniutti, who had attended the ceremony and had witnessed this enthusiasm from the balcony at Monsignor Escrivá's side, was very moved.

The next day, at noon, the cathedral was full as the Father celebrated Mass. As in Madrid, he talked to the five or six thousand people gathered around him, speaking to them *like a father, like a brother, like a mother, with his heart and soul fixed on God.*

Referring to the Gospel, *so old and so new* , and his own vocation, *his thirty-three years of vocation* in Opus Dei, he addressed not only his sons and daughters, but their parents too, those he called the *crown of Opus Dei* , asking them to continue to help their children with their prayers, that they might persevere on their path.[145]

Finally, when he had concluded the thanksgiving after Mass, during which he had said a few words, he received hundreds of people in the cathedral cloister.

The pointlessness of trying to hold the sea back

The presence of all these men and women around him, most of them fathers and mothers, was a sign of the growth of the Work in Spain. There had, however, been no lack of difficulties; and the difficulties persisted. The initiators of the same old slanders had simply changed their approach. Now some people persisted in talking of Opus Dei as if it were a political group, apparently because in 1957 two members of the Work, as a matter of personal choice and on their own responsibility, had accepted ministerial posts in the Spanish government.

This slander – which was often repeated without any bad intention – made Monsignor Escrivá suffer, for it denied one of the most essential aspects of the vocation to Opus Dei: the freedom of thought and action that each and every one of its members enjoys in temporal matters. In his own words, the bond that links each member with Opus Dei is *exclusively for the purpose of receiving spiritual aid and Christian formation as well as for helping in the apostolic activities of the Work* . Opus Dei, therefore, does not have any temporal aim; neither does it have any say in or interfere in any way with the professional, social, or political behaviour of its members. These are purely personal matters. As a consequence, a member of Opus Dei in his temporal activities will have no other limitations than those derived from the ethical principles which bind all Christians.

Anyone who sincerely believes in the existence of religious ideals and moral values that are capable of bringing together all mankind, for a common purpose which is above – far above – political and social divisions, will be able to understand the pluralism of thought and of political action of the members of Opus Dei, who come from different countries from the five continents, and from the most varied levels of society. But it will never be understood by those who have a pitiful intransigent or one-party mentality, be it within the Church or outside it.

Many people might not have been aware that Monsignor Escrivá, ever faithful to the Will of God, in very different political situations, had twice refused point blank to use his influence to help found a great "Catholic Party" in Spain – in the 1930s during the troubles of the Second Republic, and ten years later, when they were just coming out of the civil war. It was not the social success of his children that mattered to him, but their holiness; whether they make a go of their work or not is up to each one. This is what he had firmly told a Cardinal who had congratulated him one day on the nomination of a member of Opus Dei to a post of some distinction.

Everything had been foreseen to ensure that Opus Dei would never deviate from its original course, and always pursue only supernatural aims. In Spain itself, where political parties were not yet recognised, the variety of directions and positions taken by members of the Work in public life could easily be seen. Even so, no doubt some time would be needed before people freely admitted that Catholics could come together – and actually do come together – for reasons other than political ones.

But the concern to establish the truth about a central characteristic of the Work he had founded was not the main thing on the Father's mind. What really interested him was the expansion of the apostolates all over the world. This was why he made a point of passing through Paris to see his sons and daughters before returning to Rome.

The Father arrived in Paris on 29 October. He was very tired, but at the same time very happy to have seen and met so many people in such a short space of time. Three French members of the Work were there. One of them, who had been at Pamplona a few days earlier, asked him what he thought about when he saw the crowds around him. Only of their affection, the Father replied, and of their faith. *What faith they have!* [146] he repeated, referring those demonstrations of enthusiasm to God alone. Amused and surprised at the same time, he recalled several incidents from the journey. It was obvious that this meeting with large numbers of his children had had a big effect on him, and made him leave aside his embarrassment and his reluctance to be the centre of attention.

Along with the anecdotes about his trip to Spain, he also talked about life in Rome and heard news of the apostolate in France. The Father was very relaxed; as usual, he played the leading part in that family gathering.

Suddenly the telephone rang. It was for the Father ... When he returned, his face was drawn. He had just learned that three of his sons had been killed in a car accident coming back from the ceremonies at Pamplona. Among them was a Chilean recently ordained, one of the first in his country.

They said the prayer for the repose of their souls in the oratory. Then the Father complained filially, and sorrowfully, as he had done in similar circumstances once before. *Lord, why have You taken these sons away from me? When they are so needed ... But You know better. Fiat, adimpleatur ...* [147]

The tone of the family get-together changed. The Father spoke now of Heaven. He asked those with him to have recourse to the intercession of these three brothers of theirs who were now close to Our Lord, to help them in their apostolate in France.

In the afternoon, after visiting a house in the suburbs of Paris which could become a residence, he returned to the Boulevard Saint Germain. Despite his efforts to talk of other things, his mind was elsewhere and he could not stop thinking about those three sons who had gone to Heaven. It occurred to him also that the accident had happened as a result of his visit to Pamplona and this was a further cause of suffering for him.

As soon as he had heard the news, he drafted a note so that whenever they had to travel by car, the members of the Work should not forget to take the indispensable safety measures. Later that afternoon he made sure that the family of one of those who had been killed in the accident received whatever financial support it had a right to.

Soon he was unable to continue, and got up to go, leaving his sons visibly grieved at the Father's sorrow and also by the obvious efforts he was making to master his emotion and draw a more supernatural lesson from the incident. That phrase of Saint Paul which he was wont to repeat to those suffering from pain or contradiction, he himself lived to the letter. He was not without suffering: he knew it was true for him, too, that "for those who love God, all things work for good" (Rom 8:28).

12. ROME: 1961 - 1965

The visit to Spain in October, like the short journeys he had made to various countries in Europe, was a brief interlude in the busy life of Monsignor Escrivá. Since 1946, and especially since 1952, he had nearly always stayed at Villa Tevere, fully dedicated to the task of directing Opus Dei.

He was now approaching sixty, but his vitality was as great as ever. The diabetes which had caused him so much trouble had stopped in 1954, quite inexplicably and for no apparent physiological reason. On 27 April of that year, just before dinner, Don Alvaro del Portillo had given him his customary insulin injection. It was a new kind of retarded-action insulin which his doctor had just prescribed. But the effects were produced very soon. Just as he was sitting down at the table, the Father collapsed, and lay there as if he were dead. Don Alvaro, who was with him at the time, had given him absolution, for the Father before losing consciousness had asked for it. He had then tried to bring him round by making him swallow some sugar, to counter the effects of the insulin. The Father recovered consciousness about fifteen minutes later, though his sight did not return immediately and it took a few hours before he could see again.

From then on, all the symptoms of diabetes, particularly the headaches, diminished until they had entirely disappeared. He felt as if he were being liberated from a prison. You could see, he joked afterwards, that Our Lord wanted to give him the means to work harder! This was the lesson he drew from his anaphylactic shock, which according to his doctor is normally fatal after only a few minutes ...

Days well filled

He refused to think of himself as "old" when he celebrated his sixtieth birthday on 9 January 1962. Indeed, his jovial demeanour impressed not only those who lived and worked with him, but also the many visitors who came, in greater and greater numbers, to Rome to see him, even if only for a few minutes.

His hair was still black; his gestures were perhaps a little slower than before, his face and features finer as he lost weight. But he still had the rapidity of pace and urgency of action of someone who wants to make good use of time, and that vivacity which often made him speak out, with vigour or quick wit, as soon as something was said to him.

Orderly by nature, he managed to make time "last" much more (according to him, for a Christian time was not just *gold* but *glory*),[148] achieving a maximum of order in his daily work. *Virtue without order? Strange virtue!*[149] These words, which he had written in *The Way*, he lived to the letter.

He rose early, and spent a long time in mental prayer before celebrating Mass. He would frequently preach (particularly on certain liturgical feasts or anniversaries of important moments in the life of Opus Dei) to a more intimate group of his sons with whom he worked, in an oratory which was in a significant way the heart of the Work for his sons and daughters spread throughout the world. In that oratory, in front of a vast stained-glass window representing Pentecost, he had placed a tabernacle, made at a time when they were having to go without even the bare necessities. It bears the words he loved so well: *consummati in unum* – united in one (John 17:23).

Those who were lucky enough to hear his words – more a meditation spoken aloud than simple preaching – took notes from what he said to pass on to the other members of the Work.

After a frugal breakfast, the Father would have a rapid glance at the newspaper. Then he would recite his breviary and go on to deal with current matters of government, usually with Don Alvaro del Portillo, the Secretary-General of the Work. He also had brief meetings with the members of the Council who governed the Men's Section with him, or with the members of the Central Advisory – the equivalent governing body of the Women's Section. Information on the various apostolates and on matters that needed consultation came in to Rome from all over the world.

Towards the end of the morning he would frequently receive visitors. They might be members of the Work passing through Rome, often with their families, or friends who were helping with apostolic activities in different countries; sometimes they were celebrities who had asked to see him, and others who wanted to receive advice for their spiritual lives or consolation in their sorrows ... The Father could devote only a limited amount of time to each visitor. But those few minutes they spent with him left them totally satisfied, for his interest in what they told him, his sincerity and his sense of humour, and his ability to find the right words for each one, would help them to be more faithful to their Christian vocation.

The number of visitors increased every year. But he still tried to receive them whenever he could: for him it was another chance to speak about God and to do apostolate.

After lunch, which was always a very meagre affair, for he continued to eat very little, he spent a few minutes in informal conversation with those who worked with him and, as often as possible, with the students of the Roman College who lived next door.

Then he went back to his desk, seeing always souls instead of statistics behind the sheets of paper. He also worked on the preparation of homilies and meditations, or revised them for publication. He devoted some more time to mental prayer, said the Rosary and read a chapter from the Gospel and from some spiritual book.

This plan he had followed for many years. But there were also meetings with members of the Roman Curia and with Cardinals and bishops visiting or passing through Rome. They came to see him and learn the spirit of Opus Dei from the lips of the founder. The Father also spoke to them about the problems of the Church, always looking at them from a supernatural point of view.

The responsibility of the founder in governing the Work

Monsignor Escrivá had concentrated his exceptional energies on continually pressing forward the apostolate of the Work in every country, with a sense of urgency which found its counterbalance in the prudence necessary for good government. No decision was taken without its being carefully studied in a collegial way. The Father could not stand anything resembling tyranny or autocracy, be it in the direction of souls or in the government of apostolic works. He would always say, fully convinced, that he required the personal and responsible participation of all those in the decision-making structures over which he presided. And this is what he practised, while naturally reserving for himself the right to exercise his authority in determining the different matters under consideration. His interventions were thus decisive and firm, for he knew his responsibilities before God as founder. What had to be avoided was the slightest risk of deviation from the spirit that God had wanted for Opus Dei, and which had to be maintained at all costs and not be allowed to break down after his death. As a consequence, he looked after even the smallest material detail or the slightest evidence of neglect – for this would show a lack of love – because everything is great in God's eyes. *In apostolic work there is no such thing as a trifling disobedience* .[150]

He was demanding towards the others, as he had always been on himself. But when he had to correct someone on a point regarding the spirit of the Work, he was careful always to make up for his correction with some mark of special affection which won that person over, without, however, making him forget the lesson. He knew well how to form those around him, teaching them in their turn to form their brothers, with his example, his prayer and by timely indications, thus helping to ensure that everyone persevere.

Above all, he knew how to pass on his overriding apostolic concern to his children from the very beginning. The Work must go resolutely and speedily forward, without fear of the inevitable obstacles and contradictions it would encounter along the way. But this drive would not come from a purely human enthusiasm: it would come rather from a great sensitivity to God's Will, be the fruit of prayer and, also, of common sense ... The Father taught them to go *at God's pace*,[151] as he had never ceased to do himself since 1928.

The apostolates grow and consolidate

The 1960s also marked the spread of Opus Dei into new territories: Paraguay was next in 1962, and in 1963 four Americans settled in Australia.

A year later two Filipinos who had met the Work in the United States returned home. The Father, receiving them in Rome, told them that he had been praying for years for the start of the Work in the Philippines, the gateway to the Far East.

In July 1965 some members of the Work made a journey to Nigeria, which soon became the second country in Africa to benefit from the apostolates of Opus Dei, together with yet another European country, this time Belgium.

The Father was, however, just as concerned to strengthen Opus Dei in the countries where it was already established, and to ensure the perseverance and the fruitfulness of the apostolate of the first members. For the Work is, in a way, nothing other than an enormous undertaking of *permanent training* on a spiritual level, and a *great catechesis* which requires a constant dedication. He therefore urged the opening of various centres of education or technical assistance which, like the residences in Madrid before the Spanish civil war, would be instruments of apostolate and, at the same time, a service to society. These centres would also be able to count on the help of many people generous enough to understand the point and value of such undertakings. He urged his children as well to show initiative and to try to obtain vocations in other towns in the country where they might find themselves, among all levels of society.

It was, in fact, a matter of always aiming high in the apostolate, of being very demanding towards oneself in the interior life and in work, and of avoiding the slightest trace of "settling down comfortably".

All this means that, from their first contact with a Centre of the Work, the people who come to Opus Dei know that they will not receive any material benefit: they will be asked to give. Or, better, they will be expected to give "themselves". And if they are generous and do not hold back, they will soon realise that they are receiving much more than they have given, for the direction of their lives has begun to change, and is now leading them straight to God.

This is the cause of constant cheerfulness which is a consequence of constant effort and self-surrender, that people who go along to a Centre of Opus Dei find so striking. It is a contagious joy which brings one closer to God.

It was also the reason for the great affection the members of Opus Dei had for the Father, because of their gratitude as well as their concern for unity with the head. This attachment, lived at every level of the slight structure that underpinned the Work, gave it an astonishing unity. It was something difficult to explain, for it was supernatural. It was a special, unmistakeable spirit, which has become and is, now, the founder's heritage.

At Villa delle Rose

During the autumn of 1962, just as the Ecumenical Council was about to commence, some young women from different countries began to arrive in Rome to live there for two or three years, doing studies similar to those undertaken by members of the Men's

Section at Villa Tevere. The place that had been chosen was *Villa delle Rose*, the property in Castelgandolfo by then definitively ceded by Pope John XXIII for the Work to organise activities of doctrinal and spiritual formation. Now renovated, it was to be, provisionally, the *Roman College of Holy Mary*, which had already been functioning in Rome, and which meant for the women of Opus Dei a period of intense formation at Saint Peter's Chair.

On 19 December of that same year the process of beatification of a woman member of Opus Dei was opened in Barcelona. Montserrat Grases had died at the age of eighteen.

The Second Vatican Council

After an audience granted to him by Pope John XXIII on 27 June 1962, the Father wrote to all his children and asked them to offer penances, prayer and their daily work for the success of the Second Vatican Council.

In contrast to what many were saying, he considered that the Council could go on for quite a long time and that it would probably come up against unforeseen obstacles: it was what his sense of history and his knowledge of human nature led him to believe.

In all the Councils there have been difficult moments, for at times we men don't let the Holy Spirit act freely and place obstacles in His path. But from this you have to draw more love for the Church, more unity and fidelity, more obedience and submission to the Magisterium of the Church and to the Pope. And in the end the Holy Spirit is always triumphant. [152]

This was why he asked everyone to pray harder and to recite the prayer *Veni, Sancte Spiritus* often, as he did himself.

In 1961 Monsignor Escrivá was named consultor to the Commission for the Authentic Interpretation of the Code of Canon Law. By agreement with the Holy See, he did not take part as a Council Father in the work at Vatican II, but he followed it very closely. Furthermore, many bishops and some of the expert theologians and canon lawyers who were in Rome went to visit him at

Villa Tevere. Although he did not interfere in any way in their decisions, the Father, with his characteristic sense of the Church, urged
them to play an active role in the Council, answering their questions
with an alacrity and sureness which impressed them.

Two members of Opus Dei, the Bishop of the Prelature of
Yauyos and the auxiliary Bishop of Chiclayo (both from Peru), took
their place among the Council Fathers. As for Don Alvaro, who
had taken an active part in the preparations for the Council as
President of the pre-preparatory Commission for the Laity, he was
named Secretary of one of the conciliar commissions, the Commission *De disciplina Cleri et Populi Christiani*, and was also an expert
(*peritus*) with a seat on other commissions.

This meant, of course, that the Father was burdened with
extra work for the duration of the Council, for Don Alvaro was pre-
cluded from dedicating much time to his duties as Secretary-
General of Opus Dei.

Never mind, my sons, Don Josemaría said, *this is what the
Holy Father wants; and we have to serve the Church as the Church
wants to be served.* [153]

On 13 November Pope John XXIII told the Council Fathers
that he had decided to add the name of Saint Joseph to the canon
of the Mass, at the request of a group of bishops. An important
Church figure, knowing the Father's devotion to the man who had
been the head of the Holy Family, called him on 8 December –
when the Pope had just solemnly ratified the decision in his
discourse at the end of the first session of the Council. *Ralle-
gramenti!*, he said, "Congratulations! As soon as I heard, I thought
of you, and of how happy the news must make you."

For the founder of Opus Dei, what had been proclaimed was
*the immense supernatural value of the life of Saint Joseph, the value
of a simple life of work in God's sight, in complete fulfilment of the
divine Will.* [154]

The election of Paul VI

On 3 June of the following year Pope John, after a painful
deathbed agony, rendered his soul to God. The Father, surrounded
by the members of the General Council of the Men's Section of
Opus Dei, immediately said the *Requiescat* for the repose of his
soul. He then wrote to all his children asking them to do likewise
and to start praying for his successor. The priests of the Work
everywhere in the world said Masses for the deceased Pope.

The newly elected Pope turned out to be none other than Cardinal Montini, one of those who had received Father Escrivá most
warmly on his arrival in Rome in 1946. The founder of Opus Dei
knew the intelligence and kindness of the new Pontiff well. But for
him he was, from then on, above all, *the Pope*, the visible head of
the Church, Christ's representative on earth.

When he heard about the election of Paul VI, Monsignor
Escrivá prayed that his pontificate, which was beginning at a crucial
time in the history of the Church, might receive the continual assistance of the Holy Spirit.

His thoughts went with the new Pope, too, on the pilgrimage
Paul VI made to the Holy Land in January 1964.

On 24 January he had the great joy of being able to speak to
him during an audience lasting three quarters of an hour, starting
with an affectionate embrace from the Holy Father. A letter from
the Cardinal Secretary of State a few days later confirmed the senti-
ments of the Pope, expressing his pleasure at "the sight of such a
large number of people, spread over the five continents, practising
the high ideals proposed to them by Opus Dei and so apt to the
demands of these new times, and trying to serve the Church as She
wants to be served – through their vigorously Christian personal
conduct, uniting contemplation and action, and through their sub-
lime desire to incarnate and to spread in the most varied places of
work the postulates of the truth and holiness of the Gospel."[155]

Paul VI spoke in the same vein a few months later, on 10
October, in another private audience, in which he gave the founder
of Opus Dei a chalice of precious metal, similar to the one he had
presented to the Patriarch Athenagoras several months earlier, and

a hand-written letter, in which he wrote at length about the apostolate of Opus Dei, "born in this era which is our own, as an expression of the eternal youth of the Church". He also noted "with paternal satisfaction, how much the Work has accomplished for the Kingdom of God; the desire to do good which marks it out; its burning zeal for souls, which presses it towards the arduous and difficult paths of the apostolate of presence and witness in all sectors of contemporary life."[156]

The Father came away from this second audience deeply moved. He admitted as much, in words and in writing, to his sons and daughters, and underlined how these words of the Pope's had made him feel well rewarded *for so many things offered "in laetitia"* [157] over the thirty-seven years that had passed since the foundation of the Work.

Another journey to Spain

Towards the end of November 1964 Monsignor Escrivá travelled to Pamplona again. As Chancellor of the University of Navarre he was to confer on the present and former rectors of the University of Saragossa the degree of Doctor *honoris causa* .

As soon as he arrived the Father met a large group of students gathered at a hall of residence which had been founded in Pamplona a few years earlier. He spoke to them with great enthusiasm about their future responsibilities, for which they were now preparing at the University of Navarre: *You are here like good quality flour ready for the leaven, in the oven: it is going to be good bread to feed souls and minds very well.* [158] Among those responsibilities he mentioned that of being sowers of peace and joy, at the same time showing mutual respect for others.

The ceremony of conferring the doctorates took place the following day, in the presence of more than three hundred university lecturers and professors from Spain. The universities of Bordeaux, Montpellier and Toulouse were also represented. There were flags, decorating the main building, from the forty different countries that students at the University came from. In spite of the rain, a great crowd was waiting before the main balcony to cheer the Father, who was receiving one group after another: these were the academic authorities, representatives of the Navarre Council and the Municipality of Pamplona, the administrative and ancillary staff of the University, the Patrons' Committee of the Shrine of Torreciudad, the Managing Committee of the Association of Friends of the University of Navarre (members of which had flocked to Pamplona by the most varied means of transport), a group of foreign journalists and so on ...

On 29 November more than twelve thousand people had gathered in Pamplona to take part in the first General Assembly of the Association of Friends of the University of Navarre. One of its tasks was to provide financial help for the University.

The Assembly took place in the Gayarre Theatre, which could not possibly provide room for everyone. The vast majority of the men and women who filled the auditorium, a great mixture of people of all social conditions, had come first of all to see the Father, to hear him and show their gratitude by their presence and by the spontaneous applause that they could not contain, even when the Father gestured for them to stop. For it was he who, by being faithful to the grace he had received, had changed their lives, allowing them to discover their vocation to the fulness of the Christian life in the midst of their ordinary occupations.

After the usual speeches the Father came forward. He suggested replacing his intended discourse to his audience by a conversation with them all, about any subject they might choose. There was thunderous applause and, at that moment, the official nature of the ceremony changed into a family get-together. Everyone felt close to the Father, as if in a little group, although there were several thousand people present.

The questions came firing in from all directions, from the pit to the gallery. The answers came quickly back, provoking laughter or causing attentive silence from the audience when he talked with vigour about important matters of everyday life: the family, the education of their children, a life of piety, prayer, frequent reception of the Sacraments, professional problems, how to make family life compatible with an intense work ...

One of the subjects he touched on most frequently was that of the freedom of Christians.

"Father, why do you love freedom so much?" someone asked.

I love freedom because without it we would not be able to serve God: we would indeed be poor wretches. Catholics must learn to live not by merely calling themselves Catholics, but as citizens who are prepared to assume personal responsibility for their free personal acts. A short while ago I wrote to a very exalted person – imagine whoever you like, it doesn't make any difference – and told him that the children of God in Opus Dei live in spite of being Catholics. [159]

The allusion to the temptation of clericalism was clear to most of the audience. In an environment which is officially Catholic, as Spain was then, it is so tempting to take advantage of one's faith in order to gain from the State certain, sometimes very substantial, advantages. The founder took this opportunity to reaffirm as strongly as he could that Opus Dei did not and would never in any way form a pressure group. This would be utterly contrary to its nature. Besides, its members come from such an enormous variety of different backgrounds that it would be impossible to make it such.

"What stance do members of Opus Dei take in the public life of their countries?" asked someone.

Whatever stance they like! With absolute freedom. Their particular attitude doesn't interest me. I defend their freedom; otherwise I couldn't defend my own. And I come from a region where they don't let themselves be told what to do. [160]

There was a burst of laughter; people recognised the Father's reference to his Aragonese origins.

Respect for freedom, however, is rooted principally in wise Christian traditions.

Do not forget that the world is ours; the world is our home, it is the work of God and we must love it, as we must love those who are in the world. It is our business to consecrate the world to God through giving ourselves completely, as we do, in the service of Our Lord, each one of us as we carry out our ordinary work being a witness of Jesus Christ and serving the Church, the Pope and all souls there where we are. That's why we have to understand the world; we have to raise it up, we have to divinise it, we have to purify it, we have to redeem it with Christ, because we are co-redeemers with Him. [161]

The Father returned to Rome exhausted by the physical strain, but very happy to have been able to talk about God to many more people than during the days he had spent in Spain in 1960. If he felt that he had encouraged these men and women, he knew that he had also learned a lot from them and from their determination to struggle to deepen their interior lives and to give Christian witness wherever they had been placed by God: *at all the crossroads of the world,* [162] as he had already foreseen in his preaching in the 1930s ...

The Pope visits a centre of Opus Dei

A year later, on 21 November 1965, Monsignor Escrivá welcomed Pope Paul VI at the entrance of a Centre in which Opus Dei was carrying out an important apostolic work in Tiburtino, a working-class district of Rome.

Centro ELIS (*Educazione, Lavoro, Istruzione, Sport* – Education, Work, Training and Sport) – is made up of a technical training school, a residence for students, a sports club and, independent of the rest, a catering school for women.

Pope John XXIII had decided that the money collected in honour of Pius XII on his eightieth birthday should be used for a social work in some suburb of Rome which had no educational or supportive facilities. The Pope had entrusted the project to members of Opus Dei. Paul VI wanted to inaugurate the Centre in person, after celebrating Mass in the parish church dedicated, in his honour, to Saint John the Baptist and entrusted to priests of the Work.

Several Cardinals and many of the bishops present at the Council – which was due to close in a few weeks – took part in the ceremony, along with representatives of the District Council, the Province of Rome and the State of Italy, joined by a great number of people living in the Tiburtino district. In his speech, Monsignor Escrivá spoke of the specific message of Opus Dei – the sanctifying value of work – and the climate of freedom and understanding that the members of the Work tried to create, here as elsewhere.

In his answer, the Pope added a few words to the speech he had prepared, remarking how he had long known and admired the founder of Opus Dei as well as its Secretary-General, Don Alvaro del Portillo.

At nightfall, after a long visit to the training centre and the catering school, Paul VI left Centro ELIS accompanied by torch-bearers.

Before getting into the car after his two- and a half-hour visit to ELIS, the Pope embraced Monsignor Escrivá publicly, saying aloud: "Tutto qui, tutto qui e Opus Dei!" "Everything here is Opus Dei!"[163]

V

VULTUM TUUM, DOMINE, REQUIRAM!

Lord, I seek Your face!
Psalm 26:8

If I die, know that it is for love of the Church.
Saint Catherine of Siena

1. COUVRELLES: 30 AUGUST 1966

The Father opened his heart to his sons who sat around him at the foot of the double stone staircase of a small chateau near Soissons, in north-east France. It was mid-afternoon and the air was already a little fresh, owing to the misty dampness coming from a wood and a small lake nearby.

He had been working for several days in a village near Etampes, twenty-five miles south of Paris. From there he had come to have a family gathering with some of his sons who had interrupted their various professional activities in order to spend some days together at the Couvrelles International Conference Centre.

The building had been acquired by a group of co-operators and friends of the Work so that spiritual and formative activities could be organised there. It was modest in size, but elegant, with its seventeenth-century facade and compact grounds that blended into a background of surrounding woodland. As well as the French, there were members of the Work from neighbouring countries, from Germany, Belgium, the Netherlands, Switzerland, Italy and Spain.

Referring to the activities that took place there all year round – educational conferences, periods of intense doctrinal formation, courses and retreats – the Father recalled how essential it was to have material means and venues for the apostolates of the Work, even if finding them meant a serious and sustained effort, as had always been the case since the very beginning.

A centre like Couvrelles, or a students' residence, or a youth club, is not there only for the activities that take place in it. It must also help to raise the spiritual level and the human education of many who will find in it an opportunity to meet Christ and to love Him more.

Opus Dei is poor. But souls are precious, and the most adequate means should be used to serve them. These means are provided for the Work by the people who help with its apostolic activities. Besides, these instruments will never be as expensive as those used for other aims – for sport or leisure, for instance.

The Father spoke with even more energy when he explained how no member must keep the treasure of the Faith and his vocation to himself, and how all must carry out a continuous apostolate in their surroundings. Hence the duty to be well formed, not only from a religious but also from a professional point of view. *Dialogue*, something about which people talk a lot but hardly ever practise, has to be founded not only on openness to others but also on knowledge of the truth and an evident professional competence.

Concern for the Church

The Father was visibly tired. But he managed to maintain the same vigour and spiritual strength he always showed.

He was worried, too, about certain changes brought about by a widespread defective understanding of the Council – by certain attitudes of disaffection, by stubborn refusals which were, for him, though he did not judge individuals, signs of a weakening in the Faith, with the damaging and dramatic effects all this could have for souls.

Few Christians, no doubt, had been as happy as he had been on reading the texts elaborated by the Council and solemnly promulgated by Pope Paul VI on 7 December 1965. Some sentences went right to his heart: they expressed, in the name of the

Magisterium of the Church, the truths which had been at the base of his teaching since 1928.

In a document of great authority – the Dogmatic Constitution *Lumen gentium* – the universal call to holiness and apostolate is solemnly proclaimed: "The vocation proper to the laity consists in seeking the Kingdom of God precisely through the administration of temporal things, which they ordain towards God. They live in the midst of the world, that is, engaged in all the different duties and works of the world, in the ordinary conditions of family and social life from which their existence is, as it were, woven."

"The calling to the fulness of the Christian life and to the perfection of charity is addressed to all those who believe in Christ, whatever their state or form of life might be."[1]

In other texts devoted to the apostolate of the laity, the Council affirms that, when they live a contemplative life in the middle of the world, the laity "do not separate union with Christ from their lives, but grow in that union through the accomplishment of their work according to the will of God."[2]

Prayer, prayer, prayer, sacrifice, and then action ... This had been the "secret" that Monsignor Escrivá had been at pains to communicate to as many as he could since 1928.

Contemplative life is all the more necessary if one lives immersed in the world. Order the structures of the world in accordance with the divine will? *Yes: but only by first being well ordered within.* Move the world in a Christian way in order to change it? Certainly; but in order to do that, the lay person must have *a contemplative soul* ... This is what he had explained, quite vehemently, to a group of bishops and Council experts whom he had met in Villa Tevere while the texts of Vatican II were being hammered out. *Otherwise they won't change anything: on the contrary, it is they who will let themselves be changed – and instead of the world becoming Christian, Christians will become worldly!*[3]

"This spirituality of the laity," added the Council, "must take on particular characteristics, in accordance with the life of each one: conjugal and family life, celibacy, widowhood, the state of sickness, professional and social activity."[4]

"Thus these men and women who, while gaining their

livelihood and that of their families, carry out their activity so as to serve society well, are indeed justified in seeing in their work an extension of the work of the Creator, a service to their brothers and a personal contribution to the realisation of the plan of Providence in history."[5]

Far off now were the days when the young Father Escrivá had been branded a heretic for having affirmed that the laity, no less than priests or religious, are called to sanctify themselves in the middle of the world.

Finally, the decree on priests, *Presbyterorum ordinis*, worked out by the commission with Don Alvaro del Portillo as its Secretary, recognised that priests had the right to associate in order to help each other and to deepen in their spiritual lives.

Monsignor Escrivá, as a Canon lawyer, was very happy at this turn of events, for a personal natural right was thus being recognised – the right of association.

Solidity in the Faith

Even if it was obvious that the Holy Spirit had been at work in the Council, as the documents made manifest, the stir some had produced did not die down easily.

The Father's fears were only too evidently justified. For someone who knew history as he did, a Council was a milestone in the Church's teaching but at the same time could also be, indirectly, the occasion of a period of confusion. It can be compared to what happens if the water of a pond is suddenly agitated; the mud rises to the top, then sinks down to the bottom again, taking much longer to settle than it took in rising to the surface.

Shortly after the end of Vatican II, Pope Paul VI started to express his concern, in less and less veiled terms, at the erroneous interpretations of the Council, in matters of both theory and practice, that were being made by some people. The Holy Father returned often to this subject: indeed he went so far as to speak of a veritable "disintegration of the Church".

The founder of Opus Dei was very conscious of the special responsibility he had towards the members of the Work as President-General. So he devoted his best efforts to his sons and daughters during these times described by the Pope as particularly difficult for the Church. He took all necessary steps to ensure that the prescriptions of Vatican II, notably in the area of the liturgy, were applied within Opus Dei. At the same time, he took sensible precautions to ensure that the widespread disorientation did not infiltrate, as if by a process of *osmosis*, into the *little flock* under his charge. He urged his children to improve their doctrinal formation and to strengthen their life of piety, while at the same time spending no less time on their professional work and on their duty to their families.

Such an effort to intensify their interior lives was a spur members of the Work to carry out more apostolate with those around them. This apostolate of giving doctrine was something the Father had practised himself, and got those around him to practise in the 1930s. It has always been the kernel of the apostolic work of Opus Dei. More than ever he saw Opus Dei as *a great catechesis*,[6] for he was more than ever persuaded that ignorance was *the greatest of God's enemies*.[7] In the words of Tertullian, "Man ceases to hate what he ceases to be ignorant of."

He received more and more visitors in Rome, and tried to give them the right doctrinal orientation.

Groups of German students had started coming to Rome every Easter in the second half of the 1960s, to receive the blessing of the Pope and to see the Father. Soon students from other countries began to do the same.

The Father received them all. Standing in their midst, or sitting on the arm of an armchair, he answered their running fire of questions, strengthening and stimulating the spiritual restlessness many of them showed.

The students would very soon relax, or laugh, when the Father answered in his own characteristic way that avoided any possibility of his lively conversation turning into a sermon. His audience always thereafter retained the main point of his message: *Everyone, wherever he is in the midst of the world, must become a saint!*[8]

Many "good intentions" became resolutions or commitments for life on hearing these warm words of the Father. But he would not take any of the credit when he would hear of these decisions a few days later. For him the interior changes were the work of Christ, *Christ who still passes today in the streets and market-places of the world, among Christians, his disciples.* [9]

Intensifying doctrinal formation

The storm that had begun to buffet the centuries-old tree of the Church did not shake the supernatural optimism of the founder of Opus Dei, nor did it impede in the slightest his spirit of initiative. It was precisely during this time that he decided to begin carrying out a plan that had been very close to his heart, but which he had kept hidden for many years; it would be, as he put it, *his last-but-one folly.* [10]

All over the world, Opus Dei would have to develop its central organisms of direction, even if they were and would always remain very modest in scale. At the same time, members of the Work, both students and more mature men who had already exercised a profession for a number of years, were arriving in Rome in greater and greater numbers to receive part of the doctrinal and spiritual formation that is given to all the members of the Work over the course of their lifetime.

Thus, as the Father had foreseen, Villa Tevere had become too small. He therefore decided to build as soon as possible a residence for a hundred and fifty students, to be the definitive seat of the Roman College of the Holy Cross and the international centre of formation for the Men's Section of the Work.

After prolonged negotiations a site was acquired near the Via Flaminia, which goes out from Rome into the region of Umbria. Thus, by the end of 1967 the Father was asking for plans to be drawn up as quickly as possible so that they could start laying the foundations for *Cavabianca* , as the new centre was to be called.

Above: Rome, November 1965. Pope Paul VI, with Monsignor Escrivá, after officially opening the ELIS Centre.
Below: Rome, March 1970. The founder with Japanese members of Opus Dei.

Above: Mexico, June 1970. Monsignor Escrivá in a get-together with a group of farmers.

Below: Madrid, October 1972. In a get-together with diocesan priests, some belonging to the Priestly Society of the Holy Cross.

A gesture of thanks

The founder of Opus Dei was powerfully and urgently impelled to rally, spiritually, a world which was becoming inhuman because it had lost its sense of God. It was this that led him to another *folly*[11] around the same time. It was an old dream that took his thoughts back to Aragon, near the town of Barbastro where he had been born, to the shrine where his parents had taken him as a small child in 1904 or 1905, on horseback, to thank the Blessed Virgin for having cured him of a serious illness: it was the shrine of Torreciudad.

As early as 1940, or perhaps even earlier, the Father had dreamed of creating – or in some cases resurrecting – a few Marian shrines throughout the world. As the years passed he felt that God was asking him to promote the first of these places of pilgrimage at Torreciudad.

Around 1962, as the Work developed in Catalonia and Aragon, a group of people heard of his desires and decided to buy from the diocese of Barbastro the rights over the old chapel and the lands surrounding it. They had then started restoring the chapel.

In June 1967 Monsignor Escrivá received in Rome a son of his, Heliodoro Dols, who was an architect. The Father had decided to carry out a larger project, one which would allow pilgrims to come in large numbers to pray to Our Lady and use the opportunity to renew their spiritual lives. For this an entirely new shrine would be built, one which would be larger and more dignified, with a building for retreats and courses next to it, and a centre for professional training which would help the whole surrounding rural district.

A committee of Patrons of Torreciudad had been set up in 1966 so that people from every part of Spain and other countries all over the world could help in the construction of the different buildings.

The Father described to his sons the benefits he expected from this new centre of pilgrimage in the following way: *I expect a flood of spiritual graces, which Our Lord will want to grant those who have recourse to his blessed Mother before the little statue in the old hermitage so venerated over the centuries. That is why I want there to be a lot of confessionals, so that people can purify themselves in the holy Sacrament of Confession and so that – having once renewed their souls – they can confirm and renew their Christian lives, learning to sanctify and love their work, keeping alive the light and joy of Jesus Christ in their homes.* [12]

2. FATIMA: MAY 1967

Thirteen years after his previous pilgrimage, the Father found himself once again at the feet of Our Lady of Fatima. Pilgrims were arriving in huge throngs, despite the rain: in a few days, on 13 May, Pope Paul VI would be presiding over the ceremonies on the fiftieth anniversary of the apparitions. In advance, the founder of Opus Dei united his intentions to the intentions of the Roman Pontiff and prayed for the Church and for the fruits of the Council. Later he met groups of his sons and daughters in a Centre of the Work called *Enxomil* , near Oporto.

Transfiguring ordinary life

In Pamplona, on 7 October 1967, he presided at the same kind of ceremony that had brought him there in 1964. Six academics from different countries received at his hands the degree of Doctor *honoris causa* of the University of Navarre. Guilherme Braga da Cruz, professor at the University of Coimbra; Monsignor Onclin, professor of Canon Law at the University of Louvain and Secretary of the Pontifical Commission for the Reform of the Code of Canon Law; Ralph Hower, professor at Harvard Business School; Otto Roegele, professor and Director of the Institute of Information

Technology at the University of Munich; and Jean Roche, professor of the College de France and Rector of the Sorbonne. The honorary degree was also conferred posthumously on a leading light of the Spanish medical world, Dr Jiménez Díaz, who had been of great assistance to the University of Navarre from its inception.

This time more than thirty-five thousand people had come, not only from Spain but also from Portugal, France, Italy, Germany, Belgium and other countries. There were a number of special train services for that occasion.

The same kind of get-together as had taken place in the Gayarre Theatre in 1964 was repeated in other places, even in the open air, on the university campus. There was also the same type of spontaneous and lively dialogue between the Father and the audience as before: there were different meetings for students, clerical and manual workers, parents, co-operators and friends of the Work, and on the 8th they met again for a Mass celebrated by the Father in front of the university library.

In his homily he spoke of *the setting of our Eucharist, of our act of thanksgiving. We find ourselves in a unique temple. We might say that the nave is the university campus; the altarpiece, the university library; over there, the machinery for constructing new buildings; above us, the sky of Navarre ... Surely this confirms in your minds, in a tangible and unforgetable way, the fact that everyday life is the true setting of your life as Christians. Your ordinary contact with God takes place where your fellow men, your yearnings, your work and your affections are. There you have your daily encounter with Christ. It is in the midst of the most material things of the earth that we must sanctify ourselves, serving God and all mankind.* [13]

Tens of thousands of men and women listened in silence as the founder expressed, in striking words, the central message of Opus Dei: we have to sanctify ourselves wherever we are in the most ordinary situations, avoiding the temptation to *lead a kind of double life: on one side, an interior life, a life of relation with God; and on the other, a distinct and separate family, social and professional life, full of small earthly realities. No, my children! We cannot lead a double life. We cannot be like schizophrenics if we want to be Christians. There is just one life, made of flesh and spirit. And it is this life which has to become, in both soul and body, holy and filled with God. We discover the invisible God in the most visible and material things ... Heaven and earth seem to merge, my children, on the horizon. But where they really meet is in your hearts, when you sanctify your everyday lives.* [14]

At the end of 1968 this homily would be published in a book entitled *Conversations with Monsignor Escrivá*, which gathered together interviews given by the founder of Opus Dei to journalists from various countries. The Father, breaking his usual rule of conduct, for the good of souls, had accepted several requests for interviews since 1966.

He had met a number of journalists in Pamplona in 1964, including the Spanish correspondent of *Le Figaro*, who two years later asked the founder of Opus Dei for an interview for his paper. Others followed: the *New York Times*, *Time* magazine and various Spanish newspapers.

The book also contained another interview which had appeared in 1960 in the Sunday edition of the *L'Osservatore Romano*. In all these interviews Monsignor Escrivá replied to questions about the life of the Church, the position of the university, the role of woman in the world, and so on. He spoke also about Opus Dei, and defined the nature of the Work he had founded in 1928 as clearly as possible: *The purpose of Opus Dei is to foster the search for holiness and the carrying out of the apostolate by Christians who live in the world, whatever their state in life or mission in society ... Christ is present in every honest human activity ... The one and only mission of Opus Dei is the spreading of this message ... And for those who grasp this ideal of holiness, the Work offers the spiritual assistance and the doctrinal, ascetical and apostolic training which they need to put it into practice.* [15]

Referring to those who insisted on talking about Opus Dei as if it were for Spain alone, and in an area which is foreign to it – that of politics – he repeated with passionate emphasis that the Work was not attached to any country, nor to any government, any political allegiance or any ideology, and that its members *abominate any attempt to make use of religion to support political or party interests.* [16]

It was perfectly clear to him – indeed, he knew for certain – that the the members of the Work *do not act as a group. They act individually, with personal freedom and responsibility.* [17]

The founder also knew that it would take time to bring to an end the prejudices caused by slanderous campaigns against the Work. But he was confident that the journalists he met would tell the truth. He knew that the root of the problem went back to the 1940s, to a clerical way of seeing things which was characteristic of what he called *official Catholicism* .[18] He was not surprised by this, but he held it in abhorrence, because *to instrumentalise the laity for ends which are not in keeping with the ends of the hierarchy* [19] was something completely opposed to the founder's way of thinking. That was the reason for his answer to the editors of the *L'Osservatore della Domenica* when they questioned him on this point: *I hope the time will come when the phrase "Catholics are penetrating all sectors of society" will go out of circulation ... The members of Opus Dei have no need to "penetrate" the temporal sector for the simple reason that they are ordinary citizens, the same as their fellow citizens, and so they are there already.* [20]

The founder remained as non-conformist at sixty-five as he had been in the 1930s, when he had been preaching to ordinary men and women that they could sanctify their ordinary work there in the midst of the world, thus provoking annoyance, indignation and scandal amongst various churchmen who considered that the laity should be, at the very most, the *longa manus* of the hierarchy.

A symbolic gesture

In 1968 Monsignor Escriva again gave public proof of his independent-mindedness, taking a decision he was sure would be wrongly interpreted by some people, even though he was inspired only by a deep sense of justice.

The more he thought of how Opus Dei had been born and of how it had developed, step by step, the more convinced he was that God had looked after him like a father who tells his child where to put each piece of a jigsaw puzzle: 2 October 1928; then, against his expectations, the foundation of the Women's Section on 14 February 1930; finally, on another 14 February, the Priestly Society of the Holy Cross thirteen years later ...

Now he could also see more easily how the trials his parents had gone through were simply a means used by Our Lord to purify him during his youth, in order to make him freer to carry out the immense task He was going to give him. He now could gauge more accurately the meaning of those sufferings of his family – the death of his three young sisters, the sudden drastic change in his father's circumstances and his premature death, to say nothing of the direct consequences to his mother, his brother and his sister of his own gift of himself to Our Lord.

His family had always agreed to the additional sacrifices he had continually asked of them in order to be able to develop the apostolates of the Work, from selling part of the family heritage in order to open the first residence in 1934, to the untiring work of his mother and his sister in dealing with the administration of other residences, the last of which had been the house at Salto di Fondi in Italy, where Carmen had worked so hard.

At sixty-six the Father felt obliged to do something, in retrospect, for his parents who had suffered so much, and. in a certain sense, because of him. Only his brother Santiago, now forty-nine, was still alive. For him and his children and in memory of his parents, who had been shamefully treated during their last years at Barbastro, he hoped to carry out a plan which, if successful, would be a sort of symbolic repayment, though minimal compared to what he owed his family.

The initiative had come from his sons, especially from Don Alvaro del Portillo. For many years, realising the historical importance that the figure of the founder would acquire with time, they had inquired into the history of his family. Certain family links had been established – which the Father knew about but had never mentioned, for he gave them no importance – with ancient noble families of Aragon. His family had a claim to a title of nobility, that of the Marquisate of Peralta, which had been granted by Charles of Hapsburg to an ancestor of his mother in 1718. After investigating the case thoroughly, they were informed that it would be possible for the title to be re-established in Spain. After a filial struggle Don Alvaro managed to get the Father to consider the idea of re-claiming that title. If he obtained it, he could then pass it on to his brother after a reasonable lapse of time ... It was a practical way of honouring a debt to his family.

He was well aware, of course, that people would not miss the opportunity to make snide remarks, without even taking into con-sideration that at his age, and in his present conspicuous position, he had no need of such honours for himself. He knew that, even if his sons and daughters would understand, others would take advan-tage of the situation to slip sneering and detrimental comments into what they said or wrote, and might even, indirectly, sling mud at the Work.

For this reason, he was, naturally, careful to consult various prominent members of the Curia before proceeding with his plan. He also asked the Papal Secretary of State, as he felt that, being President-General of an institution of the Church, it was incumbent on him to do so. All of them considered that there was no obstacle to his going ahead with the project. What is more, one of the prom-inent figures of the Curia told him he *must* do so, for if he, who had always told his sons and daughters to fulfil their civic duties and exercise all their rights, did not do so he would give them bad example ...

Thus, at the beginning of 1968 he wrote to the Counsellor of Opus Dei in Spain, explaining the reasons for that decision, which were simply those of piety and justice towards his family, together with his desire of putting into practice *the sweetest precept of the Decalogue*, the Fourth Commandment: "Honour thy father and thy mother." At the same time the Father asked him to dissuade his sons and daughters from wanting to justify his action in the public's eyes: *I am not at all worried about the comments that may be made – though they would not be made if it was a case of any other person or of any other Spanish citizen – and I ask you to turn a deaf ear if they say or write anything unpleasant, for whatever it may be it will be unjust.* [21]

As the Father expected, the legal rehabilitation of the title was taken up and made much of by the press, with expressions of pharisaical scandal and comments in bad taste as soon as it became known. Yet no explanation of the facts was made by by Opus Dei in any country. The Father, on his part, remained completely silent until, a year later, he transferred the title to his brother so that he, in turn, could pass it on to his children.

Undoubtedly the silence of the founder was in part a sort of healthy disregard for what people might think. It was as if he had wanted, by his example, to encourage his sons to make use of their civic rights as he had always taught them, without trying to hide behind a misplaced modesty which was very different from true Christian humility. And he showed his humility by his very act, offering the ill-intentioned a pretext to insult him.

The members of the Work understood the Father instinctively, as did the many people who knew him. And they considered that in the whole affair he had borne himself, whether he possessed a noble title or not, with true nobility.

Suffering for the Church

His sufferings from the misunderstandings he had expected were as nothing compared with what was the Father's deepest concern during this part of his life.

Lord, if it is your will, turn my poor flesh into a Crucifix, [22] he had written in *The Way*. Now, it seemed as if Our Lord wanted to configure his servant to his own image, in this period of trial for the universal Church. For it *seems as if it is being influenced by the evil things of the world, by a crumbling down which is subverting and dividing everything, and stifling the supernatural sense of a Christian life.* [23] Questioning everything had given rise to doubting everything, so that what we had was no longer a crisis, but a convulsion which was sweeping the Church.

We are living in a time of madness, the Father told his closest helpers on 25 November 1970. *Millions of souls are totally confused. There is a great danger that the Sacraments will, in practice, be emptied of their content – all of them, even Baptism – and that in the end consciences won't even be able to understand the Command-ments of God's Law.* [24]

The founder of Opus Dei knew that the barque of Peter could not sink; but he also knew that God may permit times of very real and very hard trial. The slightest disclosure that showed a crack in the Faith, the least piece of news that revealed that the love of God among Christians was growing cold, cut him to the heart. He thought of it day and night, prayed, mortified himself more gen-erously still, and made reparation ... [25]

For years he had known long night-vigils in which the shadows seemed to become denser. Now he felt compelled still more to beg God to put an end to the trial.

As the crisis continued, he begged to see, if not the end, at least the beginning of the end, and besought his sons to do the same: to pray without ceasing so that the Lord, humbly and gently implored, can not but intervene.[26] The only thing he could do was abandon himself into the hands of Providence.

The Church causes me such suffering! [27] he would often say.

His faith, that *faith you can cut with a knife* ,[28] which had been his since childhood and which had continued to deepen since then, told him that the end of this collective insanity would be a great light of hope, for *the Lord knows how to draw good from evil and great goods out of great evils.* [29]

But *Sorrow is the touchstone of Love* ,[30] and the Father could not stop himself from suffering with the Church, not only as a Christian, but also as a priest, and as a man responsible before God for all the souls that He had entrusted to his care. In addition, there were reasons for him to think that the Prince of Darkness was still as determined as ever to raise obstacles to this new *divine path on the earth* [31] which was Opus Dei.

The hand on the rudder must sometimes, during the storm, bear down more heavily to keep the right course ... That is why what Monsignor Escrivá suffered for the Church was not only pas-sive, for it was accompanied by keen concern not to stray, by a sin-gle degree, from the course set by God for His Work. Indeed, he felt responsible before God for the integrity of the deposit he had received on 2 October 1928. The lay character of the Work was part of that deposit.

His sons and daughters, united around the founder and identified with his spirit, had no doubt that they were ordinary Christians. They were not not religious in the world or adapted to the world. They were exactly the same as everyone else. There was no doubt among their families and friends either. Besides, the law of the Church had recognised this secular characteristic of Opus Dei. But the Father, as founder, had been hoping for a number of years to make things even clearer if possible, by giving the Work a legal position more in keeping with its real nature than the one given to it in 1950. Things had not yet been ripe for that, and Canon Law had still not been sufficiently developed. Now, however, he thought that some proposals of the Second Vatican Council would certainly allow him to obtain the new statute.*

Have confidence, he told a group of his sons in Rome on 6 January 1970, inviting them before the crib to contemplate the mystery of the Nativity. "Ask, and you will receive." (Luke 2:9)

Taking shelter close to the Trinity on earth,[32] Jesus, Mary and Joseph, in his mind the Father took the Child in his arms; then he made acts of contrition for all the evil done and all the good not done by Christians ...

Not far from the crib, Herod had been waiting. *But they can do nothing, Lord, either against your Church, or against your Work. I am sure ... More than once the Work, too, has met Herod in its path. But rest assured, rest assured ... Not for nothing have we left aside*

---

* On 28 November 1982, His Holiness John Paul II, by the Apostolic Constitution *Ut sit*, set up Opus Dei as a personal Prelature and named Monsignor Alvaro del Portillo as Prelate.

The Prelature of the Holy Cross and Opus Dei is a personal Prelature, international in its scope and with its centre in Rome, which has as its aim the spreading throughout all sectors of society a deep awareness of the universal call to sanctity and apostolate, in the fulfilment of ordinary professional work. It is formed by a Prelate with his own clergy and by lay people, men and women, who in virtue of a divine vocation freely join the Prelature. (*Translators note*) *our own personal interests.* [33]

Those around the Father were grave. They suffered because of his sufferings. What else could they do but associate themselves with his plea, and work even harder in the direction he pointed out to them?

Two pilgrimages in the Iberian Peninsula

As in every trying predicament of his life, it was to the Mother of God – proclaimed Mother of the Church by Paul VI at the end of the Council – that he turned. It was this that took him to the feet of Our Lady several times during 1970.

I am going to visit two shrines of the Blessed Virgin , he wrote to his sons. *I am going like a pilgrim of the twelfth century: with the same love, with the same simplicity, with the same joy. I will pray there for the world, for the Church, for the Pope and for the Work ... Join me in my prayers and in my Mass.* [34]

These two shrines were Torreciudad, in Spain, and Fatima, in Portugal.

At the beginning of April the founder of Opus Dei flew to Spain. He found the statue of the Virgin of Torreciudad was in the process of being restored at the old house on Diego de León Road in Madrid. It was a traditional representation of the Virgin and Child, of the type seen in many shrines in Europe at the end of the eleventh century. The wood was bare; it had been stripped of the layers of paint from more recent centuries, and was awaiting the gold leaf that would restore its primitive appearance.

Realising how the Father would feel, they left him alone before the statue. He kissed the feet of the Virgin and the feet of the Child in filial gratitude, speaking to the Virgin with heartfelt words, telling her of his joy on seeing her, like a son who finds himself with his mother after a long absence.

A few days later, after a stop to see the Virgin of *El Pilar* at Saragossa, he arrived at Torreciudad. About a quarter of a mile from the shrine, at a bend in the road, which was still under construction and not yet properly surfaced, the Father stopped the car, took off his shoes, and continued on foot, while he said the Sorrowful Mysteries of the Rosary. It was a grey, drizzly day, but twice the Father refused to put his shoes on once more.

There are plenty of shepherds who go barefoot every day over the rocks. I'm not doing anything extraordinary. [35]

Having finished the Sorrowful Mysteries, and after a few minutes of silent prayer, the Father continued with the other two parts of the Rosary. When they arrived at the chapel he went up to the altar to sing the *Salve Regina*, then knelt and recited a prayer to Our Lady which he had learned as a child. Only then did he go into another room to remove the stones embedded in the soles of his feet and put his shoes back on.

Soon he was out again in the rain, in the middle of the foundation works for the new shrine, a few hundred yards from the old chapel. Standing over a vast excavation, which was where the crypt with the confessionals would be, he blessed it, making the Sign of the Cross over it. His dearest wish was that many would receive, at Torreciudad, the most precious of gifts: the grace of God.

The great love that God has for his Mother will make his omnipotence and mercy shine there also. We shall ask and seek for miracles to be wrought in souls. [36]

On 14 April he was again barefoot as he walked towards the *capelinha* of Fatima surrounded by some of his Portuguese sons. Next to the statue commemorating the visit of Pope Paul VI in 1967, which was also the year of his last pilgrimage, he prayed for the Pope.

He was pleasantly struck by the piety of the pilgrims around him. At a time when the faith seemed to be weakening in many places and devotions to Our Lady were being put in doubt, certain manifestations of piety moved him now. That is why he often said that he would give a great deal to be able to express his faith with the sincerity of a little old woman sighing in the shadows of a corner in the church. That is why he was also very pleased when one of his Portuguese sons wrote to him, a few days later, saying that he had noticed at Fatima that the Father had kissed the medals on his rosary, just the way his own grandmother used to do ...

These pilgrimages were an evident proof of the great faith of the Father and, at the same time, made him more convinced than ever that the Church would soon find peace and unity again. "If God is with us, who can be against us?" (Rom 8:31), he repeated with the Apostle Paul.

In Mexico, at the feet of Our Lady of Guadalupe

But he was still very concerned about the Church. Thus, shortly after his return to Rome on 1 May, the Father suddenly decided to undertake a third Marian pilgrimage.

This time he would go further – to America, where never before had he spoken about going. His children in Mexico had indeed for a long time been asking him to come to their country. But perhaps he would never have decided to cross the Atlantic if he had not been compelled by such a strong motive as his concern for the Church.

On 14 May 1970 he boarded a plane that would take him to Mexico.

One of his first visits was to the *Villa* , which is where the Mexicans flock in great numbers every day to pray before the famous painting of the Virgin of Guadalupe. She has been the Patroness of Mexico and the whole of Latin America since the apparition of the Mother of God to a poor Indian, Juan Diego, in 1531. Her image had been miraculously imprinted on the rough cloth Juan Diego used as an overcoat.

The Father knelt at the sanctuary, his eyes fixed on the picture of the Lady, whose face shows the same racial features as those of the inhabitants of that land blessed by her presence. Inside the basilica many people come up to the painting all day long, often on their knees.

An hour and a half later he rose and left. A large number of members of the Work, who had started to arrive on hearing that the Father was there, had surrounded him with their silent and loving presence. The same thing happened again for eight days in succession, from the 17th to the 24th. But then, so as not to attract attention, the Father went up to a gallery to the right of the sanctuary where, without being seen, he was immediately opposite the famous image. No one could possibly know the intensity and depth of that prayer. Only those who were very close to him could hear his words *daring and childlike* [37] ... *which the pen cannot and should not write.* [38] They were words which expressed his constant concerns: the Church, the Pope, his sons and daughters.

Every day his plea was made aloud. Those next to him, among them Don Alvaro and Don Javier Echevarría, another of his closest collaborators, were overcome by the simplicity of this dialogue of a son with his Mother. Perhaps it was with the same words that little Josemaría addressed Mary in the month of May in Barbastro, when bringing his flowers and presenting his requests to the Virgin like all the other children.

The Mexicans, too, men as well as women, brought roses all year round to lay at the feet of "their" Virgin of Guadalupe and the Father wished to join in with them too. On the fifth day of the Novena he addressed the following words to the Mother of God: *Our Lady, I bring you – for I have nothing else – thorns, the ones I have in my heart, but I am sure that with you they will turn to roses ...*

Grant that we may have in us, in our hearts, little roses blooming all the year round; the roses of daily life, ordinary roses, but filled with the perfume of sacrifice and love. I have said little roses, on purpose, because it suits me better, for in my whole life I have only been able to do ordinary, everyday things, and even then I often haven't been able to finish them; but I am sure that it is in this, my everyday, ordinary behaviour, that you and your Son are waiting for me. [39]

After this the Father formulated his request with the *holy shamelessness* [40] he had always recommended to souls who wanted to work for God: *Here I am. Because you can do everything! Because you love! My Mother, our Mother ... , keep us from everything that stops us from being your children, everything that is trying to obstruct our path and spoil our vocation. I won't let it, because I don't want to be condemned; but don't let the forces of evil act. Against you the Devil can do nothing! How çan I not rely on that certainty? Hail*

Mary, Daughter of God the Father; Hail Mary, Mother of God the Son; Hail Mary, Spouse of God the Holy Spirit; Hail Mary, Temple of the Most Holy Trinity: greater than you, no one but God! Show us that you are our Mother! Show what you are able to bring about! [41]

The audible prayer continued. From his position up in the balcony where he was speaking to Our Lady, the Father heard the songs of the faithful, addressed to her who is their Patroness, and his heart beat in unison with their praises. He kept on praying insistently:

I love you as much as I know how and can. I have been wrong so many times in my life, but I love you with all the strength of my soul. Tell us what we have to do, and with your grace we will do it ... Hear us: I know that you will! [42]

Between a creature, even one infinitely faithful, and his Creator, bargaining would seem almost unthinkable – unless the supernatural outcome had already been decided in the divine Plan, as Abraham finally realised after negotiating inch by inch with Yahweh for the salvation of a handful of people from a nearby town ...

The fact is that, from 20 May 1970 onwards, Josemaría Escrivá showed greater confidence and peace. He was unshakeable, though he did not cease to suffer, to make reparation and to pray for the Church. When the time came, everything would be set right. It was as if Mary, in her basilica where the Father had come to pay her honour, had wanted to show him the obstacles removed, though not the day or the hour of their removal. What did it matter if he did not see it with his earthly eyes? The great river of the Church would return to its normal course ...

Before leaving the balcony, the Father made a promise to Our Lady of Guadalupe, an *unconditional* [43] promise like the promise he had made many years earlier in Madrid, when he had invoked Saint Nicholas of Bari to ask him to solve the apparently insoluble financial problems facing him at the time. In thanksgiving for the grace he had just obtained, he would place a mosaic replica of the image of the Virgin of Guadalupe, and a commemorative plaque, in one of the chapels of the crypt of the as yet unfinished shrine at Torreciudad.

The race of the children of God

When he arrived in Mexico, the Father had said with a smile to his children that they were only the second reason for his trip: the first reason was Our Lady of Guadalupe. But seeing their joy at his being in their midst, he realised that the second reason was practically identical to the first.

The Father visited *Montefalco*, an old hacienda in the State of Morelos which his sons had reconstructed and used for different educational projects, particularly as a rural training centre for the country people of the region. He was as much at ease among these Indian peasants as among the town-dwellers of Mexico City or any of the other great cities of the country. In those gatherings there were many who had come from other countries, from Costa Rica, Guatemala, El Salvador, Venezuela, Puerto Rico, Colombia, Argentina and even from the United States and Canada. To all of them he said:

No one is better than anybody else. No one! We are all equal! Each of us is worth the same: we are worth the blood of Christ. What a marvellous thing this is. For there are neither races nor tongues; there is only one race: that of the children of God. [44]

This direct way of speaking was understood by everybody. The city dwellers and the country people heard it, people from all the different walks of life, and it loosened the tongues of even the most taciturn of the peasants. They all wanted to ask questions of that priest who always had a ready answer that lifted their spirits and gave dignity to their lives. Everyone wanted to come near the Father, to greet him, to receive a word or a smile from him, or at least touch him.

In Mexico D.F., at a Centre of the Women's Section of the Work, a little wrinkled Indian woman had remained in a corner of the entrance hall. They told the Father that four of her children were in Opus Dei. The Father went towards the old lady, and she without further thought as to what would happen, fell on her knees before this man of God. While her daughter tried in vain to raise her up, she saw to her great emotion the Father in his turn kneel before her to be at her height, and murmur things that she heard with tears in her eyes. *We are the same, my daughter. We are children of God* ... [45]

My children, I have come here to Mexico not to teach but to learn. [46] He had come to learn from the Mexicans, from their unwavering faith and from their sincere love for the Mother of God ...

But the Father also spoke of the apostolate which they could carry out in all the Spanish-speaking countries of their Continent: *How much good you can do! If there were more of us, and if I were better and you too, and you; if we were all better, what wonders we could work!* [47]

During his forty days in Mexico the Father met over twenty thousand people. In his spontaneous conversations with them, like those he had held in Spain and Portugal, he spoke again about the sanctification of ordinary occupations, about married life; about friendship and apostolate; about prayer, the Church, the Sacraments, and particularly about the Eucharist and Penance. In fact, about all the means which nourish that personal exchange between the soul and God which is the secret of all apostolic fruitfulness.

The Father, in spite of his age, stood up to this physical trial surprisingly well. One day, however, on 16 June, while he was speaking to a group of priests not far from Lake Chapala in the north-west of Mexico, he had to rest for a while in another room, for the suffocating heat of the afternoon had begun to make him feel ill. He gazed at a picture hanging on the wall representing the Virgin of Guadalupe giving a rose to the Indian Juan Diego.

That's how I'd like to die , he had said quietly, lost in his habitual contemplation, *looking at the Blessed Virgin, while she hands me a flower* ... [48]

3. LOURDES: 3 OCTOBER 1972

The Father had just landed at Tarbes airport, not far from Lourdes. A few of his French and Spanish sons had come to meet him there before he went on to Hendaye and from there into Spain. He intended to spend several weeks in the Iberian peninsula and meet a large number of people. First, on 7 October, he would preside at a ceremony during which he was to award honorary doctorates of the University of Navarre to a German professor of medicine, Erich Letterer, a Spanish art historian, the Marquis of Lozoya, and a French legal historian, Professor Ourliac, a member of the Institute of France.

Soon, as they passed in front of the basilica of Lourdes, the Father spoke of the miracles that were starting to happen at Torreciudad, on the other side of the Pyrenees, even before the shrine and the other buildings were finished: confessions, conversions, decisions to give more to Our Lord ... all the miracles he had thought of when he gave the word for the construction work to begin.

The Father walked briskly to the grotto. As always in Lourdes, he stopped to drink the spring water. Then he went towards the site of the apparitions, where a ceremony was about to start. As soon as he saw the statue of the Virgin of the Rosary, he knelt on the ground; after a short and intense moment of prayer, he rose and returned across the esplanade.

The Father said farewell to his French sons and got back into the car.

Before drinking the miraculous water, he had remarked to those around him that he was asking nothing of the Blessed Virgin for himself, not even for his health. But his sons were not surprised, for they were well aware of the motive for this detour to the place where on 11 December 1937 he had said Mass after his memorable crossing of the Pyrenees. It was the same motive as on the previous pilgrimages he had made to Lourdes, to Sonsoles in Avila, to El Pilar in Saragossa, to the Basilica of Our Lady of Ransom in Barcelona, to Our Lady of Willesden in London, to Einsiedeln in Switzerland and to Loreto in Italy. And to Torreciudad, in 1970, to Fatima in Portugal, to Guadalupe in Mexico ...

Praying in these famous places of pilgrimage, he had asked Our Lady for peace for the Church, peace for the world, for the perseverance of his sons and daughters and the fruitfulness of the apostolates of the Work.

Now, more than ever, the Church was his first concern, urging him as it did towards further plans for making reparation and for strengthening the faith of his children, both when they visited him in Rome and when he met them on his journeys. Previously, he had customarily avoided talking to very large groups, but now he felt a burning desire to speak about God directly to the largest possible number of people, to set them on the way to deepening their Christian lives. But for him the apostolate would always be, as he had written long ago in *The Way*, the fruit of *prayer, which grows in value with sacrifice.* [49] He frequently repeated the words of a liturgical prayer he had often used when he was young: *Ure igne Sancti Spiritus* ... "Lord, burn us with the fire of Your Holy Spirit; burn our hearts and our innermost being ..."

This plea to the Holy Spirit was prompted by his desire to be constantly close to the Holy Family of Nazareth, *the trinity on earth*, [50] as he called it.

If we want to become intimate friends with Our Lord and our heavenly Mother, we must listen to Joseph. [51]

At Saint Joseph's side his soul came closer to Mary, and

through her to Jesus, God made Man. And Jesus introduced him into the mystery of the Blessed Trinity. This was how, according to his own words, he went from the trinity on earth to the Trinity of heaven, by the *way of childhood*[52] of which the great mystics have spoken. It is a path *whose difficult easiness demands that the soul start and continue led by the hand of God*, and which demands *the submission of the understanding, more difficult than the submission of the will.*[53]

Christ is passing by

The themes of his recent preaching were a faithful reflection of the key points in his interior life: the Church, her supernatural end, the need for her children to be loyal, and abandonment into the hands of God.

Some of the homilies he had given on various liturgical feast-days had been published in different languages over the previous few years. A collection of eighteen previously unpublished texts in one volume was planned for the beginning of 1973, bearing the title *Christ is passing by*.

Monsignor Josemaría Escrivá was indeed constantly trying to take Our Lord to every street and square of the towns and villages of this world. He was very much aware that in these times in which we are living the people who are walking in them experience a great spiritual emptiness and sometimes obstinately refuse to find, in Christ, the true answer to the questions they ask themselves.

The experience of our weakness and our errors; the sorry sight of how small-minded and even niggardly those who call themselves Christians can be, and the unedifying result of this meanness; the apparent failure or irregularity of some apostolic undertakings; all this, the result of man's sins and shortcomings, may be a test for our faith, permitting temptation and doubt to infiltrate our minds. Where, we cry, is the power and might of God? Be, always and in everything, the sign held aloft before the eyes of nations, a sign announcing to mankind the benevolence and love of God ... The arm of God has

*not been shortened (Is 59:1). God is no less powerful today than he
has been in ages past, and his love for men is no less real. Our faith
assures us that the whole of creation, the wheeling of the planets, the
stars in their courses, the right behaviour of the things He has made,
all that is positive and admirable in the long unfolding of history – in
a word, everything – comes from God and is directed towards
Him.* [54]

An act of confidence

Although he was in continual distress at the harm done to
souls by the doctrinal deviations which were now commonplace
throughout the world, the founder of Opus Dei found reinforce-
ment for his active optimism in his faith. To him, the great
moments in history had always seemed *like so many calls by God to
men to face the truth, and like so many opportunities given to Christians to announce, by word and deed and with the help of God's
grace, the Spirit to whom they belong (Luke 9:55). Each generation of
Christians must redeem and sanctify its own times* ... [55]

Two years after speaking these words, Monsignor Escrivá consecrated the Work to the Holy Spirit on Whit Sunday, 30 May 1971,
in the oratory of the General Council. It was there, behind the
tabernacle, that the stained-glass windows portrayed the Holy Spirit
descending upon the Apostles. *God the Holy Spirit ... who have
given always to the Church your peace, your joy and your consolation
amid so many contradictions, confirming our faith, sustaining our
hope and kindling our love: give us Your sevenfold gifts so that,
throughout our lives, in our acts, our thoughts and our words, we may
be pleasing to Our Father who is in Heaven, the eternal God, One
and Three* .

*We pray also that You aid Your Church always, and in particular
the Sovereign Pontiff, that he guide us with his word and his example,
and that he obtain eternal life together with the flock entrusted to him;
that we never be without good shepherds; and that all the faithful
serve You with the holiness of their lives and the courage of their faith,
so as to come to the glory of Heaven.* [56]

The only thing the Father could do was to *pester* the Lord day and night, to beg Him to act, and to make reparation with additional penances for all the harm he saw being done. He felt the urgent need to form his children even better, and to spur them on to extend their personal apostolate more and more. He took part in this effort as often as possible, talking directly to groups of all sizes who were ready to listen to him.

Two months of catechesis

The Father's visit to Spain, at first for the ceremony at the University of Navarre on 7 October 1972, would give him the opportunity to recall the essential truths of the Faith once again to many people. For him, *all the apostolates of Opus Dei boil down to just one: the giving of Christian doctrine.* [57]

Leaving Pamplona on 10 October, the Father travelled all over Spain and Portugal; in two months he met around one hundred and fifty thousand people, of all ages and situations, in Bilbao, Madrid, Oporto, Lisbon, Jerez, Valencia, Barcelona ... No two meeting places would be the same; one would be a gymnasium specially transformed into a lecture hall; another would be an auditorium; elsewhere a concert hall ... And in Jerez, it was a kind of marquee on the site of an old wine-press.

Everywhere there was the same warm greeting from the members of the Work, their families and their friends, the same joy to hear the Father strengthen their faith and encourage them to aim more and more each day for that sanctity to which every Christian is called from the time of his baptism.

When he arrived there would be applause: it was the only way the audience had of showing him their affection. He would cut them short with a gesture:

You've applauded, but I don't want you to; because if people see us they might think that we're a crowd. But here we are a family, a very united family. [58]

He would go straight into a commentary on a passage from the Gospel or on some aspect of the life of a Christian, before suggesting to his audience that they ask him questions.

The right atmosphere had been established and people would

ask advice on personal worries or uncertainties; the Father was always very moved, for he could see from these straightforward questions that the person in front of him was truly concerned about living his faith in a more demanding way. The young asked him how to persevere in the interior life without giving up, how better to offer their hours of study, how to bring their friends really to live their Christianity, how to sanctify human love ... Husbands or wives expressed their concern for the sanctification of married life, for their children's education, for their efforts to make their professional duties, the apostolate and their family responsibilities all compatible with one another ...

It was clear that the apostolic work of Opus Dei had influenced every level of society and every age-group. The Father saw that those around him – many of whom did not belong to the Work – tried to live their faith without complexes, but at the same time without being ostentatious or aggressive, with the resolution to become better and to share the supernatural riches they had gained.

In his answers he strengthened their good dispositions with his *gift of tongues*,[59] putting himself on a level with each one, using the right words, the phrase that hit home. Everyone felt involved, not just the person who had asked the question, although each was answered more fully and precisely than he had expected – especially if he had not known the Father before.

At the end, everyone felt his faith strengthened, ready to go deeper instead of remaining content with a so-called "simple faith"; resolved too, to go to the Sacraments more often and more fervently, and to take part more wholeheartedly in the Holy Sacrifice of the Mass, the *centre and root of the interior life*,[60] where he would find the strength to use that "royal priesthood" (as the expression of Saint Peter has it) proper to all the faithful.

The Father often used examples and anecdotes drawn from real life to ensure that his message was understood.

We have ... prayer, which provides a direct link with God Our Lord, an opportunity for a personal relationship, the opposite of anonymity. When they speak about the special hot-line telephone which exists between the Russians and the Americans, I just smile, because we, you and I, we've got one made of platinum. And if we're not close to the tabernacle to speak to Jesus Christ Our Lord, who is truly present there, all we have to do is to go right inside ourselves; or better still, go above ourselves. Josemaría goes on top of himself, tramples on himself, because he knows that he is nothing, he is worth nothing, he has nothing. But in my heart, if I don't drive Him out with mortal sin, I know that I have the Holy Spirit, and also the Father and the Son. We are the tabernacles of the Most Holy Trinity; we can immediately be in touch with Our Lord without anyone else realising it, saying words of love to Him, making acts of reparation and, as we are so weak, asking Him for help. I am so weak, more so than anyone else; that's why I lean on you all the time.

When I go to pray for a while, I say to Our Lord: "Ne respicias peccata mea!" Don't look at my sins but see the virtues of all my children; see those thousands of souls all over the world given to You ...[61]

A treasure to share

What the Father was doing in these family conversations was revealing part of his own interior life, showing, in their simplicity, some of the "tricks" he used all the time to keep up his union with God. Everyone realised this: that was the reason for their complete silence as they listened. It was all to encourage his audience to follow him along the same path.

Often he would give a precise piece of advice to someone who had put a question to him. When, for instance, someone asked him how to keep up a contemplative dialogue with God throughout the day, the Father would invite him to go within himself, without letting anything show, while he was working, or walking down the street, or with his wife and children. Better still, he advised him to seek intimacy with the Holy Spirit, by the route of humility. This would lead to his getting 'on top of himself' –: *treading on yourself in your thoughts*, he told him, *for you and me, what are we, my son, if not the potter's clay? We're worth nothing, we can do nothing, we are nothing. But we are also the throne of God, of the whole Trinity.* [62]

Another family man had asked him how he could increase his faith in the Eucharist. The Father, at the end of quite a detailed explanation, added:

The second Person of the Most Holy Trinity, taking on mortal flesh – the same as ours, except for being sinless – with a heart of flesh that beat so strongly, wished to stay among us to be our food … so defenceless, hidden in the sacramental species, at the mercy of everyone. But he is waiting for your love and mine. Isn't that a spur to love Him truly, to want to approach all the tabernacles in the world to tell Him: 'Lord, here I am, I love You'? Tell Him with all the strength of your strong, vigorous man's heart! Don't search for words, just as you don't look for words when you're speaking to your wife or your children, or to someone you love, or when you spend a few moments in prayer each day. Consider: never has Jesus in the Most Holy Sacrament of the Altar been mistreated as He is today. And let your prayer flow … [63]

Prayer, interior life. The more *active* one is, by reason of one's position in the world, the more *contemplative* one must be, thus transforming one's life, *the prose of every day, into heroic verse.* [64]

In Barcelona, the Father urged a surgeon to keep constantly in the presence of God during his work, from the moment he carefully puts on his surgical gloves to the moment he takes them off. To give a better understanding of the supernatural height to which this work can be raised, he compared each action of the surgeon, who is so involved with human suffering, to those of the priest.

The surgeon acquiesced with a smile, thanking the Father for this advice, which was equally applicable the work of the nurse, the manager of a firm, the housewife. For all work that is useful to society is noble, and thus by its nature can be sanctified. That was why the Father's teaching concerned everyone, from the housemaid proud of her work, making it a true profession, to the university lecturer who had to find, in preparing his classes, the best way of bringing his students, normally sensitive to the seriousness and prestige of those who taught them, closer to God.

Thus, in the interlinking of these constant themes, the apostolic march of the founder of Opus Dei went on from one city to another, in Portugal as in the Spain which he had already travelled from end to end in the first beginnings of the apostolate.

Times had changed, but the needs of souls were still immense. Monsignor Escrivá seemed indefatigable. Hardly had he finished one get-together than he was thinking of the next. He wanted to put these few weeks he spent away from Rome to as good use as possible.

Loyalty to the Church

The Father begged his listeners to be faithful to the Church and the Pope, to their own vocations, at this time when disobedience was common coinage:

We live at a time which is characterised by disloyalty, treason and heresy. And the heresies come out of mouths that should be speaking the truth; those who should show faith but show doubt; those who should be the strength of others and are only their weakness; souls who, according to the Gospel, should be the salt of the earth and are instead the corruption of the world. [65]

It was obvious that he suffered from the attitude of some priests. However, as he was careful to clarify, he didn't know any bad priests – perhaps some who were a little "sick". *There are priests who instead of speaking about God – the only subject which is their own – speak about politics, sociology or anthropology. And as they don't know the first thing about them, they make mistakes. Besides, Our Lord is not happy with them. Our ministry consists in preaching the doctrine of Jesus Christ, administering the Sacraments and teaching others how to seek Christ, to find Christ, to love Christ and to follow Christ. Everything else is out of our field.* [66]

In Bilbao he asked a group of priests, sons of his, to treat Jesus Christ in the Eucharist with the greatest respect, and to pass on their own feelings and attitude to the laity:

For the love of God, be priests, seek intimacy with Christ. Have you seen how some priests go in shirt-sleeves or dress any old way? You must dress in all the vestments – clean vestments – and celebrate the Holy Sacrifice without rushing, even if everyone around you is in a hurry. For they're not in a hurry when it comes to eating, or enjoying themselves, or doing the things they like, but only when it's a matter of the things of God. If we go about it properly we shall be doing a magnificent work, for this is how we shall know ourselves to be acting "in persona Christi", doing a work both priestly and pro- found. [67]

To these same priests he said the very things he had already said on many occasions, and which he would repeat over the weeks to come to men and women of all ages:

My brothers, if we try to be united through prayer and mutual affection, with the charity of Christ, everything will be all right. Love the Pope, the present one and the one who will come after him ... [68]

He referred to Paul VI's words about those who were destroy- ing the Church from the inside, but he also gave reasons for hope:

The things that are happening in the Church and in the world at the moment we can hardly understand; but it will ultimately be for the good of mankind. And I like to think that in the same way as the light of day comes after the darkness of the night, we are already very close to the dawn .

And revealing a prayer he would often say when he was think- ing of the situation of the Church, he added: *My mother, deign to shorten the time of trial!* [69]

Each time he spoke those words his soul was filled with peace, confirmed in its conviction that, as Christ had said to Peter, "the gates of hell will not prevail" (Matt 16:18).

The apostolate of Confession

One source of suffering for the Father for a long time had been the cold-shouldering by many people of the Sacrament of Penance.

A God who draws us out of nothing, who creates, is admirable. And a God who lets himself be fixed with nails to the wood of the Cross to redeem us, is a God who is truly all Love. But a God who pardons is father and mother a hundred times over, a thousand times, an infinity of times. [70]

For people who are normal from a psychological point of view, Confession – a gift from God, because it is a Sacrament instituted by Jesus Christ – is also a motive for joy, happiness, peace and comfort. [71]

The Father asked each person listening to him to keep urging his friends to go to Confession frequently. Some will say they have lost their faith, he would tell them. But isn't it rather that they have a layer of grime on their souls, which is preventing them from being sensitive to the promptings of the Holy Spirit? In the Sacrament of Penance they will receive *the good bath* [72] which will clean them and give them the strength to take up their Christian lives again.

Speaking to the young, to the "anti-establishment" generation, he encouraged them to rebel against everything that seeks to degrade man and bring him down to the level of the beasts. He invited them to fight every day, with the help of God's grace, in the little details that strengthen their will, like the sportsmen who begin again and again without giving up, so as to improve their performance. The Olympic Games which had recently been held in Munich had provided him with examples that really hit the mark. When he explained that the spiritual life is a struggle, and that just as any sport requires effort and training to overcome obstacles, or when he imitated the athlete limbering up for the pole-vault, the attention with which his audience followed his every movement showed that they had understood him perfectly.

The Father continued the conversation in each of these family get-togethers – as he called them – for three quarters of an hour, sometimes more. At the end, before leaving, stretching out his hands, he would ask them to pray for him:

Pray for me, I need it badly ..., pray for me as if you were giving me alms. [73]

It was so that Our Lord would mould him into what he wanted to be: a good and faithful servant, a good channel of the grace of God.

Seventy years? No, seven!

Monsignor Escrivá returned to Rome showing no signs of tiredness in spite of all the work he had done, and was happy to have been able to breathe more strength and optimism into thousands of men and women.

He had also been able to see for himself the expansion of the apostolates of the Work. Closing his eyes, he could see all those new faces beside the ones he knew already, so many intentions for which he offered each day the apparently monotonous labour which was his lot, in the heart of the great family of Opus Dei.

Since his seventieth birthday on 9 January, he thought of himself less and less as being old. He joked about his age, saying that the zero did not count and that all he would keep was the *seven* . *In the history of the Church there have been many holy souls who knew how to remain children, by various means, when they were old. Doesn't it seem natural to you that I only want to be seven? I cherish the hope that Our Lord will grant this request in my interior life* ...[74]

Since then, whenever he had to refer to his age he would only admit to being seven years old, to the delight of his audience.

The death of an elder son

Shortly after his return to Rome, the Father's heart was to suffer another blow. For several months he had been expecting the news: it was the death of Don José María Hernández de Garnica, one of the first members of Opus Dei, who had helped to start the Work in Ireland, England and France, and had then also gone to Germany and Austria.

A cancer of the brain had given him a long and progressive paralysis, which had got worse over the last few months. The Father had been thinking about him continually during his stay in Spain, asking Our Lord for a miracle. When he went to his bedside at a Centre of Opus Dei in Barcelona, the Father had to make an effort not to start crying in front of him.

Don Jose María died offering his sufferings for the Church

and for the Work, in great peace, confirming what Monsignor Escrivá liked to repeat: that Opus Dei is the best place to live and *the best place to die* .[75]

Don José María had been one of the first three to be ordained priest in 1944, the first generation of a line which has continued, uninterrupted, increasing in number year by year.

New ordinations

In the summer of 1973 fifty-one members of the Work were ordained priests. They were all holders of degrees in some academic secular subject, like their predecessors, and they were all men who had worked in some profession for a considerable time. Thinking of them, of those who had gone before and those who would follow after, he preached on the theme of the priesthood on Friday of Passion Week.

He wanted priests to be *priests a hundred per cent* . Some authors say nowadays that priests have to seek their identity. But for the founder of Opus Dei, the identity of a priest is *that of Christ* .[76]

All Christians can and must be not only "alter Christus", but "ipse Christus"; other Christs, Christ Himself! But with the priest this is realised immediately, in a sacramental way. [77] This is what the "ministerial priesthood" is.

What did he ask of the priest? *To learn not to get in the way of Christ's presence in himself.* [78]

*   *   *

On 12 June 1973, soon after Pope Paul VI had announced the next Holy Year, the Father spoke of these future ordinations to the Pope. The audience lasted almost an hour and a quarter. Monsignor Escrivá was aware that the Holy Father suffered greatly from the tensions that were all too evident in the Church. This was why, as a good son, he tried to bring him comforting good news, relating anecdotes illustrating how the apostolates of the Work were developing, and the good being done to souls in all the countries where his sons and daughters were to be found. And indeed, over the last few years he had been receiving extremely encouraging news from the five continents. Some came from the countries where Opus Dei had recently arrived, from Nigeria, which was still recovering after the Biafran war, from Belgium and Puerto Rico ...

The fruitfulness of the apostolates of Opus Dei did not make the founder forget his responsibility to keep those in his care faithful to Christian doctrine and to the Magisterium of the Church.

A time of trial, he wrote to his children on 28 March 1973, the anniversary of his priestly ordination, *is all the days a Christian must spend on this earth! A time destined, by God's mercy, to purify our faith and prepare our souls for eternal life. We are passing through a time of hard trial in these days.* [79]

Nevertheless, the Father did not let himself give way to discouragement. All that had to be done was to look carefully at fashionable innovations and currents of thought. *Let us live face to face with eternity ... Our days down here are counted, and we must not lose a minute in the work of salvation, drowning evil in an abundance of good.* [80]

His responsibility in the tasks of government was to ensure that his children were not swept away by the confusion felt by many of the faithful.

But he was not satisfied with simply taking the necessary measures in this direction. Seeing the confusion increasing, he longed to carry out in other lands the catechesis he had started a few years before, and which he continued in his meetings with groups of students from many different countries during Holy Week and throughout the whole year, receiving large numbers of people of all races. Thus on 22 May 1974, a few days after conferring Doctorates *honoris causa* at the University of Navarre on Monsignor Hengsbach, Bishop of Essen, and on Doctor Lejeune, Professor of Fundamental Genetics at the University of Paris, Monsignor Escrivá set off for South America.

4. RIO DE JANEIRO: 22 MAY 1974

"I have come to bring fire on the earth ..." (Luke 12:49) These words of Our Lord, which Don Josemaría had repeated during his years at the seminary at Saragossa, had been the inspiration of all his apostolic work since the foundation of Opus Dei.

The fire had for a long time had remained hidden in the undergrowth; then, slowly and surely, it had spread, sometimes with sudden flarings which surprised and delighted him, even though he had in some way foreseen them.

This was the case with many countries in Latin America. Scarcely twenty years after the the first members of the Work had arrived to work there – so few in number and with such meagre material means – the apostolates had really exploded.

Between 22 May, the day he arrived in Brazil, and 31 August, the date he left Venezuela for Europe, the Father was to meet thousands and thousands of people, in six countries in South America where the Work was present.

Many of the meetings that were held were really family get-togethers in which an intimate conversation was maintained with not very large groups. Other meetings drew enormous crowds; however, they all became personally involved in the conversation with the Father for, as is well known, he had the singular gift of being able to change "the audience" into a family gathering with his very first words.

So many people wanted to see him and hear him that it was necessary to organise several get-togethers each day, and to look for big places because the centres of the Work were not large enough. Large assembly areas had to be hired, such as the Conference Hall of Anhembi Park in Sao Paulo, or the Coliseo Theatre in Buenos Aires, both of which can accommodate four and five thousand people respectively. Even so, they had to have repeat meetings so that everyone could hear the Father at least once ...

People invited their friends; they would come with their whole families. The quickest off the mark might be lucky enough to capture a microphone and start one of those amazing conversations with the Father, where the sincerity of the question and the directness of the answer made one forget the size of the gathering.

Everywhere it was the same extraordinary kind of dialogue. A young man spoke of his possible vocation, a father, of his concern for his children, a businessman or a labourer of his desire to sanctify his work more and more; a bookseller, a dressmaker, a journalist, an actress, spoke of what they were doing to bring a Christian influence to bear on their professional surroundings.

The Father listened carefully and replied without hesitation, as if he had already guessed the person's worries before the question had been asked, taking fully into account the questioner's age, family situation and social condition. His whole attention was given to the speaker. He seemed, however, to be carrying on a private conversation with everyone there, and they all had the impression that the Father was also speaking to them personally.

It was more than a natural affinity between the audience and the lively black-clad figure moving from one end of the stage to the other, depending on where the questions came from. It was a familiarity in Christ, which drew their hearts close together and breathed a new desire in them to hurl the dynamism of Christian joy to the four winds.

Sometimes the questions discreetly brought up private hardships: the parents of abnormal children, the widow left with a big family to look after, professional people who found themselves out of work ... There was that mother of a priest who had not been faithful to his vocation, who was overcome with tears as she was reading out her question and had to get someone else to finish it. Then the silence was even deeper, charged with charity as the Father spoke, putting all his priestly heart into the answers where each word lifted and encouraged, and referred every sorrow to the triumphant pain of the Cross of Christ, that Cross which, if carried with nobility, is no longer *just any cross but the Holy Cross.* [81]

The tears which many people wiped furtively from their eyes were not born of sentimentality; they came from that impulse which moves every Christian when God gives him the grace to feel more of a Christian and more of a person.

As in Mexico in 1970, and Spain and Portugal in 1972, Monsignor Escrivá said more than once that he himself had learned a lot from the questions, especially about the love of God and of others that they revealed.

In other answers the Father made the atmosphere more relaxed, talking about important matters in an amusing way which provoked a spontaneous laughter. Then faces would become serious again as he spoke of the mystery of the Communion of Saints, or the treasures of God's mercy which are poured out in the Sacrament of Penance.

Sometimes the Father would say that he would consider his trip a success if he convinced as much as one of those listening to him to go to Confession. *Take your friends, your relatives, the people you love, to Confession!* [82] It was one of the things he repeated most often, raising his voice to provoke specific resolutions in his audience.

Frequent Confession, he insisted, even if the Sacrament was sometimes passed over in silence by preachers and catechists. Even for children. It was not true that they would be "traumatised" by being taken to Confession too young.

In support of what he had just said, the Father quoted the example of his first Confession in Barbastro and the extraordinary – and certainly hardly "traumatising" – penance imposed by the good monk his mother had taken him to – to eat a fried egg. *That man was worth his weight in gold!* [83] he added to better convince his listeners, who smiled at the anecdote (though some of them learned the lesson and found the path back to the confessional, or helped friends to find it, as a result of hearing those words).

The message was the same for all the six countries in South America as it had been in Mexico, Spain and Portugal and in the various countries in Europe the Father had visited. It was an invitation to constant dialogue with Our Lord in prayer, in daily work; it was an encouragement to seek union with God through the grace given by the Sacraments – notably Baptism, which opened the doors of the Christian life, thous pointing up the necessity of baptising new-born children as soon as possible. He spoke also of Confession, and of the Eucharist.

There is Christ Our Lord, he would repeat, *hidden in the Sacred Host. He is there really, truly and substantially present, with His Body, with His Blood, with His Soul and with His Divinity.* [84]

It was not difficult to realise that the Father's advice was the advice of an experienced guide of souls, as full of common sense as of supernatural wisdom. He often made his audiences laugh, and his vivid phrases stuck in their minds. Thus he advised women to take particular care after a certain age to *restore the facade a bit* [85] with the usual cosmetics. This would be a gesture of charity for everyone, and a way to keep themselves always young for their husbands!

As everywhere, with the necessary prudence when there were children in the audience, the Father reminded couples very clearly about the doctrine of the Church on certain points of morals for married people, asking them *not to stop up the sources of life*, [86] which would make them not husband and wife but accomplices. Besides, *every child arrives with a loaf of bread under his arm.* [87] This was a saying in his own country which he was fond of repeating, for he found it sound and eminently practical.

As for abortion, he had no hesitation about calling it assassination, separating the syllables so that no one could miss the point.

But the Father's words also had a different nuance in each country, as if he had caught its essential characteristic at first glance. In Brazil, for instance, a country the size of a continent, he urged his listeners – a mixture and blend of every race – to prepare to go out into the whole world; to pray and work at the apostolate which they would have to carry out *in Brazil and from Brazil.* [88]

He repeated his invitation in Argentina from 7 June onwards, speaking at the end of his get-togethers about the vast lands of the Pampas. In Chile, which had recently emerged from violent political upheavals, he asked those who came to listen to him, between 28 June and 9 July, not to be *passive Christians* ,[89] to love the Church, to be good citizens and to love their fellow-countrymen *without any exceptions. Have a heart large enough to treat everyone, I insist, with affection.* [90]

That was what he asked from Our Lady in all the shrines he had visited: *Lo Vásquez* , between Santiago and Valparaiso; *La Aparecida* , in Brazil, and Our Lady of Luján in Argentina ... In all these places he asked the grace of fidelity and of loyalty for himself, for his children, for priests and for all Christians.

Loyalty to the Church [91] was again to be his central theme in these countries of America, as it had been in the Iberian peninsula two years earlier. *You can't tear a stone from the Church of God without bringing the whole of the Church down. One task I recommend and you can do it as well as I can – even better, because you are better and so you have more love. When you see that they've pulled a stone out of the Church, go to it, kneel and kiss the stone, take it on your shoulders and put it back in its place. But, Father, how can we put it back in its place? By desire, I reply, because for one thing we have no other strength in the Church than that. But on the other hand, we have our desires to be saints, our desires to do good to souls, to be faithful to our Good Mother, to ensure that not one drop of the Blood of Christ is lost. What a wonderful job you have there!* [92]

The pilgrimage to *Lo Vásquez* took place on 8 July, the day before the Father left Chile. The news had spread by word of mouth, and many of his sons and daughters had gone to the shrine and were there before the Father arrived. They all said the Rosary together. He knelt on the ground, in the sanctuary, his eyes fixed on the life-sized statue of Our Lady which, dressed in beautiful robes, presides over the altar. Then they sang the *Salve Regina* together.

Touched by this manifestation of their faith, the Father repeated several times before leaving Chile that *Chileans know how* to pray.[93] Many times the Father urged those who had come to listen to him not to abandon the traditional devotion of the Rosary. He took up and complemented what he had written at one sitting in 1934, after Mass in the church of Saint Elizabeth in Madrid:

The Rosary is something for men. It is something very human to say the Rosary! What is not human is not to pray ... Only the beasts do not pray ... A son of God, a daughter of God, a man worthy of the name, addresses himself to God, speaks to Him, commends himself to Him, asks Him for help. [94]

And the better to convince them, the Father did not hesitate here, either, in front of large crowds, to take his rosary out of his pocket and kiss each one of the medals hanging from it, which provoked applause from his listeners, driving the lesson home more readily than a long speech would have done.

* * *

Brazil, Argentina, Chile ... The get-togethers continued without a break despite the fatigue they entailed for the Father. He was ready to continue his apostolic journey, maintaining the same relentless rhythm of work.

He landed at the airport in Peru on 9 July, the twenty-first anniversary of the arrival of the first members of the Work in that country. He was delighted with the apostolic works of Opus Dei, which he saw for himself, in Lima itself, and also in Cañete, the central seat of the Prelature of Yauyos which had been entrusted to the Work by the Holy See in 1957.

Hundreds of Andean peasants from the mountains and valleys for miles around had walked for hours and hours, day and night, to be with him for a while in *Valle Grande Rural Centre* or in the *Condoray School for Women*. Indians, mestizos and creoles, peasants and businessmen, students and teachers, everyone mingled in the get-togethers which recalled the talks Our Lord had with His disciples "about all manner of subjects" (Acts 3:1); the Acts of the Apostles thus describe the last days of the risen Jesus among men.

The Father had the same words for all, because in the Church everyone has the same dignity: *there are no rich and poor; there are just the children of God.* [95]

Speaking to a domestic worker in Lima, he told her that her work was like that of Mary and that it could be divine, not only because she should carry it out like an art and a science for the well-being of the families she helped, but also, and particularly, because *there are no jobs which are not noble, holy and divine.* [96]

The value of work, after all, does not reside in its greater or lesser glamour but in the love of God that is put into it, whether the worker is at the top of the social ladder or on the lower rungs.

For we find God in our everyday life, in the moments of our day which seem so similar, today the same as yesterday and tomorrow, and the day before yesterday and the day after tomorrow. He is at our lunch and our dinner, in our conversations, in our sorrows and in our smiles: He is in everything. God is our Father; if we want to go to Him, He will always be there. [97]

*   *   *

During his stay in Peru, in the third week of July, the Father fell ill with pneumonia. This did not stop him from receiving fifteen hundred people in the grounds of *Miralba Cultural Centre*, near Lima, and then other groups, one of them of priests, in the days that followed.

He had a nasty surprise waiting for him during his stay in Ecuador, however – altitude sickness. It is a frequent complaint afflicting people arriving in Quito, the capital, which is at an altitude of more than ten thousand feet. The sickness dogged him and forced him to leave earlier than planned, without being able to see those who had awaited his arrival so impatiently – many members of the Work, with their families and their friends ... although he did manage to have three or four small gatherings.

The founder of Opus Dei, who had been so much looking forward to continuing in Ecuador the family teaching he had started in Brazil, Argentina and Peru, was not feeling at all well. But he took advantage of all circumstances to be more and more in union with God. He spoke with difficulty. (He had to breathe oxygen before two of the get-togethers with small groups). His voice was faint, which was unusual with him, but he was still able to joke about himself, saying:

I am not a man for heights ... [98] (which in Spanish also has the meaning of "man of stature").

Then, in a more serious tone he went on, saying that the Lord plays with us men the way a father plays with his little child. *He has said to Himself: this son, who loves the life of childhood so much, of a special life of childhood, I Myself will make him feel what it is like. And He has made me become a little child ... But now I have to preach with my smile and the example of my poor behaviour, for I feel within me the protest of the child who has to walk, holding the hands of his father and mother ... when I should like to run around ... Quite a humiliation, isn't it?*

Jesus, I accept that I must live under whatever conditions, during these days and during my whole life, whenever you like. You will give me my sense of humour, my joy, my good spirits to enjoy life, to serve you, and to accept these little troubles, turning them into a prayer filled with love. [99]

For his sons and daughters, disappointed to have seen him for such a short time, and, if it were possible, all the more attentive to his teaching, this fortnight, which had been difficult for the Father but which he had accepted with so much submission as God's Will, was a lesson which did not need words, a most beautiful catechesis.

*   *   *

When he landed at Caracas on 15 August, the founder of Opus Dei was still extremely tired from his altitude sickness. This did not stop him from meeting large groups, especially in his two last days in Venezuela, the 29th and 30th August. His greatest suffering was not to be able to lengthen and multiply these get-togethers. One day when the Father was very tired, one of his sons heard him murmur a few words in Latin: *Vultum tuum, Domine, requiram!*

These words from the eighth verse of psalm 26 had vivified his conversation with God for some time; they were a way of offering Him his acceptance of these new limitations, and of telling Him that he desired to be finally united to Him at the end of a long life of service.

Lord, I seek Your face! I want to gaze in wonder at Your countenance, to contemplate You. I love You so much, I long for You so much, Lord! [100]

* * *

When he returned to Rome Monsignor Escrivá could still see in his mind's eye the amazing sight of those apostolic initiatives and the throngs of thousands in those six countries of South America where twenty years previously Opus Dei had been unheard of.

He had given his all and even more to pass on his greatest treasure to those souls – the teaching of the Church and the spirit he had received from God. Now he was counting on his sons and daughters to take up the reins.

The letters he had received since his return from America confirmed that the apostolate had received a new impetus. Our Lord really knows how to do things well; and in these fertile lands He had surpassed Himself in generosity.

I thank You Lord, for having made me realise so clearly that it's all Yours: the flowers and the fruit, the tree and the leaves, the clear water that gushes up in a fountain to everlasting life. [101]

Gratias tibi, Deus!

* * *

What did the Father think of when he found himself at the front of one of those great halls filled with people?

"Aren't you afraid to get up there and speak to so many people?", his eight- or nine-year-old niece asked him one day with all the boldness of her age.

And it is true that the idea of making a spectacle of himself did not at all appeal to him. The only thing that impelled him to continue was his passionate desire to confirm the faith of all those souls who had already benefited from the Work's spiritual influence in some way or other, but who heard the most elementary truths questioned every day in the troubled world in which they lived.

What did the Father think of when he saw those thousands of men and women listen to him with rapt attention, with that immediately perceptible affection? Perhaps when he opened his arms at the end of the get-together to trace the Sign of the Cross over them, Josemaría Escrivá could see those three students bowing their heads before the monstrance in the old chapel of Porta Coeli that January day in 1933. No doubt he could also see behind them those who were with him now, with so many others already in America, and the millions of souls who would follow in their footsteps, opening the same furrow of peace in the world.

And his traditional blessing for a journey developed as the days went by, to the measure of the vast continent, becoming "patriarchal" ...

In Brazil: *May you multiply like the grains of sand on your beaches, like the trees on your mountains, like the flowers of your fields, like the aromatic grains of your coffee* ... [102]

In Argentina: *For all the land of Argentina, for the wonderful woods of Paraguay, for the land that lies beyond the River Plate (Uruguay), for your homes, for your children, for your children's guitars and for the joy in your hearts.* [103]

In Chile, the Father ended: *Now I bless your good and noble loves, your pure friendships, your great scientific and apostolic enthusiasm, and also your amusements* ... *And your future homes, and your parents* ... *In the name of the Father, and of the Son, and of the Holy Spirit.* [104]

5. ROME: 27 MARCH 1975

Sitting at the back of the oratory of the General Council of Opus Dei, the Father spoke out loud and clear about his fifty years as a priest, which he would celebrate the next day.

I don't want any solemnities, he had written two months earlier, *because I would like to celebrate this jubilee in conformity with what has always been my rule of conduct: to pass unnoticed and disappear, that is what is right for me, so that Jesus alone may be in the limelight.* [105]

He only asked that his children be united to him on that day, which would fall on Good Friday: *Help me to thank God for the immense treasure of the calling to the priesthood and of that other divine vocation, to the Work, and also for all his mercies and all his favours, including those which I may not have been able to perceive.* [106]

He had had even more reason for giving thanks recently in America.

The year before, he had promised to return to Venezuela, when health problems had forced him to cut short his visit. Now he had just fulfilled his promise. He had been in Venezuela and also in Guatemala, but was again forced for health reasons to end his trip earlier than planned.

Other family get-togethers

The visit had lasted eighteen days – eighteen days that seemed like a dream when he saw the wonders God had worked in those lands in so few years. Everywhere, between happy periods of laughter and singing (most often the love songs of those tropical countries, which he used in a very natural way to feed his prayer), he had received thousands of people, often in the open air under awnings. Among them were very many young people to whom he had spoken about God, because, in his own words, *I do not know how to speak about anything other than God.* [107] But it was precisely to hear him talking on this subject that men and women had come to listen to him, particularly from every corner of the two countries, Venezuela and Guatemala, but also from Ecuador, Mexico and Colombia, Puerto Rico, Trinidad and the United States ...

Seeing their enthusiasm, he thought of Alexander the Great's comment before a decisive battle, when he divided all his goods among his astounded generals, saying "What is left for me is hope!"[108]

The Father's hope was in the rapt attention of the youth of so many countries in the get-togethers from which he had to tear himself away after long conversations during which he tried to set them alight with the love of Christ.

Surely God's Love is worth any love! [109] he would say to them repeatedly, years after writing the same thing in *The Way* with people such as they in mind, and many others. Thus the Father played *God's fool*,[110] as he put it, in an expression he liked to repeat to explain how he felt in these circumstances, recalling the legend of Our Lady's Juggler. But what many of his listeners did not realise, however, was that as a result of his 'performance' he was utterly exhausted by the end of each day.

He was surprised to see, on landing in Guatemala on 15 February, the Archbishop of the diocese, Cardinal Casariego, among the people waiting for him at the airport. At his departure he saw several thousand people applauding him as he boarded the plane. They were all those he had not been able to meet due to his having to leave earlier than anticipated because he felt weak and tired. As in Ecuador at the end of his previous trip there, when Our Lord had asked for this self-denial, he abandoned himself in His hands, like a child in the arms of his father.

Looking back

Like a faltering child ... [111] This was the theme of his prayer in Rome on that morning of Holy Thursday, 27 March. The Father opened his heart before his sons, asking them to help him with their prayers, to give thanks for his fifty years as a priest.

A glance backwards ... What an immense panorama! So many sorrows, so many joys. But now, all is joy, all joy ... because experience teaches us that the sorrow is the chiselling of the divine sculptor, who is eager to make of each of us, of this shapeless mass that we are, a crucifix, a Christ, the "alter Christus", that each one of us is called to be. My Lord, thank you for everything. Many thanks! ... The life of each of us ought to be a hymn of thanksgiving! Just look how Opus Dei has come about. You, Lord, have done it all, with a handful of good-for-nothings ... You have laid hold of instruments that were utterly illogical and in no way suitable, and you have spread the Work all over the world. People are thanking you all over Europe, and in places in Asia and Africa, and in the whole of America, and in Australia. Everywhere they are giving you thanks ...

You are what you are – perfect goodness. And I am what I am – the filthiest rag in this rotten world. And yet, you look at me ... and you seek me ... and you love me ... Lord, may I seek you, look at you, love you! To look is to turn the eyes of the soul towards you, yearning to understand you, insofar as – with your grace – human reason can come to know you. I accept my littleness. [112]

Vultum tuum, Domine, requiram! (Ps 26:8) Lord, I seek your face! For months now the Father had continued to repeat this Biblical invocation, which so well expressed his heart's yearning: the Pope, the peace of the Church, the apostolates of the Work, which he would like to see extending still farther, like that *shoreless sea* [113] he had spoken of in the 1930s to those to whom he tried to pass on his faith.

Lord, that I may see! [114] he added now. The exclamation of the blind man asking Jesus to cure him on the road to Jericho (Lk 18:35-43) had, since a few months ago, taken on a very different meaning from the one he had given it before, when he had asked light from Our Lord before the foundation of Opus Dei. For now he had started to lose his sight. Having consulted a specialist in the first week of January, he knew that his cataract, a result of his old diabetes, was inoperable. He could see very little; but only those who lived with him had realised it. But, as always, he did not ask for his physical cure, for he abandoned himself entirely in the hands of God.

He carried this new trial, which hampered him greatly since it reduced considerably the amount of work he could do, into his interior life. He asked all his children as the new year began, often to make this request of Our Lord, taking it, as he did, in its higher sense: *Let us say together: "Domine ut videam!", that each one of us may see. "Ut videamus!", that we may remember to ask that others may see. "Ut videant!", that we may ask that divine light for all souls without exception.* [115] *May they see! That we may see the things of the earth clearly, with the light of the soul, with supernatural sense.* [116]

Defections had, thank God, been the exception during the forty-seven years of the Work's history. The unity of all his children was no less comforting: more than sixty thousand men and women, all over the world, were living with the spirit that the Father had received from God to pass on to them in every human situation.

It was true that he had tried with all his heart to do the will of God, despite his own failings. But the Lord had been faithful to His promises, and had paid handsomely by allowing him to see, during his own lifetime, a part of what He had shown him, by a special grace, on 2 October 1928. It was like the vast progeny of a patriarch.

As in a relay race, it would soon be time for him to *pass on the baton* . But that would not present any problems either.

You are the continuity , [117] the Father would say to those around him. Through them he was speaking to all the members of the Work, to those whom he had always called *co-founders* , [118] because they had been allowed to see with him the marvellous adventure of the expansion of Opus Dei all over the world.

In the eyes of the visitors he received in Rome almost every day, in the eyes of the young men and women who were being formed in Cavabianca and Castelgandolfo, or of those who came to see him in greater and greater numbers each year during Holy Week, he could read affection, the desire to be faithful, the will to give themselves more to Our Lord, with the certainty that they would be richly rewarded after their time on earth. What moved him more than anything else, though, was the faithfulness of his eldest sons who, like him, had begun now to grow grey and who carried on their souls the scars of all the big supernatural battles which had led to an advance in their interior lives. Among them were many who had devoted their experience and their faithfulness to keeping the heart of Opus Dei – that is, its government – beating steadily, either in different parts of the world or, like Don Alvaro del Portillo, by his side.

The prayer of 27 March was coming to an end. Once more Monsignor Escrivá reminded his sons of the meaning of their vocation *in Heaven and on earth, always. Not "between" Heaven and earth, because we are of the world ... In Heaven and on earth, divinised; but knowing that we are of the world and made of clay, with the frailty that is typical of clay ...* [119]

Then another liturgical act of thanksgiving: *Gratias tibi, Deus!* There followed an invocation to the Blessed Virgin, to Saint Joseph and the Holy Guardian Angels who were the privileged witnesses of that divine calling on 2 October 1928, and the prayer was over.

On Good Friday, 28 March, the anniversary of his ordination, the Father spent some time in the morning with some of his sons who had come to greet him. In one of his remarks he made reference to the fifty years of his priesthood: *I wanted to add up these fifty years, and I must say I couldn't help laughing. I laughed at myself, and I was filled with gratitude to Our Lord, because it is He who has done it all.* [120]

At Torreciudad

The construction of the new Roman College of the Holy Cross at Cavabianca was almost finished. The centre had been operating normally since September. There were several final touches that needed to be added, but soon it would be possible to lay the *last stone* of this new *folly* which the Father had dreamed of for so many years.

On 23 May he arrived at the shrine of Torreciudad from Madrid, where he had been for a week after passing through Saragossa. He consecrated the altar, after gazing for long minutes at the great alabaster reredos which he had suggested should be placed there, in a similar style to the reredos of Barbastro Cathedral, to those of *La Seo* and the Basilica of *El Pilar* in Saragossa.

Only the madmen of Opus Dei could have done something like this. And we are very happy to be madmen ... Well done! You've worked very well. You've put a lot of love into it ... but now it has to be finished. We have to reach the end ... How well people will be able to pray here! [121]

The shrine and the adjacent buildings were built in a modern and original style, and the Father liked them very much. He told the architects and all those who had taken part in the construction:

With the humble materials of the earth, you have made a work of God. [122]

Faithful to his motto – *to pass unnoticed and disappear* [123] – he would not, he explained to those listening, be present at the opening of the shrine the following June. He had in his own way already inaugurated it by consecrating the high altar and by going to confession with Don Alvaro in the crypt of the confessionals.

Before his return to Rome, the municipality of Barbastro wanted to present Monsignor Escrivá with the gold medal of the town. Hardly had he begun his speech of thanks when the Father had to stop, choked with emotion. It was not so much the ceremony, he explained very simply, but rather a thought which he could not get out of his mind. Just the previous evening he had learned that Don Salvador Canals, whom he had sent to Rome in

1942, a member of the Tribunal of the Sacred Roman Rota, had died in Rome. Once more God had called to Himself one of his sons, who could have served Him generously for many more years. Once more the Father had to submit his heart and his intelligence, without really understanding ...

He himself had been long prepared for that same last summons. His eagerness to work still more for the Lord over the last few years had no other explanation. He often said now that the night was coming for him. But the foreknowledge of his death did not make him sad: *Sudden death* , he had said one day, *is as if the Lord surprised us from behind, and turning round we found ourselves in his arms.* [124]

On 25 June the Father celebrated the thirty-first anniversary of the ordination of the first three priests of Opus Dei, in the relative privacy of his home at Villa Tevere. In the *memento* of the Mass he also remembered the fifty-four members of the Work from different countries who were to be ordained at Barcelona in a few weeks' time. It was a large number, but not nearly big enough in comparison with the needs of the Work.

The next day, after saying Mass early, he left for Castelgandolfo to spend some time with his daughters before leaving Rome for the Summer.

It was 26 June, and the weather was rather sultry.

At half past ten the Father and those who had gone with him arrived at Villa delle Rose, which had for some years now been an international centre of formation for the Women's Section of Opus Dei. The newest arrivals were from Kenya and the Philippines. All of them showed their joy in their noisy greeting for the Father. Slowly and gravely he spoke to them of the central concerns of his prayer. He explained to them yet once more about that priestly soul held in common by all Christians, whether they are men or women, priests or lay people:

You have a priestly soul, as I always say when I come here ... And with Our Lord's grace, and with the ministerial priesthood of the priests of the Work, our work will be effective. [125]

He asked them to pray for those who were due to be ordained on 13 July, and also for the Church, *which is so much in need, going through such a time of trial as it is today.* [126] *We have to have a great love for the Church and for the Pope, whoever he may be.*

After twenty minutes or so the Father felt unwell and had to conclude the get-together and go off to rest in another room. A few minutes later, despite the advice of those with him, who asked him to wait a little, he decided to return to Rome. He intended to go to Cavabianca that afternoon to say good-bye to his sons at the Roman College.

The return journey was very quick. The car arrived at Villa Tevere shortly before noon. The Father greeted Our Lord in the Blessed Sacrament with a profound genuflection, accompanied as was his custom with an act of love. Then he took the lift to go up to the office where he normally worked. As soon as he opened the door he glanced, as always, at the little picture of the Virgin of Guadalupe.

Javi!

Don Javier Echevarría, who was accompanying the Father, had stayed behind a moment to close the door of the lift.

Javi! I don't feel well ... [127]

This time his voice was weaker. Don Alvaro del Portillo and Don Javier Echevarría were close at hand when the Father collapsed on the floor.

6. ROME: 26 JUNE 1975

That night in Europe and, as the hours went by, over the rest of the world, thousands of men and women lay sleepless, repeating to themselves over and over again, without being able to believe it: the Father is dead!

After spending an hour and a half trying to revive him his sons realised that any further attempt to bring him round would be in vain. Don Alvaro del Portillo had administered Extreme Unction and given him absolution several times. They knelt in prayer, without trying to hold back their tears.

A few minutes later, near one of the doors of Villa Tevere, two members of the Work knelt as the Father's body was carried past on a board towards the oratory of Our Lady of Peace.

Don Alvaro informed Pope Paul VI, who retired into his private oratory on hearing the news.

He also sent a message, by telephone or telegram, to the Counsellors in all the countries in which the Work was present.

From that Thursday afternoon civil and church figures came to pray before the body of the founder of Opus Dei, who now lay on a black pall before the altar, dressed in a lace alb through which could be seen the Prelate's purple.

Masses were said continuously in the oratory. Don Alvaro celebrated the first, and he too celebrated the last Mass *corpore insepulto* at six o'clock on the Friday evening.

One of the Cardinals who presented his condolences said that it was a day of mourning not only for Opus Dei but for the whole Church. Another exclaimed: "How much good he will do for the Church from Heaven!"

Monsignor Deskur, President of the Pontifical Commission for Social Communications, spoke of his gratitude to the Father and to Opus Dei for all they had done in the field of the apostolate of public opinion, adding that he wanted to be among the first bishops to ask for his beatification.

Many other messages of condolence arrived at Villa Tevere on the Thursday and the Friday.

On the afternoon of Friday, 27 June, after the last Mass *corpore insepulto*, Monsignor Escrivá de Balaguer was buried under the dark green marble slab he had had placed in the crypt of the oratory of Our Lady of Peace.

On Saturday, 28 June, a solemn Requiem Mass was celebrated in the Basilica of San Eugenio, in the presence of six cardinals and a number of bishops and prelates. The nave was packed. The distinguished visitors present, among them several ambassadors, were much impressed by the number of communicants and by the recollection of the congregation.

After the Mass a telegram signed by Cardinal Villot, the Papal Secretary of State, arrived at the central offices of Opus Dei. It contained the assurance of the prayers of Pope Paul VI, and of his fervent suffrages that Our Lord grant the founder of Opus Dei "an eternal reward for his priestly zeal." The same afternoon a letter arrived from the Holy Father, addressed to the Secretary-General of Opus Dei, saying that he had celebrated Mass for the repose of the soul of Monsignor Escrivá the day before, and that he would continue to pray for him, aware of the loss to the Church. He asked God that all the members of Opus Dei remain very faithful to the spirit that, by God's will, the founder had left them.

Monsignor Benelli, the Substitute Secretary of State, had come on the Thursday afternoon to pray before the body of Monsignor Escrivá. And it was he who represented the Holy Father at the Requiem in San Eugenio.

Requiem Masses were said, almost at the same time, in churches in many places all over the world. Reports of these ceremonies appeared in the world's newspapers. In Kenya, just as in Japan and the Philippines, in London, Paris and Washington, observers were struck by the piety and expression of serene sorrow of those who attended.

More or less everywhere in the world these events produced a number of impressive spiritual results: there were sudden interior conversions, confessions, and a return to the practice of their faith by many who had drifted away from the Church for years. Meanwhile, in Rome, at 75 Viale Bruno Buozzi began the unending procession of people from all walks of life making their way to the crypt where the remains of the Father lay. Sometimes it was whole families who came in for a few minutes to pray at the marble slab where only two words are carved: EL PADRE – The Father – together with two dates, those of his birth and death: 9-I-1902, and 26-VI-1975. They came to pray in silence, entrusting their worries and preoccupations large or small to the founder of Opus Dei, or giving thanks for favours he has already obtained for them in Heaven.

During the weeks after his death, and over the whole summer, thousands of testimonies witnessing to the outstanding life and heroic virtues of Monsignor Escrivá came in to the central offices of Opus Dei. Stacks of letters requested that his cause of beatification be opened. The varied origins and widely differing styles of these letters were a reflection of the way in which the spirituality of the Work had made headway in a large number of countries and among all levels of society.

These "letters of postulation" were signed by young people and old, humble and distinguished; from persons attending clubs or institutions promoted by members of Opus Dei, by well-known figures in public life – statesmen, academics, writers and so on – as well as by very many cardinals, archbishops, bishops (a third of the entire episcopate worldwide), priests and members of religious orders.

On 15 September 1975, two and a half months after God had called Monsignor Escrivá de Balaguer to himself, the electors who represented the eighty nationalities of the members of the Work unanimously elected Don Alvaro del Portillo as his successor on the first ballot.

For Opus Dei the period of continuity, faithful to the spiritual heritage of its founder, was now beginning.

EPILOGUE

Even though, as one French writer put it, death turns all lives into destiny, it sometimes happens that, while sharing in a common lot, the special destiny of some men is revealed to those around them in their own lifetimes by a single moment that gives their life its meaning. For Josemaría Escrivá de Balaguer, and for the many thousands of people who knew him, that moment was the instant of the foundation of Opus Dei – 2 October 1928; it had been the first "dying to himself" for which Our Lord had been preparing him for a decade or more, ever since he was old enough to understand what it meant to give one's life.

The many public testimonies throughout the world since that twenty-sixth day of June 1975 have only confirmed what a growing number of men and women had already realised, that the founder of Opus Dei played the role of a pioneer in the effort to give the laity, the simple faithful, their rightful place in the economy of the Redemption. Monsignor Escrivá appears now as a precursor of the Second Vatican Council, which solemnly called all men to the fulness of the Christian life in the midst of their ordinary occupations.

This important role has been attested by the last five Popes: Pius XII, who gave Opus Dei its first legal standing; John XXIII and Paul VI who constantly encouraged it; and after the brief pontificate of Pope John Paul I, who also encouraged it, Pope John Paul II has provided Opus Dei with its definitive juridical structure.

And yet the founder of Opus Dei never desired "to shine",

from the time when he was building the first foundations of the
Work in the suburbs and hospitals of Madrid, to the long years in
Rome, entirely given over to the work of directing Opus Dei, to
writing and to preaching. The few exceptions that he allowed himself towards the end of his life, in his journeys to the Iberian peninsula and America, had no other motive than the exercise of his
priestly zeal and his concern for the Church. It would have been
easy to act otherwise. It would have been easy to make the Work
develop in a more "spectacular" fashion. But the Father was quite
certain, from the very beginning, that his mission was strictly supernatural, that it was a matter – as he used to say – of being at *the
service of the Lord and of all souls.* [1] This conviction was the origin
of the phrase which he used in some way as his motto: *to pass
unnoticed and disappear, so that Jesus alone may be in the
limelight.* [2]

He had to carry out an apostolate in depth: to invite a number
of Christians to give themselves entirely to God without looking for
any human reward, following the model of Jesus Christ in the hidden part of His earthly life.

It would have been easy, for example, in the 1930s when he
was just a young priest, to accept the offer made to him to undertake the formation of the future generations of chaplains of
Catholic Action. He would have been famous; he would have gone
far. But the Work of God would not have been done.

It would have been simple, too, at the very start, to have given
in to the temptation of speeding things up by amalgamating Opus
Dei with other associations whose ends were, apparently, similar.
Clearly, this would have damaged the growth and the very nature of
the spiritual family that Our Lord had asked him to found.

His constant concern, in every stage of the growth of Opus
Dei, was to seek the Will of God and to follow it. No doubt that is
why, to the great surprise of many people, the Work has developed
amazingly fast. By the end of his life, Monsignor Escrivá had succeeded in getting more than 60,000 men and women to commit
themselves to strive for holiness in the midst of the world, and had
brought almost a thousand of them to the priesthood. The editions
in various languages of his writings can be counted in hundreds of

Above: With some African members of Opus Dei visiting Rome.

Below: Buenos Aires, June 1974. Monsignor Escrivá at the Coliseo Theatre during his catechetical journey to Argentina.

Above: Torreiudad, Spain. An interior view of the Church.

Below: Torreciudad, May 1975. Contemplating the altarpiece at the Shrine of Our Lady.

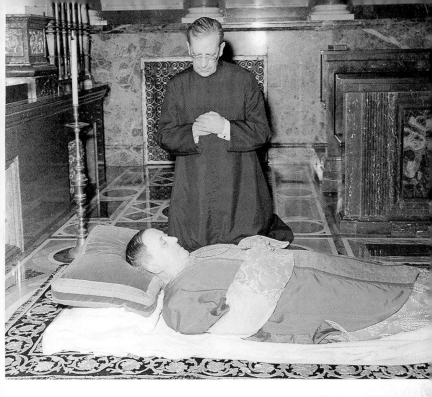

Above: Rome, 26 June 1975. Don Alvaro del Portillo seen in prayer beside the mortal remains of the founder of Opus Dei.

Right: Monsignor Escrivá is buried in the Crypt of the prelatic Church of Our Lady of Peace, in the central offices of Opus Dei in Rome.

Pope John Paul II in an audience granted to Monsignor Alvaro del Portillo, the Prelate of Opus Dei. Opus Dei was established as a personal prelature of the Catholic Church on 28 November 1982.

thousands of copies – and over three million copies of one book, *The Way*, alone – bringing the message of the sanctification of temporal realities to millions of people. As for the apostolates of the Work, they have spread a Christian spirit over the five continents.

How has it all happened so quickly? Is it because of the urgency with which the founder acted from the very beginning, in order to start carrying out as quickly as possible the divine Will which had been communicated to him, by a very special grace, on 2 October 1928?

Certainly he did not spare his efforts in the midst of countless problems, both during the first steps and in the years of growth and development of the Work all over the world. His plans often gave the impression that he wanted to run before he could walk: the opening of the DYA Academy, for instance, in 1933, with hardly any financial support, as well as the Ferraz Street Academy-Residence in 1934; the plans to extend the work to Valencia and Paris on the very eve of the Spanish civil war; the expansion, again without any financial help, in countries which were just emerging from the Second World War ... And so it continued, one could say, right up to the days before his death, when he was still urging forward the apostolate of the Work.

And yet, he who had done all this was wont to tell his children that he often felt that he was holding them back when they wanted to go too fast. At the beginning, although he had always acted with the approval of the ecclesiastical authorities, he had been in no hurry to ask for the various necessary canonical approvals, diocesan and Papal, for the Work. This was just the opposite of what one might have expected from a young founder, because he knew that the pastoral concept which Opus Dei represented would of necessity pose problems for the corpus of Canon Law then in force. It needed real and persistent campaigns of slander and defamation against Opus Dei to persuade him to ask for the official approvals earlier than he would have liked.

They have kicked us around, that is why we have spread,[3] he would say towards the end of his life, remembering the way God had used indirect causes – that is to say, an unsought publicity – to speed up the growth of the Work.

When all was said and done, he had followed his own recommendation and gone *at God's pace*.[4] His sons and daughters, in the twilight of his life – and still more when they learned that God had called him to Himself – had come to realise how extraordinarily fast that pace had been.

What is the secret of this breath-taking spiritual adventure?

It remains a mystery if one looks only at the simple, exterior facts which can explain the lives of men of action, without regard to the supernatural trail trodden by men of God. But it is as clear as day for the Christian, who knows that nothing goes forward, nothing lasts, without that meeting, made operative by obedience to grace, of the human will and the plans of God.

With the perspective of time we can contemplate the very real action of God in the world, through a few men who have followed his plans with special fidelity. It is like the currents that move the oceans, heating or cooling whole continents more effectively and more deeply than the storms which only stir up the surface.

The secret of the fruit borne by the life of Josemaría Escrivá de Balaguer is, without any doubt, the concern that he had, before the foundation of Opus Dei, but even more afterwards, to second the least indication of the action of the Holy Spirit with all his strength. That divine Will he sought with constancy and, at times against the grain, with total generosity in prayer and penance. His was a prompt obedience from the moment he had *seen* what had to be done, holding to the foundational spirit, not turning aside when he had to swim against the current, with the very clear conscience that the exceptional graces he had received gave him a grave responsibility.

It was, paradoxically, this unshakeable attitude that drew criticisms from some people who insisted on seeing in Opus Dei a human undertaking shaped to the measure, perhaps, of their own earthbound ambitions.

When some of his sons, exercising their basic rights, accepted public offices in Spain and other countries, he could easily have silenced the slanders – fruit of old campaigns of persecution – which attributed to Opus Dei a role that did not belong to it. It would have been enough to ask these members of the Work to resign from their posts. But he could not have done so without himself contradicting the lay nature and spirit of the Work which he had founded, for each member assumes his own responsibilities in society without having to give an account to anyone except those who appointed him, for in his professional job he represents neither Opus Dei nor the Church.

Hence Monsignor Escrivá never dreamed of limiting the freedom proper to his children. If he had acted otherwise, the Work would not have been the Work of God but that of the devil:[5] its goal and its means would have ceased to be strictly supernatural.

He had no need to establish rules for the fulfilment of that foundational spirit. He had the absolute and logical certainty that if it were to happen – unlikely though it might be – that the Directors of Opus Dei should attempt to impose a uniform way of thinking or acting in temporal matters, not only would they be acting against the legitimate personal freedom of its members but against the very essence of the Work. Opus Dei would have no reason to continue, and its members no reason to persevere.

A fine fool I would look, he said to some of his sons in 1969, *if I had spent my life – my youth, my manhood and now my old age – for something purely human!*[6]

If anyone had asked him for the secret of Opus Dei's rapid spread, the founder, without any hesitation, would have attributed it to the concern he had always felt – he who considered himself *a clumsy tool*[7] – to implore more help from God, through the powerful intercession of His Mother and of the angels and saints, for every step of the way. Then there was his work, and the work and prayer of his sons and daughters and of many other people, all carried out with continual mortifications offered for the development of the apostolates of the Work, and for the Church.

Knowing the supernatural character of the undertaking, he was sure that the means should match the end: they, too, should be supernatural.

* * *

It was only after his death that his children learned what none but a few of those close to him had known. Suffering all that could be suffered on account of the state of the Church, feeling himself powerless to do anything other than what he was already doing – praying, offering reparation, strengthening the faith of his sons and daughters – he had offered his life to God for the Church, so as to be of greater service to those he left behind, if God granted him the grace to be able to *hurdle Purgatory*.[8]

His sudden transit, and his peaceful face, striking to those who came to kneel before his body, made many think that the Mother of God, whose portrait – a reproduction of Our Lady of Guadalupe hanging on the wall of the office he usually worked in – was the last sight to meet his eyes on earth, had obtained for him, from Almighty God, this last grace.

*   *   *

In reading this book, you have followed me thus far. I ask you now for the alms of a prayer for Monsignor Josemaría Escrivá, as he would do himself, stretching out his hands *like God's beggar*.[9]

If, like the many who knew him, you believe that his life given to God permits him even now to contemplate Him face to face, do not hesitate to confide to him your most intimate concerns, from the most material to the most spiritual.

And do not forget to pray for those who, following in his footsteps, have undertaken to open a path of joy and peace in the world.

Couvrelles, 23 August 1982.

NOTES

Notes to Section I
[1] Historical Records of the Founder (HRF), 21500, nos. 6 & 7.
[2] Blaise Pascal, *Memorial*.

Notes to Section II
[1] HRF 20760, p. 748
[2] Letter, 24 March 1931
[3] cf. HRF 20754, p. 261
[4] cf. HRF 20771, p. 397
[5] HRF 21500, no. 9 and HRF 20159, p. 1071
[6] cf. HRF 20754, p. 263
[7] *The Way*, 742 evokes this scene, but no precise correlation can be established. The anecdote is widely known in Spain.
[8] HRF 20164, p. 222 and HRF 20771, p. 398
[9] HRF 20164, p. 222
[10] cf. HRF 20165, pp. 856 & 944 and HRF 20771, p. 399
[11] cf. note 8
[12] cf. note 10
[13] cf. HRF 20165, p. 446
[14] cf. HRF 21502, note 106
[15] cf. J. Escrivá, *The Way*, 801, Scepter, London 1986

[16] cf. HRF 20164, p. 358
[17] HRF 21501, no. 90

Notes to Section III
[1] cf. HRF 20158, p. 31
[2] HRF 21500, no. 7
[3] *Conversations . . .* , 32
[4] *The Way*, 82
[5] HRF 20770, p. 64
[6] *The Way*, 412
[7] *Ibid.* , 218
[8] HRF 21784, p. 212
[9] cf. J. Escrivá, *Friends of God* , 154
[10] cf. *The Way*, 811
[11] *Ibid.* , 72
[12] HRF 21504, no. 48
[13] *The Way*, 304
[14] HRF 21510, no. 17
[15] *The Way*, 535
[16] *Ibid.* , 537
[17] HRF 21500, no. 6
[18] *The Way*, 335
[19] *Ibid.* , 279
[20] *Ibid.* , 29
[21] *Ibid.* , 30
[22] *Ibid.* , 626
[23] cf. J. Escrivá, *The Way of the Cross* , Third Station

[24] *The Way*, 204
[25] HRF 20755, p. 298
[26] cf. *The Way*, 88
[27] *The Way*, 762
[28] J. Escrivá, *Letter*, 11 March 1940
[29] *Conversations* ... , 57
[30] HRF 20754, p. 117
[31] HRF 20755, p. 298
[32] HRF 5360
[33] J. Escrivá, *Letter*, 9 January 1959
[34] HRF 20119, p. 13
[35] *Ibid.*
[36] J. Escrivá, *Letter*, 9 January 1959
[37] HRF 20119, p. 13
[38] J. Escrivá, *Letter*, 9 January 1959
[39] *The Way*, 267
[40] *Ibid.*, 892
[41] cf. HRF 20169, p. 1208 and HRF 5362
[42] *The Way*, 291
[43] cf. *The Way*, 903
[44] cf. HRF 21500, nos. 1 and 47
[45] HRF 20587, p. 400
[46] cf. HRF 175
[47] cf. HRF 4197
[48] *The Way*, 606
[49] *Ibid.*, 982
[50] *Ibid.*, 94
[51] *Ibid.*, 961
[52] *Ibid.*, 1
[53] HRF 20165, pp. 1635-1636
[54] *Letter*, 9 January 1932
[55] *Letter*, 24 March 1930
[56] *The Way*, 353
[57] *Letter*, 9 January 1932
[58] *The Way*, 301
[59] HRF 3381
[60] HRF 20165, p. 845
[61] *The Way*, 774
[62] *Ibid.*, 864
[63] *Ibid.*, 758
[64] *Ibid.*, 726
[65] J. Escrivá, *Consideraciones espirituales*, Cuenca, 1934, p. 5
[66] *Conversations* ... , 55
[67] *Consideraciones espirituales*, p. 88
[68] *Ibid.*, p. 31
[69] *Ibid.*, p. 94
[70] *Ibid.*
[71] *Letter to Diognetus*, V-VII
[72] *Consideraciones espirituales*, p. 75
[73] *Conversations* ... , 57
[74] *The Way*, 347
[75] cf. HRF 4202
[76] HRF 21504, no. 35 and note 25
[77] HRF 162
[78] *The Way*, 808
[79] *Ibid.*, 479
[80] cf. HRF 162
[81] *The Way*, 934
[82] *Ibid.*, 970
[83] *Ibid.*, 920
[84] *Ibid.*, 820
[85] *Ibid.*, 821
[86] HRF 21500, no. 1
[87] *Ibid.*, no. 42
[88] *Ibid.*, nos. 6-7
[89] *Ibid.*, nos. 14-15
[90] J. Escrivá, *Holy Rosary*, Preface
[91] *Ibid.*
[92] *Ibid.*
[93] cf. *Ibid.*
[94] *The Way*, 558
[95] *Ibid.*, 804
[96] cf. *Letter*, 14 February 1951
[97] HRF 5827
[98] HRF 20167, p. 10
[99] *Ibid.*
[100] *The Way*, 978
[101] *Ibid.*, 372
[102] *Ibid.*, 338
[103] *Ibid.*, 796
[104] HRF 3696
[105] HRF 20157, p. 447
[106] *Ibid.*
[107] *Letter*, 2 April 1935
[108] *The Way*, 537
[109] *Ibid.*, 543
[110] *Ibid.*, 12
[111] *Friends of God*, 162

[112] *Ibid.*, no. 256
[113] *The Way*, 27
[114] *Ibid.*, 360
[115] *Ibid.*, Prologue
[116] *Ibid.*, 939
[117] *Ibid.*, 946
[118] *Conversations ...*, 55
[119] *Letter*, 31 May 1943
[120] HRF 21500, no. 21
[121] HRF 162 and 4152
[122] *The Way of the Cross*, Ninth Station
[123] cf. *The Way*, 788
[124] HRF 20165, p. 200
[125] *Friends of God*, 223
[126] cf. HRF 21505, no. 2
[127] HRF 21501, note 67
[128] *Letter*, 11 March 1940
[129] cf. HRF 184 and 4151
[130] cf. HRF 20166, p. 1148
[131] HRF 4152
[132] HRF 20165, p. 883
[133] *Ibid.*, p. 885
[134] *The Way*, 728
[135] *Letter*, 17 December 1937
[136] *The Way*, 697
[137] cf. HRF 4197
[138] HRF 8246
[139] cf. HRF 4152

Notes to Section IV
[1] HRF 20165, p. 455
[2] *The Way*, 977
[3] *Ibid.*, 380
[4] *Friends of God*, 65
[5] *The Way*, 311
[6] HRF 20020, p. 67
[7] HRF 3691
[8] *The Way*, 903
[9] *Ibid.*, 926
[10] *Ibid.*, 964
[11] HRF 20168, pp. 251-252
[12] HRF 20165, pp. 1122-1124
[13] HRF 20760, p. 746
[14] HRF 2210

[15] HRF 20164, p. 673
[16] HRF 4417
[17] *Letter*, 9 January 1932
[18] *Letter*, 11 March 1940
[19] *Letter*, 9 January 1959
[20] *The Way*, 7
[21] *Ibid.*, 764
[22] *Ibid.*, 525
[23] *Ibid.*, 689
[24] HRF 2922
[25] HRF 21502, note 118
[26] *The Way*, 452
[27] HRF 20770, p. 642
[28] HRF 20751, p. 471
[29] *The Way*, 659
[30] *Christ is passing by*, 43; *Josemaría Escrivá − A Profile of the Founder of Opus Dei*, S. Bernal, Scepter, London
[31] HRF 21500, note 45
[32] *Letter*, 6 May 1945
[33] *Ibid.*
[34] HRF 4696
[35] *The Way*, 685
[36] *Ibid.*, 688
[37] *Ibid.*, 178
[38] HRF 20165, pp. 756-758
[39] cf. HRF 21504, note 126
[40] HRF 3545
[41] cf. HRF 20165, pp. 1172-1173
[42] HRF 20171, pp. 1298-1299
[43] HRF 21505, note 126
[44] HRF 8075
[45] cf. HRF 20160, p. 312
[46] *Letter*, 29 July 1965
[47] *Letter*, 8 August 1956
[48] *Ibid.*
[49] *Ibid.*
[50] HRF 20760, p. 474
[51] *The Way*, 691 and cf. *Letter*, 8 August 1956
[52] HRF 20165, p. 265
[53] HRF 4417
[54] HRF 21502, note 134 and HRF 20165, p. 200
[55] HRF 3870; 4417

[56] cf. HRF 20170, pp. 1360-1362
[57] cf. *Holy Rosary*, Preface to the fourth edition
[58] *Ibid.*
[59] *The Way*, 928
[60] HRF 20751, p. 366
[61] HRF 20512, p. 9
[62] *The Way*, 185
[63] HRF 20168, p. 627
[64] *Conversations ...*, 114
[65] This refers to a tapestry in Molinoviejo, with these words of the Father worked in it.
[66] *Letter*, 9 January 1959
[67] *Letter*, 24 October 1942
[68] *The Way*, 573
[69] *Ibid.*, 520
[70] HRF 212
[71] *Letter*, 14 February 1944
[72] HRF 20165, p. 959
[73] HRF 20164, p. 1561
[74] *Letter*, 7 March 1947
[75] cf. *L'Osservatore Romano*, 29 January and 5 February 1949
[76] *The Way*, 972
[77] *Ibid.*, 961
[78] HRF 21503, no. 1
[79] HRF 6139
[80] *Christ is passing by*, 22
[81] *Friends of God*, 294
[82] HRF 21503, no. 9
[83] *The Way*, 27
[84] HRF 21502, no. 65
[85] HRF 20165, p. 836
[86] HRF 20162, p. 565
[87] *Letter*, 11 March 1940
[88] HRF 20559, p. 9
[89] HRF 21781
[90] *Letter*, 25 December 1949
[91] HRF 20016, p. 72
[92] HRF 20070, p. 63
[93] HRF 21502, note 10
[94] *The Way*, 825
[95] *Letter*, 11 March 1940
[96] HRF 20811, p. 1
[97] HRF 20760, p. 765
[98] HRF 20158, p. 114
[99] *Holy Rosary*, Fourth Glorious mystery
[100] Apostolic Constitution, *Munificentissimus Deus*, no. 18
[101] *Conversations ...*, 35
[102] HRF 21504, note 23
[103] HRF 20823, p. 3
[104] HRF 21502, note 151
[105] HRF 20750, p. 304
[106] cf. HRF 21502, note 149
[107] HRF 20750, p. 307
[108] HRF 20165, p. 203
[109] HRF 1177
[110] *Christ is passing by*, 12
[111] HRF 20755, p. 131
[112] HRF 20074, p. 55; cf. hymn *Ave maris stella*
[113] HRF 3360
[114] HRF 20165, p. 205
[115] HRF 3360
[116] HRF 20755, pp. 411-412
[117] HRF 21503, no. 172
[118] HRF 20850, p. 3
[119] HRF 20770, p. 64
[120] *Ibid.*
[121] *Letter*, 15 October 1948
[122] HRF 21500, no. 28
[123] *Letter*, 29 September 1952
[124] *Letter*, 18 December 1954
[125] *Letter*, 6 November 1954
[126] *Letter*, 2 March 1954
[127] *Letter*, 22 February 1955
[128] *Letter*, 31 January 1971
[129] HRF 21502, note 57
[130] *Letter*, 18 April 1956
[131] *Letter*, 30 April 1946
[132] *The Way*, 691
[133] HRF 20166, p. 659
[134] HRF 20165, p. 902
[135] HRF 20162, pp. 585-586
[136] HRF 20075, pp. 18-19
[137] HRF 20075, p. 17
[138] HRF 21503, note 152
[139] *Ibid.*
[140] *The Way*, 387

[141] HRF 20541, p. 21
[142] cf. HRF 5840 and 5871
[143] HRF 20541, p. 23
[144] *Ibid.*, pp. 24-29
[145] *Ibid.*, pp. 32-33
[146] HRF 5239
[147] *Ibid.*
[148] *The Way*, 355
[149] *Ibid.*, 79
[150] *Ibid.*, 614
[151] HRF 21501, p. 90
[152] HRF 21144, p. 73
[153] *Articles of the Postulator*, Rome, 1979, no. 209
[154] *Christ is passing by*, 44
[155] HRF 20121, p. 18
[156] HRF 20128, pp. 18-19
[157] *Letter*, 24 October 1964
[158] HRF 20565, p. 24
[159] *Ibid.*, pp. 36-39
[160] *Ibid.*, p. 40
[161] *Ibid.*, p. 45
[162] HRF 20512, p. 9
[163] HRF 20571, p. 20

Notes to Section V
[1] Second Vatican Council, Dogmatic Constitution, *Lumen gentium*, nos. 31, 40
[2] Second Vatican Council, Decree, *Apostolicam actuositatem*, no. 4
[3] *Articles of the Postulator*, Rome, 1979, nos. 212 & 213
[4] Second Vatican Council, Decree, *Apostolicam actuositatem*, no. 4
[5] Second Vatican Council, Pastoral Constitution, *Gaudium et Spes*, no. 34
[6] HRF 20760, p. 651
[7] *Letter*, 9 January 1951
[8] HRF 20157, p. 452
[9] *Christ is passing by*, 71
[10] HRF 20161, p. 164
[11] HRF 20166, pp. 212-213
[12] HRF 20582, p. 129
[13] *Conversations* ... , 113
[14] *Ibid.*, 114-116
[15] *Ibid.*, 60
[16] *Ibid.*, 65
[17] *Ibid.*, 60
[18] *Ibid.*, 2
[19] *Ibid.*, 12
[20] *Ibid.*; 66
[21] *Letter*, 26 January 1968
[22] *The Way*, 775
[23] *Letter*, 28 March 1973
[24] *Articles* ... , no. 217
[25] cf. J. Escrivá, *The Supernatural Aim of the Church*, Scepter Booklets, New York
[26] *Ibid.*, p. 19
[27] *Articles* ... , no. 294
[28] *Ibid.*, no. 281
[29] These are words of Pius XI which Monsignor Escrivá quotes in HRF 21500, no. 40
[30] *The Way*, 439
[31] cf. HRF 20153, no. 1
[32] HRF 20161, pp. 1012 & 1017
[33] HRF 20161, pp. 1009-1017
[34] HRF 20159, p. 501
[35] HRF 20159, p. 505
[36] HRF 20582, p. 129
[37] *Holy Rosary*
[38] *Ibid.*, Fifth Joyful Mystery.
[39] HRF 20166, pp. 788-90
[40] *The Way*, 387
[41] HRF 20166, p. 790
[42] HRF 20166, p. 791
[43] HRF 20166, p. 793
[44] HRF 20159, p. 950
[45] *Ibid.*, p. 1047
[46] *Ibid.*, p. 889
[47] *Ibid.*, p. 936
[48] HRF 20165, p. 692
[49] *The Way*, 81
[50] *A Profile* ...
[51] HRF 20771, p. 244
[52] *The Way*, 132
[53] *Ibid.*, 855-856
[54] *Christ is passing by*, 128, 130

[55] *Ibid.*, 132
[56] HRF 21511 p. 14 *et seq*
[57] HRF 20166, p. 227
[58] HRF 20760, p. 535
[59] *Christ is passing by*, 132
[60] HRF 21510, no 17
[61] HRF 20760, p. 94
[62] *Ibid.*, p. 206
[63] *Ibid.*, p. 225
[64] *Conversations ...* , 116
[65] HRF 20760, pp. 513-4
[66] *Ibid.*, p. 132
[67] *Ibid.*, p. 100
[68] *Ibid.*, p. 94
[69] *Ibid.*, p. 27
[70] *Ibid.*, pp. 537-8
[71] *Ibid.*, p. 670
[72] *Ibid.*, p. 214
[73] *Ibid.*, p. 845
[74] HRF 20161, p. 11
[75] HRF 20770, p. 502
[76] cf. J. Escrivá, *A Priest for ever*, Tamezin Booklets, London.
[77] *Ibid.*,
[78] *Ibid.*,
[79] *Letter*, 28 March 1973
[80] *Ibid.*
[81] *Holy Rosary*, Fourth Sorrowful Mystery
[82] HRF 20771, p. 210
[83] HRF 20760, p. 761
[84] HRF 20771, p. 210
[85] cf. HRF 20760, p. 340
[86] *Ibid.*, p. 776
[87] *Ibid.*
[88] HRF 20770, p. 72
[89] HRF 20771, p. 70
[90] *Ibid.*, pp. 135-6
[91] cf. J. Escrivá, *Loyalty to the Church*, Scepter Booklets, New York.
[92] HRF 20760, pp. 659-60
[93] HRF 20771, p. 144
[94] *Ibid.*, p. 421
[95] *Ibid.*, p. 368
[96] *Ibid.*, p. 190

[97] *Ibid.*, p. 82
[98] *Ibid.*, p. 496
[99] *Ibid.*, pp. 496-8
[100] *Ibid.*, pp. 114-15
[101] HRF 20164, p. 762
[102] HRF 20770, p. 255
[103] *Ibid.*, p. 700
[104] HRF 20771, pp. 122-3
[105] HRF 20164, p. 792
[106] *Ibid.*, p. 793
[107] HRF 20760, p. 200
[108] HRF 21835
[109] *The Way*, 171
[110] *Friends of God*, 152
[111] HRF 20164, p. 809
[112] *Ibid.*, pp. 810-812
[113] *Conversations ...* , 57
[114] *Ibid.*, p. 780
[115] *Ibid.*, p. 782
[116] *Ibid.*
[117] HRF 20165, p. 1308
[118] HRF 20128, p. 64
[119] HRF 20164, pp. 812-13
[120] *Ibid.*, p. 809
[121] *Ibid.*, pp. 820-2
[122] *Ibid.*, p. 819
[123] *Ibid.*, p. 792
[124] HRF 5074
[125] HRF 20164, p. 673
[126] *Ibid.*, p. 674
[127] *Ibid.*, p. 9

Notes to Epilogue

[1] *Letter*, 31 May 1954
[2] HRF 20164, p. 792
[3] *Ibid.*, p. 149
[4] HRF 21501, p. 90
[5] HRF 20099, p. 14
[6] HRF 20158, p. 1115
[7] HRF 21500, p. 7
[8] HRF 20164, p. 664
[9] HRF 20760, p. 555

SELECT BIBLIOGRAPHY

Published Works of Monsignor Josemaría Escrivá

The Way, Scepter, London, 1986.
Holy Rosary, Scepter, London, 1985.
Conversations with Monsignor Josemaría Escrivá, Sinag Tala, Manila 1984
Christ is passing by, Scepter, London, 1985.
Friends of God, Scepter, London, 1982.
The Way of the Cross, Scepter, London, 1981.
Furrow, Scepter, London, 1987.
The Forge, Scepter, London, 1988.
In Love with the Church, Scepter, London, 1989.
La Abadesa de las Huelgas, Rialp, Madrid, 1981.

Published Works on Monsignor Josemaría Escrivá
a) Books
Berglar P., *Opus Dei. Leben und Werk des Grunders Josemaría Escrivá*, Otto Muller, Salzburg 1983
Bernal S., Monsignor J. Escrivá – A Profile of the Founder of Opus Dei, Scepter, London 1977
Portillo A. del, F. Ponz and G. Herranz, *En memoria de Mons. Escrivá de Balaguer*, EUNSA, Pamplona, 1982.

Portillo A. del, et al, *Mons. Josemaría Escrivá de Balaguer y el Opus Dei* , EUNSA, Pamplona, 1982.

Seco L.I., *The Legacy of Monsignor J. Escrivá* , Sinag Tala, Manila, 1978.

Vazquez de Prada A., *El Fundador del Opus Dei* , Rialp, Madrid, 1983.

b) Articles

Fabro C., *Mons. Escrivá de Balaguer, maestro di libertà cristiana* , L'Osservatore Romano, Vatican City, 2 July 1977.

Helming D., *Footprints in the snow − A Pictorial biography of Monsignor J. Escrivá* , Scepter, New York, 1985.

Illanes J.L., *On the Theology of Work - aspects of the teaching of the Founder of Opus Dei* , Four Courts Press, Dublin, 1982.

Lecaro Cardinal G., *Significato della la presenza dei cristiani nel mondo* , Corriere della Sera, Milan, 25 June 1976.

Luciani Cardinal A., *L'essempio di Josemaría Escrivá, fondatore dell'Opus Dei. Cercando Dio nel lavoro quotidiano* , Il Gazzettino, Venice, 25 July 1978.

Portillo A. del, interviews with *La Vanguardia* , Barcelona, 1 January 1978; *La Libre Belgique* , Brussels, 3 October 1978; *Deutsche Tagespost* , Wurzburgo, 10 October 1978.

Rodriguez A., *The Way - A spirituality of Christian Life* , Sinag Tala, Manila, 1974.

Thibon A., *La saintete du quotidien* , Le Figaro, Paris, 25 June 1976.

Gran Enciclopedia Rialp, Madrid, entry *Escrivá de Balaguer* .

Newsletter on Monsignor Escrivá, founder of Opus Dei , published by the Office of Vicepostulation:

in Australia and New Zealand: 9 Findlay Avenue, Roseville, N.S.W. 2069.

in Britain: 6 Orme Court, London W2 4RL;

in Ireland: Harvieston, Cunningham Road, Dalkey, Co. Dublin.

in Kenya: P.O.Box 66956, Nairobi

in Nigeria: P.O.Box 72484, Victoria Island, Lagos State.

in the Philippines: P.O.Box 553, Greenhills Post Office, 1502 Metro Manila.

in the United States: 330 Riverside Drive, New York, NY 10025

Published Works on Opus Dei

Byrne A., *Sanctifying Ordinary Work – on the Nature and Spirit of Opus Dei* , Scepter, London 1984.

Fuenmayor A. de, Gomez-Iglesias V., Illanes J.L., *El Itinerario Júridico del Opus Dei – Historia y Defensa de un Carisma* , EUNSA. Pamplona, 1989.

Horrigan J., *Opus Dei: Its ideals and the unseen influence* , The Times, London, 23 January 1981

Le Tourneau D., *What is Opus Dei* , Mercier Press, Dublin, 1988.

Opus Dei – A Personal Prelature , Sinag Tala, Manila 1983

Portillo A. del, interviews with *ABC* , Madrid, 29 November 1982; *Il Tempo* , Rome and *Ya* , Madrid, 30 November 1982; *L'Osservatore Romano* , Vatican City, 25 March 1983.

Shannon M. & T., *Christianity in everyday life* , Catholic Truth Society (Australia), 1979

Shaw R., *The Secret of Opus Dei* , Columbia, New Haven (USA), 1982

Stetson R. H., *Opus Dei : the first personal Prelature* , Homiletic and Pastoral Review, New York, July 1983

Torello J. B., *The Spirituality of Lay People* , The Furrow, Dublin, 1966

West W., *Opus Dei – Exploding a Myth* , Little Hills Press, Sydney, 1988.

Wheeler Bishop G., *Christianising the civilisation of our times* , Scottish Catholic Observer, Glasgow, 23 April 1982